Financial Management for Human Service Administrators

Financial Management for Human Service Administrators

Lawrence L. Martin

Columbia University

Allyn and Bacon

Boston ▪ London ▪ Toronto ▪ Sydney ▪ Tokyo ▪ Singapore

Editor-in-Chief, Social Sciences: *Karen Hanson*
Editorial Assistant: *Alyssa Pratt*
Executive Marketing Manager: *Jackie Aaron*
Production Editor: *Christopher H. Rawlings*
Editorial-Production Service: *Omegatype Typography, Inc.*
Composition and Prepress Buyer: *Linda Cox*
Manufacturing Buyer: *Julie McNeill*
Cover Administrator: *Jennifer Hart*
Electronic Composition: *Omegatype Typography, Inc.*

Copyright © 2001 by Allyn & Bacon
A Pearson Education Company
160 Gould Street
Needham Heights, MA 02494

Internet: www.abacon.com

Between the time Website information is gathered and published, some sites may have closed. Also, the transcription of URLs can result in typographical errors. The publisher would appreciate notification where these occur so that they may be corrected in subsequent editions.

Library of Congress Cataloging-in-Publication Data

Martin, Lawrence L.
    Financial management for human service administrators / Lawrence L. Martin.
        p.   cm.
    Includes bibliographical references and index.
    ISBN 0-321-04949-7 (alk. paper)
    1. Human services—Finance.   2. Social service—Finance.   3. Social work administration.
    4. Fund raising.   I. Title.

HV41 .M283 2001
361'.0068'1—dc21   00-028869

Printed in the United States of America

10 9 8   09 08

*To Peter Kettner, who showed me the way,
and to Lella Martin, who supported me during the journey*

CONTENTS

PREFACE

The idea for this book was born out of a sense of frustration. The source of my frustration was the challenges and problems associated with trying to teach financial management to social work and human service students and professionals with textbooks written for other professional disciplines. At the time of this writing, no comprehensive financial management text exists that covers the basic topics that social work and human service students and professionals need to know. This book attempts to fill the void.

In putting this book together, an attempt has been made to emphasize conceptual understanding as opposed to skill mastery. It is probably safe to assert that most social work and human service students and professionals are not interested in becoming accountants and auditors. What they are interested in becoming is knowledgeable about how to use financial information to better manage their agencies and programs. I can still remember (with a certain horror) taking a course in financial accounting as a graduate student many years ago. After long hours of working on a complex assignment, my answer would invariably be off by a few cents or an odd dollar. In my defense, I hasten to add that this was in the days before the advent of computerized spreadsheets, when accounting and financial management exercises involved a lot of what we called "stubby pencil work." I remember thinking at the time (and I still feel this way today) that overly complicated and intricate financial management assignments place too much emphasis on process, frequently to the detriment of understanding. With my own personal experience in mind, I designed the examples, tables, case studies, and exercises in this text to tend more toward the simplistic than the complex.

The book also attempts to demystify the subject of financial management. While the use of some accounting and financial management jargon is necessary, I try to keep it to a minimum. Where possible, various ways of thinking about financial management subjects are provided that may be more meaningful to the average non–financially-management-oriented social work or human service student or professional.

Yet another major consideration in the writing of this book was the desire that it not be terminally dull. Many students and professionals have commented to me that the texts used in most financial management courses are better than sleeping pills. Just read two pages before bedtime and you're guaranteed a good night's sleep. There is no way to make the subject of financial management sexy, but I have tried not to make the topics mind numbing.

Some comments on the topics covered in this text are warranted. The idea of the book is to expose the reader to the basic financial management concepts and tools that one needs to know to successfully manage a human service agency or program today, without repeating topics that are generally available in other social work and human service texts. Consequently, this book does not spend a lot of time discussing such topics as writing grant proposals and fund-raising. These topics are covered well in existing texts, so little would be gained by replowing these fields here. The topics that are covered in this text (such as understanding financial statements, cost analysis, break-even analysis, forecasting, risk management, and auditing) represent critical content knowledge that is generally not addressed in existing social work and human service texts. Even when this book does address topics that are covered in the existing literature (such as budgeting and budgets, fund development, and grants and contracts), the discussion and analysis extend beyond that in other texts.

The writing style employed here tends to be concise and redundant. This approach is consciously chosen. As a general rule, the more words used to explain something, the greater the chance that the topic will be clouded rather than clarified. The judicious use of redundancy is employed in an attempt to ensure consistency in the use of terms. Imprecision and variation in the use of terms tends to create unnecessary confusion in the minds of readers. Consequently, terms are defined when first encountered and then consistently applied throughout the remainder of the text.

Like any book that finally appears in print, this author is indebted to a number of people for helping this book become a reality. My special thanks to Professors Ronald Nyhan and Clifford McCue of the School of Public Administration at Florida Atlantic University and to George Miller, lead auditor of the Maricopa County Internal Audit Department, for their reviews and comments on sections of this book. I would also like to thank the following reviewers: Theresa J. Early, Ohio State University; Rick Hoefer, University of Texas at Arlington; John Poertner, University of Illinois at Urbana-Champaign; and Diane Vinokur-Kaplan, University of Michigan.

L.L.M.

1 The Importance of Financial Management

For far too long, the financial management skills of human service administrators have been considered to be of secondary importance. Because of the second-class status historically assigned to financial management, many human service and social work professionals have little formal education or training in this important area. Schools of social work, for example, are not exactly noted for their financial management curriculums. The financial management knowledge and skills that human service administrators do possess are usually learned on the job. Historically, a stigma has been attached to being concerned with financial management issues. Any human service administrator concerned with financial management issues ran the risk of being labeled a bean counter.

With the benefit of hindsight, it is interesting to ponder how the human services have been able to get away with ignoring the importance of financial management for so long. Today, human service administrators who ignore the importance of financial management do so at their own peril. While caring and compassion will always be essential attributes of human service administrators, competency in financial management is of equal importance today.

What Is Financial Management?

In its broadest sense, financial management deals with "the translation of financial matters into meaningful and relevant information for management and policy leaders" (Hildreth, 1991:153). At its core, financial management is concerned with the "basic pursuit of economy, efficiency and effectiveness in the mobilization, allocation, and utilization of monetary resources" (Premchand, 1993:88). With specific reference to the human services, Lohmann (1980:292) defines financial management as "the control and use of money and other scarce resources to further organizational goals consistent with law, ethics, and community standards." Financial management then is concerned with much more than just developing budgets and writing grant proposals. Financial management involves a variety of concepts, principles, and tools designed to improve the use of resources to accomplish in an efficient and effective manner the mission, goals, and objectives of human service agencies and programs.

Why Financial Management Is Important Today

The importance of financial management in human service agencies today is related to several factors. Some of these factors are directly related to the human services themselves, while others represent changes in society, government, and technology (see Figure 1.1).

The Maturation of the Human Services

Perhaps the most important factor accounting for the increased importance of financial management today is sheer size of the human services. Estimates of the amount of government funding allocated annually to the human services now exceed $200 billion; a similar estimate is made for the amount of private sector funding spent on the human services (Martin, 1999:13; Melia, 1997:2).

Many government and private nonprofit human service agencies that were started by small government grants in the 1960s and 1970s are today multimillion-dollar operations that require considerable financial management expertise on the part of human service administrators. The human services today really constitute big business! The two terms *human services* and *business* have traditionally not been used together, but in the future they perhaps should be.

Societal Productivity and Economic Growth

Productivity improvement has always been a key component of U.S. economic growth and a major determinant of our country's basic level of economic prosperity. As our economy continues to move from manufacturing to services and information technology, economic growth in the future will become less dependent on the productivity of the manufacturing sector and more dependent on the services (including the human services) and the information technology segments (Drucker, 1999). Because social welfare, broadly defined, constitutes such a substantial pro-

---

FIGURE 1.1   Why Financial Management Is Important

1. The maturation of the human services
2. Societal productivity and economic growth
3. The accountability movement
4. Competition
5. The contract environment
6. Managed care
7. Maintaining stakeholder trust and confidence
8. The nature of nonprofit organizations
9. The nature of service organizations
10. Advances in computers and information technology

portion of the services sector, the productivity of the human services is increasingly important. This is a roundabout way of saying that the human services must become more productive. In order to become more productive, human service administrators must become better financial managers. "Faster, better, cheaper" will necessarily become part of the lexicon of human service administrators just as it has become part of the lexicon of business and government.

The Accountability Movement

The accountability movement is a term that can be used to describe several different, yet related, performance measurement initiatives. These performance measurement initiatives require government-funded programs and services to account for and report information about their outputs (efficiency), quality, outcomes (effectiveness), and related costs (Martin, 1998). These initiatives directly affect government human service agencies (federal, state, and local) and indirectly affect private nonprofit human service agencies due to the reliance of the latter on purchase of service contracts with government agencies (Kettner & Martin, 1996; Kramer, 1994).

At the federal government level, *the Government Performance and Results Act of 1993* (GPRA) (Public Law 103–62) now requires all federal departments and agencies to annually report performance and cost data to the U.S. Congress. In addition to GPRA, most state and local governments either have some type of performance measurement initiative already in place or intend to implement such a system in the near future. In order to collect and report the information required by the various federal, state, and local government performance measurement initiatives, human service agencies (both government and private nonprofit) must adopt such financial management tools as performance budgeting, program budgeting, and cost analysis.

Competition

For far too long, human service agencies have maintained that they do not compete with each other. Let's put this myth to rest. As Weinbach (1998:37) suggests, in reality most human service agencies today actively compete for funding, programs, and clients. This competition takes several forms, including (a) competition between and among nonprofit human service agencies, (b) competition between human service agencies and for-profit business firms, (c) competition between various societal needs, and (d) competition between professions (e.g., social work, business, and public administration).

Competition between Nonprofit Human Service Agencies.　While public and private funding for the human services have been increasing, so too have the number of private nonprofit human service agencies. The result is increasing competition. The abundance of private nonprofit agencies that are willing to provide services under government contracts and grants has turned the human services into a "buyer's market." Government agencies expect a great deal more than before in terms of cost consciousness on the part of their private nonprofit human service contractors and grantees.

Competition between Nonprofit Human Service Agencies and For-Profits.   Private sector for-profit businesses now view the human services as a large potential untapped market. For-profits, such as Lockheed-Martin and Electronic Data Systems (EDS), are providing welfare-to-work and information technology services to state, county, and city human service agencies. Various other for-profit businesses are providing such services as child support enforcement, child day care, home-delivered meals, specialized transportation for the elderly and disabled, adoptions, and residential treatment (GAO, 1997; Garland, 1997; Martin, 2000a; Wayne, 1998).

One by-product of the increased competition between nonprofit human service agencies and for-profit businesses is the need for better financial management information on the part of the former. As a general rule, most for-profit businesses are much better at determining the true costs of service delivery and managing service delivery costs than are nonprofits. In order to compete with for-profit businesses, nonprofit human service agencies and administrators must become more cost conscious and much better at the practice of financial management.

Competition between Competing Societal Needs.   An issue that is frequently overlooked in discussions about competition is that the human services compete with other societal needs such as health care, education, housing, transportation, infrastructure, and the environment. If human service agencies, both government and private nonprofit, fail to use resources efficiently and effectively due to the absence of sound financial management practices, policy makers may decline to provide new funding and may even reallocate existing human service funding to other societal needs.

Competition between Professions (Social Work, Business, and Public Administration).   Yet another aspect of competition is competition for jobs. In particular, social work professionals are in competition with business and public administration graduates for jobs as human service administrators. Without a firm grounding in financial management, social workers will continue to lose ground to business and public administration graduates as they have done since the 1980s (Ghere, 1981).

The Contract Environment

For some time now (Kettner & Martin, 1996; Kramer, 1994), contracts have been the principal funding mechanism used when state and local government human service agencies transfer funds to private nonprofit human service agencies. Lauffer (1997:74) estimates that by the year 2010 as much as 80 percent of all human service funding will involve contracts.

Recently, state and local government human service agencies have begun utilizing performance contracts whereby private nonprofits are paid a fixed fee per output (or unit of service) provided or per client outcome achieved (Martin, 2000b). Unlike the more traditional cost reimbursement contracts, whereby private nonprofits were reimbursed for their actual expenses involved in providing human services, the new performance contracts place greater financial responsibility for performance or nonperformance on private nonprofit human service agencies (Kettner & Martin, 1993, 1995). Unless private nonprofit human service agencies have accurate cost data, including overhead costs and rates, they may underprice their services and actually lose money on government contracts. The contract environment requires that human service administrators be well grounded in performance budgeting, program budgeting cost analysis, the determination of overhead rates, and the pricing of their agency services.

Managed Care

Managed care is yet another factor that makes financial management so important to human service administrators today. *Managed care* is an umbrella term used to cover a variety of approaches designed to control service delivery costs while maintaining a defined level of quality (Martin, 2000a; NASW, 1997). Managed care is now the norm in health care and is moving rapidly into the area of mental health and into such human service delivery areas as adoption services, child day care, and residential services (GAO, 1997; Martin, 2000b). At its core, managed care is about controling costs. Human service agencies that become affiliated with managed care companies must necessarily be able to generate timely and accurate cost information and be able to analyze that data in ongoing efforts to improve service quality and control service delivery costs.

Maintaining Stakeholder Trust and Confidence

A major national study of Americans conducted in 1998 found that 30 percent disagreed with the statement "Most charitable organizations are honest and ethical in their use of funds" (Stehle, 1998:12). While only a relatively small number of human service agencies ever have problems involving the misuse of funds, the few that do inevitably cause problems for the many. Past problems at the United Way of America (Johnson, 1998; Weiner, 1994) and with Goodwill Industries (Billitteri, 1998) in particular received considerable attention in the national news media. The situation with the United Way of America is particularly instructive. Because of the negative publicity that surrounded the misuse of funds by a former president of the United Way of America back in the mid-1990s, total giving to the 1,300 local United Ways nationally still remains at a lower figure than it was in the middle 1990s when adjusted for inflation (Billitteri, 2000:23).

Every human service administrator has a fiduciary responsibility to ensure that public and private funds are used only for their intended purposes. Without adequate financial controls and accurate, timely financial information, human service administrators cannot be assured that they are accomplishing these goals.

The Nature of Nonprofit Organizations

Financial management is perhaps more important to nonprofit organizations (including both government and private nonprofit human service agencies) than it is to business organizations. Why? Because nonprofit organizations do not have the profit test and because the scope of their activities is restricted by government.

Absence of the Profit Test.   As Peter Drucker (1990:107) is fond of saying, "What is the bottom line where there is no bottom line?" The bottom line for a business organization is the profit test. If a business is making a profit and earning a satisfactory rate of return for its stockholders, than its financial management practices (assuming, of course, they are legal) may be of little interest to most people.

By definition, a nonprofit organization does not have a profit test. In a nonprofit organization, performance in accomplishing agency mission, goals, and objectives replaces the profit test. In order to accomplish its mission, goals, and objectives, a nonprofit organization needs to manage its financial resources in the most efficient and effective manner possible. Stakeholder perceptions of the performance of nonprofit organizations are influenced, at least in part, by their financial management practices.

Restrictions on Activities.   Unlike most for-profit businesses, nonprofit organizations have restrictions imposed on their activities by government regulatory bodies. Most private nonprofit organizations are *nonprofit corporations* (meaning they have been granted a corporate charter by the federal government or one of the fifty states). Corporate charters granted to for-profit corporations allow the conduct of any legal business activity. Charters granted to nonprofit corporations restrict the activities that can be engaged in to those that are in keeping with their nonprofit mission. In exchange for the restrictions placed on their activities, however, nonprofit corporations do enjoy certain government benefits. Most nonprofit corporations are exempt from paying state income tax, property tax, sales tax, and some use taxes (such as the tax on gasoline).

The Nature of Service Organizations

Most nonprofit organizations are also service organizations. Individuals who study service organizations (e.g., Murdick, Render, & Russell, 1990) point out that financial management is perhaps more important to these types of organizations than it is to manufacturing organizations. Two major examples of how the nature of service organizations affects financial management are (1) services cannot be carried in inventory and (2) pricing options are more elaborate than in manufacturing organizations.

Services Cannot Be Carried in Inventory. Unlike the products produced by a manufacturing organization, services cannot be placed in inventory to meet customer demand. Translating this statement into human service terminology, a human service agency providing counseling services cannot store hours of counselor time to meet the needs of clients. The supply (or amount) of a human service that an agency makes available must be closely matched with the community demand (or need) for the service. Too much supply means that the agency is spending more money on staff salaries than it needs to. Too little supply means that clients who need services cannot be helped. Being able to correctly forecast program/service demand is a critical financial management skill needed by service organizations including nonprofit human service agencies.

Pricing Options Are More Elaborate. Manufacturing organizations generally have a simple pricing structure. A single fixed price is usually established for a product, although bulk purchase discounts may apply. Pricing structures in service organizations are generally more variable and more difficult to establish and manage. For example, a private nonprofit human service agency may have one fee (or price) that it charges under government grants and contracts, another fee that it charges clients who can afford to pay full cost, a sliding fee scale for clients who cannot afford to pay full cost, and even no fee for some poor clients. The ability to establish variable prices and to analyze and manage their impact on agency revenue is a critical financial management skill needed by service organizations including nonprofit human service agencies.

Advances in Computers and Information Technology

Only a few years ago, the prices of computers and the necessary software to track and report sophisticated financial information were beyond the purchase ability of many human service agencies. Today, personal computers and financial and accounting software are relatively inexpensive. Thus, one of the major arguments, "we can't afford to automate," is no longer valid. Having timely, accurate financial information is no longer a question of cost for human service agencies, but rather a question of will.

Adopting a Financial Management Perspective

Adopting a financial management perspective to the administration of human service agencies and programs is not a zero-sum game. In other words, human service administrators do not have to give up something (e.g., the client perspective) in order to adopt a financial management perspective. Financial management simply represents another way of looking at the operations of a human service agency or program. Just as policy analysis, social planning, casework, and program evaluation are important perspectives for human service administrators, so too is a financial management perspective. Each perspective provides different and important insights into the administration of human service agencies and programs. An effective human service administrator today is one who can view the operations and management of a human service agency or program from a variety of perspectives.

Financial Management Concepts, Principles, and Tools

The basic concepts and principles of financial management tend to be fairly consistent across various professional disciplines (business, government, and human services). For example, regardless of the professional discipline, financial management concepts and principles are concerned with the control of cash, costs, funds, and accounts (Hildreth, 1991). The relative importance of various financial management tools, however, frequently varies across professional disciplines.

In this text, a specific set of financial management concepts and tools basic to the efficient and effective management and control of human service agencies and programs have been selected for presentation and discussion. Specifically these financial management concepts and tools include

- Creation of a program structure and responsibility centers (Chapter 2)
- Basic financial statements, including the statement of cash flows, the statement of activities (or the profit and loss summary), the statement of financial position (or the balance sheet), the statement of functional expenses, and the Internal Revenue Service 990 form (Chapter 3)
- The basics of accounting, including transactions, debits and credits, t-accounts, the journal, the general ledger, and the trial balance (Chapter 4)
- Assessment of financial condition using financial analysis (Chapter 5)
- Performance measurement and the development of output, quality, and outcome performance measures for human service programs (Chapter 6)
- Various approaches to budgeting, including line-item budgeting, performance budgeting, and program budgeting (Chapter 7)
- Cost analysis, including the identification of direct and indirect costs, the allocation of indirect costs, and the determination of the full cost or total cost of human service programs (Chapter 8)
- Various forecasting techniques (moving averages, weighted moving averages, exponential smoothing, and regression) used to estimate agency case loads, revenues, and expenses (Chapter 9)
- The determination of fixed and variable costs and the use of differential cost analysis to compute break-even points and to make decrease/terminate decisions (Chapter 10)
- Establishment of fee and sliding fee schedules and assessment of the effect of sliding fee schedules on agency revenues (Chapter 11)

- The differences between contracts, grants, and cooperative agreements and the requirements they place on human service agencies together with the two major types of government procurement strategies and the three major types of government human service contracts (Chapter 12)
- Some of the major approaches to fund development including traditional approaches (foundation grants, United Way affiliation, annual campaigns, and special events) and more entrepreneurial approaches such as affinity marketing, bequest programs, life income programs, commercial ventures, and the creation of for-profit corporate subsidiaries (Chapter 13)
- The essentials of risk management, such as managing agency risk factors to minimize liability exposure (Chapter 14)
- The various types of audits, government auditing requirements, how to interpret audit findings, and suggestions for how to select an independent outside auditor to conduct a financial audit of a human service agency or program (Chapter 15)

Summary

This chapter has delineated the many reasons why financial management is so important today for the human services and for human service administrators. An overview was also provided of the financial management concepts, principles, and tools presented in subsequent chapters. The mastery of the concepts, principles, and tools introduced in this text will provide human service administrators with the foundation they need to improve the financial management of their human service agencies and programs.

In Chapter 2, some of the basic building blocks (programs, program structures, program managers, and responsibility centers) of financial management are introduced and discussed.

2 Programs, Program Structures, Program Managers, and Responsibility Centers

In many human service agencies, particularly small- to medium-sized private non-profits, financial information is often treated as top secret. Frequently, the only persons who have access to a human service agency's financial information are members of the board of directors, the executive director, and perhaps one other person who may go by the title of business manager, budget director, finance director, or some such appellation. Other agency employees have little knowledge or understanding of the financial management of the agency.

Valid reasons exist for treating as confidential certain types of agency financial information. For example, good reasons exist for safeguarding information about individual employee salaries and personal contributions to retirement plans. However, sound reasons also exist for expanding access to agency financial information and for making financial management the responsibility of more, rather than fewer, agency administrators. Having more administrators, rather than fewer, responsible for at least some portion of the financial management of a human service agency should be the rule, not the exception. Such an approach is not a case of too many cooks spoiling the soup. Rather, expanding the job responsibilities of agency administrators to include a financial management component decreases the probability that some important aspect of the agency's finances will be overlooked. Broadening financial responsibility also provides opportunities (with appropriate oversight, of course) for younger administrators to gain hands-on experience developing and managing budgets, dealing with cash flow problems, and resolving various other financial management issues and problems. The more administrators in a human service agency who are familiar with and understand the financial management side of the operation, the stronger the agency's financial management becomes because it has a cadre of staff capable of assuming greater financial responsibility when the need arises.

This chapter deals with some basic tasks of financial management: (1) the identification of programs, (2) the creation of a program structure, (3) the assignment of program managers, and (4) the designation of responsibility centers. These four actions can be thought of as the basic building blocks of financial management in human service agencies. Many of the more sophisticated financial management concepts and tools that human service administrators have at their disposal presuppose that these four basic building blocks are in place.

The Identification of Programs

Much of what we call the "financial management perspective" in human service agencies is actually the way in which the accounting profession views the operations of nonprofit organizations. For example, the accounting profession has decided to divide all organizations into two groups: commercial organizations (businesses) and nonprofit organizations. Included in the category of nonprofit organizations are both government agencies and private nonprofit organizations. For this reason, basic nonprofit accounting texts usually address issues related to both government and private nonprofit organizations (e.g., Hay & Engstrom, 1993).

One of the basic tenets of the accounting profession is that nonprofit organizations (both government and private nonprofit) exist for the primary purpose of carrying out programs. For example, the Governmental Accounting Standards Board (GASB) in its service efforts and accomplishments (SEA) reporting initiative (see Chapter 6) makes programs its basic unit of analysis. Likewise, the Internal Revenue Service 990 Form submitted annually by all 501(c)(3) tax-exempt private nonprofit organizations (see Chapter 3) requires that the amount of an organization's revenue devoted to program operations be separately identified.

What Is a Program?

Various definitions of *program* have been proposed over the years. For example, Weinbach (1998:91) states that a program is a component of an organization, with its own "goals, policies, procedures, rules, and frequently its own budget." Rapp and Poertner (1992:29) remind us that a social program is "how people are helped." Swiss (1991:367) augments these definitions by suggesting that a program is "a grouping of organizational activities directed toward a single group of outputs." Swiss's definition implies that a program produces something (a specific product or a service). For Kettner, Moroney, and Martin (1999), organizational permanency is also important to an understanding of the concept of a program. They define a program as a set of relatively permanent agency activities or services designed to accomplish a specific set of goals or objectives. When these various definitions are synthesized, we arrive at the consensus definition shown in Figure 2.1.

FIGURE 2.1   Definition of a Program

A major ongoing agency activity or service with its own sets of goals, objectives, policies, and budgets that produces a defined product or service.

A small private nonprofit agency might operate only one program, but most human service agencies operate two or more. Large government and private nonprofit human service agencies might operate dozens of programs. A few large human service agencies, such as the U.S. Department of Health and Human Services and some state human service agencies, operate several hundred programs.

A program can be comprised of a single activity or service or multiple activities or services. For example, services such as adoption, case management, child day care, and counseling are frequently treated as a single program. But in the case of adoption services, one could make the argument that an adoption agency actually operates two programs (a home study program and an adoption placement program). Likewise, a complex service such as adult day care could be considered one program or it could be broken down into its component parts (e.g., transportation, congregate meals, recreation and socialization, health screening) and each individual component could be treated as a separate program.

The Creation of a Program Structure

The creation of a program structure simply means determining how many programs a human service agency has. For some human service agencies this is a relatively simple task; for others it may be more complicated. While no hard and fast rules exist governing how to create a program structure for a human service agency, Starling (1993:16) suggests that each identified program should represent "a major organizational endeavor." Following Starling's suggestion, a program structure should include the major services and activities provided by a human service agency, but need not necessarily cover 100 percent of an agency's services and activities.

Thinking about programs and program structures requires looking at a human service agency from a different perspective. The traditional way of viewing a human service agency is as a collection of organizational units. For example, a large municipal human service agency (Figure 2.2) might consist of two or more divisions that are themselves comprised of multiple bureaus.

The creation of a program structure involves reconceptualizing a human service agency, not as a collection of organizational units, but rather as a collection of programs. This perspective (see Figure 2.3) enables apparently separate and semi-independent organizational units in a human service agency to be viewed as parts of one or more programs (Rapp & Poertner, 1992:30).

The Assignment of Program Managers

Each program in a human service agency's program structure should be headed by a program manager. The job duties of a program manager should include both programmatic and financial responsibilities. Many human service agencies have staff that are called program managers. Unfortunately, all too often the job duties and

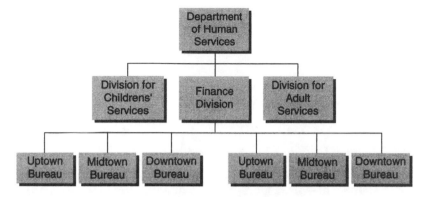

FIGURE 2.2   A Human Service Agency as a Collection of Organizational Units

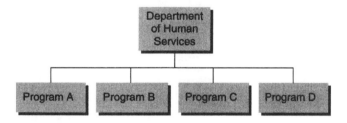

FIGURE 2.3   A Human Service Agency as a Collection of Programs

responsibilities of these individuals are exclusively of a programmatic nature (e.g., planning, coordinating, supervising, monitoring, reporting), while the financial management of the program is the responsibility of someone else. It hardly seems necessary to suggest that separating programmatic management and financial management is not an optimal way of structuring the job of a program manager. In order to ensure that a human service program provides efficient, effective, high-quality products and services, financial management responsibilities should not be divorced from programmatic responsibilities and vice versa.

The Designation of Responsibility Centers

Responsibility centers deal with financial accountability. Different types of responsibility centers are concerned with differing types of financial accountability. A program (Figure 2.4) can be designated as an *expense center*, a *revenue center*, a *profit center*, an *investment center*, or any combination thereof. From a financial management perspective, all programs should be treated as responsibility centers. The financial management question is what type of responsibility center?

FIGURE 2.4   Types of Responsibility Centers

- Expense centers
- Revenue centers
- Profit centers
- Investment centers

Expense Centers

Being designated as an expense center means that programs—and, by extension, program managers—are responsible for managing their own expenses. The practical implications of programs being designated as expense centers means that budgets are developed for each individual program (see Chapter 8). Once budgets are developed, it becomes the responsibility of the program managers to oversee and monitor them and sometimes to even approve program expenses in order to ensure that the budgets are not exceeded.

When program managers know that they are responsible for living within a budget, behaviors start to change. Before their programs were designated as expense centers, the finances of the programs were somebody else's responsibility. Now they have become the responsibility of the program managers. Program managers suddenly become interested in such issues as the cost of supplies, the amount of staff travel, the monthly telephone charges, and copying and duplicating expenses. Note that when programs are designated as expense centers, it does not mean that total financial management responsibility is simply dumped into the laps of the program managers. Agency executive directors and finance persons and other agency staff are still significantly involved in the financial management of the programs. What designation as an expense center really means is that the program managers are asked to take financial responsibility for the day-to-day expenses of their programs.

Perhaps the single most important action that can be taken to improve the financial management of a human service agency is to designate programs as expense centers. With this simple action, responsibility for the financial management of the agency is broadened as agency administrators become more interested in, concerned with, and knowledgeable about financial management.

Revenue Centers

Being designated as a revenue center means that programs and program managers are responsible for helping to generate either a portion, or all, of the revenue necessary to cover proposed expenses. Now the behaviors of program managers really change. Program managers can ill afford to simply sit back and let others worry about where the revenues are coming from to support their programs. Program managers necessarily have to start demonstrating financial management leadership in helping to develop and submit grant proposals to foundations, in responding to requests for proposals announced by state and local governments, and in determining fees and establishing client sliding fee schedules and client donation policies.

Program managers heading up revenue centers also become interested in monitoring their programs' revenue streams, usually on a monthly basis. If revenues fall short of expectations, program managers must take steps to help identify new revenue sources or they must put on their other hat as the program managers of expense centers and take steps to control and reduce expenses.

Being designated as a revenue center means that program managers are asked to take financial responsibility for assisting the larger agency in generating sufficient revenues to adequately fund their programs.

Profit Centers

Some programs designated as revenue centers are also designated as profit centers. As the name suggests, programs designated as profit centers, as well as their program managers, are held financially accountable for generating revenues in excess of expenses (earning a profit). In reality, many human service programs generate revenues in excess of expenses. Take the case of many visiting nurse service programs. It is not unusual for a visiting nurse service to divide its clientele between full-pay patients and partial-pay patients. The service price charged to full-pay patients generally covers the full cost of care plus a little something extra. The little something extra, the excess revenue over expenses (the profit), is then used to offset the cost of providing care to partial-pay clients. From a financial management perspective, what these visiting nurse service programs are really doing is creating a *de facto* program structure and designating one program (the one that provides services to full-pay patients) as a profit center that is expected to generate revenues in excess of expenses.

Not all human service programs are candidates for designation as profit centers, but many may well be. Designation as a profit center means that program managers are being asked to become more entrepreneurial and businesslike in their thinking and actions.

Investment Centers

An investment center is a program that manages the endowment, investments, and other assets of an agency. In many human service agencies, the management of agency endowment, investments, and other assets is the responsibility of the board of directors, the executive director, the finance person, or perhaps a committee representing all of these people. Many human service agencies are too small in terms of endowment, investments, or other assets to warrant the creation of an investment center. However, if a human service agency has sizable assets, it might well benefit from having the responsibility placed in the hands of a trained professional on a full-time or part-time basis. This trained professional, the program manager, would be financially responsible for earning a reasonable rate of return on the agency's endowment, investments, and other assets while safeguarding the principal.

Multiple-Responsibility Centers

An individual program can have multiple responsibility center designations. All programs should be designated as expense centers. Some programs can be designated as both expense and revenue centers. And still other programs can be designated as expense, revenue, and profit centers. It is not uncommon for a program designated as an investment center to also be designated as an expense center, a revenue center, and a profit center.

Summary

The identification of a human service agency's programs, the creation of a program structure, the assignment of program managers, and the designation of responsibility centers are the basic building blocks of financial management. The Miami Cuban-American Service Center case study that follows emphasizes this point.

EXERCISE 2.1

The Miami Cuban-American Service Center was founded in 1962 as a place for older Cuban Americans to meet and socialize. Over the years the agency became increasingly involved in providing human services and other support activities. The agency expanded to include the operation of three senior centers and one adult day care center.

In the 1980s, the Miami Cuban-American Service Center also became involved in the operation of a child day care center. In addition to providing a much-needed service to the community, the child day care center provided volunteer opportunities for older Cuban Americans and provided a bridge between the oldest and the youngest members of the community. A few years later, the agency also began sponsoring a federal Head Start program. By the late 1990s, the annual operating budget of the agency had grown to nearly $6 million. Agency revenues are derived from a variety of public and private sources.

On December 31, 20XX, the former executive director of the agency retired. The new executive director, a woman with an MSW degree and several years of experience working for the City of Miami's Department of Human Services, came on board on January 1, 20XX. She quickly discovered that when it came to the financial management of the agency, all responsibility was centralized in her office. The former executive director had directly handled the agency's finances including budget preparation and monitoring and had even handled the agency's endowment fund.

The new executive director decides that for the long-term fiscal health of the organization, more agency administrators need to become involved in the financial management of the center. She informs the agency staff that it is her intention to create a program structure for the center, assign a program manager to each program, and designate the programs as responsibility centers.

Assignment

You have been appointed by the new executive director to chair a committee of agency administrators charged with (1) conducting an inventory of the agency's various services and activities, (2) recommending a program structure, and (3) recommending responsibility center designations for each program. The committee has completed an inventory of agency services and activities (see the following list), including the number of clients served and an approximation of annual expenditures. Based on this inventory, the committee must now make a recommendation to the executive director on a program structure and the designation of responsibility centers. As chairman, what will be your committee's recommendation? How many programs will be in your program structure? What are they? What is the rationale for each program? What type of responsibility center designation (expense, revenue, profit, investment) will you assign to each program?

Inventory of Services and Activities
The Miami Cuban-American Service Center

Senior Services

The agency operates four facilities including three senior centers and one adult day care center. The three senior centers provide a hot noon meal, socialization and recreation services, and transportation to and from the facilities. About 250 seniors are served each week at the three senior centers. The combined total operating costs for all three senior centers are about $3,500,000 annually. The funding sources include the local area agency on aging, the United Way, the City of Miami, donations from the seniors themselves, and some endowment income.

The adult day care center provides the same services as the senior centers (hot noon meal, socialization and recreation, and transportation), but because of the frail nature of most clients, the facility also provides health services including routine physician screening and administration of medications under the supervision of a registered nurse. The adult day care center can serve a maximum of 40 clients a day; many clients attend five days per week. The annual budget is approximately $500,000. The major sources of revenue for the adult day center are payments from insurance companies and managed care companies plus fees from family members. The adult day care center also derives revenue from two small government contracts and as well as some revenue from the endowment fund.

Children's Services

The agency operates two child care facilities. One facility is exclusively funded by the federal Head Start program. The other facility, a regular child day care center, is funded by a combination of city contracts and private donations. Some endowment income goes to both facilities. The combined cost of operating both facilities is estimated to be about $1,500,000 per year.

The children served in the Head Start facility must be from low-income families. The children served in the other day care facility come from families with higher incomes including some families that pay the full cost of care themselves. The two facilities serve a combined total of 150 children per school year: 75 children at each center in classes of 25 children each. In addition to traditional preschool activities, a hot noon meal and transportation to and from the center is provided for children at both facilities. Children in the Head Start program also receive dental and health services and their parents participate in structured parent involvement activities.

Endowment

The agency's endowment fund stands at $22 million.

3 Understanding Financial Statements

A variety of fiscal reports and documents exist that assist in the financial management of a human service agency or program. These include budget formats, revenue projections, monthly and quarterly expense reports, bank statements, and funding source reports. One particular class of fiscal reports is called *financial statements*. The purpose of financial statements is to provide a comprehensive overview of the financial condition of a human service agency. The review and analysis of a human service agency's financial statements can provide important insights into its operations, management, and fiscal health.

Financial statements have several classes of end users including human service administrators, members of an agency's board of directors, funding sources, and the general public. The ability to review and analyze financial statements is a critically important skill for human service administrators. Human service administrators need to be aware at all times of the fiscal health of their agencies in order to make informed management decisions. Members of the board of directors of private nonprofit human service agencies frequently review the financial statements as part of their fiduciary responsibility to safeguard the financial resources of the agency. Government and private funding sources as well as the general public also may from time to time review financial statements to discern if agencies are utilizing their resources in furtherance of their missions and their private nonprofit organizational status.

In this chapter we will discuss several types of financial statements as well as their purposes, content, and appearance. The focus of this chapter is on the financial statements of private nonprofit human service agencies. If one knows how to read and interpret the financial statements of private nonprofit human service agencies, then this understanding can be applied to the analysis of the financial statements of government agencies. Before proceeding with the discussion of financial statements, some prepatory comments are in order concerning generally accepted accounting principles and Internal Revenue Service status.

Generally Accepted Accounting Principles (GAAP)

Generally accepted accounting principles (GAAP) are basic sets of rules governing how the financial books and records of an organization are to be maintained; how revenues, expenditures, and expenses are to be accounted for; and how financial statements are to be prepared. A private nonprofit human service agency's financial statements are reviewed as part of a financial audit. The auditors comment on the extent to which the financial statements are prepared in accordance with GAAP and note any deviations (see Chapter 15).

Generally accepted accounting principles for both for-profit organizations and private nonprofit organizations are established by an organization called the Financial Accounting Standards Board (FASB). GAAP for state and local governments are set by a different organization, the Governmental Accounting Standards Board (GASB). Finally, GAAP for the federal government is established by the Financial Accounting Standards Advisory Board (FASAB). While coordination between these three standard-setting boards does take place, GAAP for governments, for-profit businesses, and private nonprofit organizations are not always in accord.

Internal Revenue Service (IRS) Status

The Internal Revenue Service (IRS) recognizes several classifications of nonprofit organizations (see Figure 3.1). Nonprofit organizations recognized by the IRS are referred to as "exempt" because they do not pay federal income taxes on their earnings. Designation by the IRS as a 501(c)(3) nonprofit charitable organization, a special class of nonprofit organization, is the most highly sought after status. Charitable contributions made to 501(c)(3) nonprofit organizations are usually tax deductible to the donor for federal income tax purposes.

FIGURE 3.1   Internal Revenue Service Classification of Nonprofit Organizations (Partial Listing)

501(c)(1)	Corporations organized under an Act of Congress
501(c)(2)	Title-holding corporations
501(c)(3)	Charitable and religious
501(c)(4)	Social welfare
501(c)(5)	Labor and agriculture organizations
501(c)(6)	Business leagues
501(c)(7)	Social and recreational clubs
501(c)(8)	Fraternal beneficiary societies
501(c)(9)	Voluntary employees' beneficiary associations
501(c)(10)	Domestic fraternal beneficiary societies
501(c)(11)	Teachers' retirement funds
501(c)(12)	Benevolent life insurance associations
501(c)(13)	Cemetery companies
501(c)(14)	State-chartered credit unions
501(c)(15)	Mutual insurance companies

Source: U.S. Department of the Treasury (1998b).

Section 501(c)(3) of the Internal Revenue Code defines a nonprofit organization as one that is not intended to provide any monetary gain for its members, directors, or officers as a result of its operations except for reasonable compensation including salaries for services rendered. To receive the 501(c)(3) status, a nonprofit corporation must file certain paperwork with the IRS and meet the following tests. First, the nonprofit corporation must be organized exclusively for a charitable purpose as stated in its articles of incorporation. Second, none of the earnings of the nonprofit corporation can go to any director, officer, or other individual. Third, the nonprofit corporation must not attempt "to influence legislation as a substantial part of its activities and it may not participate at all in campaign activity for or against political candidates." (U.S. Department of the Treasury, 1998a:1). Fourth, upon dissolution of the nonprofit corporation, any remaining assets must be transferred to another 501(c)(3) private nonprofit organization (U.S. Department of the Treasury, 1998a).

A widely held myth is that a private nonprofit human service agency cannot make a profit. Any nonprofit organization, including those with IRS 501(c)(3) designations, can have an "excess of revenues over expenses" (a profit), but the excess revenues must be used in furtherance of the agency's mission. Any human service agency that does otherwise runs the risk of being penalized by the IRS and perhaps even having its 501(c)(3) status revoked.

Having completed our short detour to cover the topics of GAAP and IRS status, let's now return to the main topic of this chapter, financial statements.

Financial Statements

As just noted, the Financial Accounting Standards Board establishes generally accepted accounting principles for private nonprofit organizations. One of the FASB's many rules, statement of financial accounting standard (SFAS) No. 117, requires that all private nonprofit organizations periodically prepare what it refers to as "general purpose external financial statements." For the sake of brevity we will adopt the term *financial statements*. For FASB purposes, financial statements must be prepared at least once each fiscal year and must be reflective of the organization's overall financial activities in their entirety during that fiscal year. Note that for financial management purposes, financial statements can be prepared more frequently (e.g., each fiscal quarter and in some instances perhaps even monthly).

A fiscal year is a period of time (usually twelve months) for which the financial and accounting books and records of an organization are maintained. The fiscal year of the federal government begins on October 1 of each year and ends on September 30. The fiscal years of most state and local governments (cities and counties) run from July 1 to June 30. Private nonprofit agencies, including human service agencies, can usually select any twelve-month period as their fiscal year, but most choose January 1 to December 31 to coincide with the calendar year.

A question frequently asked is Why do these fiscal years differ? The short answer is history and tradition. These varying fiscal years can present financial accounting challenges for private nonprofit human service agencies. For example, a private nonprofit human service agency may keep its financial books and records on a January 1 to December 31 fiscal year, but may have to report to state funding sources on a July 1 to June 30 basis and to federal funding sources on an October 1 to September 30 basis.

Types of Financial Statements

We will discuss five types of financial statements required of private nonprofit organizations (including human service agencies). Four are required by FASB; one is required by the Internal Revenue Service.

Under SFAS No. 117, private nonprofit organizations, including human service agencies, are required to annually prepare (1) a statement of activities, (2) a statement of financial position, and (3) a statement of cash flows. SFAS No. 117 also requires that all voluntary health and welfare organizations, which includes most private nonprofit human service agencies, also prepare (4) a statement of functional expenses by both functional and natural classifications. In addition to the four financial statements required by FASB, the Internal Revenue Service requires that every 501(c)(3) nonprofit organization annually prepare and submit a financial report called the IRS 990 Form.

Phoenix Specialized
Transportation Services (STS)

As an aid in discussing the various types of financial statements, we will use a case example, Phoenix Specialized Transportation Services (Phoenix STS). Phoenix STS is a 501(c)(3) nonprofit corporation that operates two programs: a transportation program and an escort program. Both programs provide transportation services to elderly and disabled clients in need of medical and social services. The transportation program uses paid drivers who operate twelve passenger vans owned by Phoenix STS and transport clients in a group mode. The escort program uses volunteers who transport individual clients requiring more personal assistance. Escorts use their own vehicles and are reimbursed for mileage.

The Statement of Activities

Table 3.1 presents the statement of activities for the Phoenix STS for the fiscal year ended December 31, 20XX. It should be noted that this is only one of several formats that could be used. FASB specifies the content of a statement of activities, but not the

TABLE 3.1   Phoenix Specialized Transportation Services

Statement of Activities
(Profit and Loss Summary)
January 1, 20XX–December 31, 20XX

	Total	Unrestricted	Temporarily Restricted	Permanently Restricted
Revenues				
Operating revenues				
City of Phoenix	$250,000	$240,000	$ 10,000 (a)	
Maricopa County	100,000	100,000		
United Way	50,000	50,000		
Area Agency on Aging	75,000	75,000		
UMTA	90,000		90,000 (b)	
Subtotal	$565,000	$465,000	$100,000	
Other revenues				
Rider donations	30,000	30,000		
Contributions	44,000	34,000		$ 10,000 (c)
Investments	6,000	6,000		
Subtotal	$ 80,000	$ 70,000	$ 0	$ 10,000
Total revenues	$645,000	$535,000	$100,000	$ 10,000
Expenses				
Program services	$378,000			
Supportive services				
Management and general	90,400			
Fund-raising	46,600			
Total expenses	$515,000			
Excess of revenue over expense	$130,000			
Net assets Beginning of year	$343,000	$343,000	$ 0	$ 0
Changes in net assets	$130,000	$ 20,000	$100,000	$ 10,000
Net assets End of year	$473,000	$363,000	$100,000	$ 10,000

Notes: (a) Matching funds for Urban Mass Transportation Administration (UMTA) grant.
(b) UMTA grant for vehicles.
(c) Fund for driver recognition awards.

format. The statement of activities for a private nonprofit human service agency represents an accounting for all agency revenues and expenses for the fiscal year. The statement of activities also includes some additional information required by SFAS No. 117; these additional features will be discussed later. In the world of business, the statement of activities is called the profit and loss summary. Despite the fact that the term *profit* is generally not used in nonprofit accounting, thinking of the statement of activities as a human service agency's profit and loss summary does help put the purpose of this financial statement in perspective. The statement of activities answers the question, Is the agency breaking even, making money, or losing money?

Before delving further into the topic of the statement of activities itself, a few terms need to be defined: *assets, liabilities, net assets, revenue, expenses, expenditures, accounts receivable, accounts payable, cash accounting, accrual accounting, permanently restricted, temporarily restricted,* and *unrestricted.*

Assets

In the language of accounting, *assets* are anything that a private nonprofit organization owns that has economic value. Classes of assets include cash, accounts receivable, equipment, and property.

Liabilities

Liabilities are obligations to pay somebody something, usually in cash.

Net Assets

Net assets are what is left over (if anything) when liabilities are subtracted from assets.

Revenues

Revenues represent an increase in the net assets of a private nonprofit human service agency. Revenues usually take the form of cash coming into the agency. The term *cash* here is used generically to include actual cash, checks, money orders, and so on. Revenues can come from many different sources including, for example, government payments for providing services under contracts and grants, donations, client fees, and third-party payments from insurance companies and managed care firms. However, not all cash that comes into a human service agency constitutes revenue. For example, if a human service agency takes out a loan (say, $15,000), the loan represents cash coming into the agency, but the loan must eventually be paid back so an offsetting liability (a debt) in the amount of $15,000 is also incurred. The $15,000 in cash coming into the agency is offset by the new liability in the amount of $15,000, so the net assets of the human service agency are not increased.

Expenses and Expenditures

Expenses are resources consumed (used up) by a human service agency. *Expenditures* are cash out transactions (cash that goes out of the agency). Expenditures and expenses are not the same thing.

All cash out transactions in a human service agency are expenditures, but not all expenditures are expenses. The difference depends upon whether the expenditure represents resources that are consumed (used up). For example, when a human service agency has a cash out transaction for salaries or wages, the asset (cash) is used up; it goes to the agency's employees. But when an agency purchases a new computer, some office supplies, food for a senior center, or playground equipment for a child care center, the asset (cash) is not used up but rather is exchanged for another type of asset. One can think of transactions of this nature as "asset swaps."

The difference between expenditures and expenses is why accountants depreciate equipment (because the purchase of equipment represents an expenditure, but not an expense), why inventories of supplies are routinely taken (to determine how much of the asset "supplies" has been used up), and why accountants treat some cash out transactions (such as prepaid insurance) in special ways. For example, in the case of a prepaid fire and liability insurance policy covering a building occupied by a human service agency, when the annual premium is paid (let's say the premium is $12,000), it constitutes an expenditure but not at expense. Why? Because the agency now has a year's worth of insurance coverage. The asset (cash) has not been used up; it has simply taken a new form (prepaid insurance). What usually happens in the case of an expenditure such as prepaid insurance is that the agency accountant would expense one-twelfth ($1,000) each month of the expenditure ($12,000) made for the annual insurance premium.

Accounts Receivable

Accounts receivable are revenues earned by a human service agency, but not yet received. For example, a human service agency provides homemaker/home health aid services under a managed care contract. At the end of the month, the human service agency bills the managed care firm (say $25,000). The service has been provided, the revenue ($25,000) has been earned, but the cash has not been received. Accounts receivable can be thought of as a type of "temporary holding account." The dollar value of the revenue ($25,000) is considered an account receivable. When the actual cash is received, the account receivable ($25,000) is removed.

Accounts Payable

Accounts payable are monies owed by a human service agency to someone else, but not yet paid. For example, a human service agency makes a large purchase of office supplies and is billed (invoiced) by the office supply store for $1,500. The human service agency owes the $1,500 but has not yet paid it. In the language of accounting, the agency has an account payable in the amount of $1,500. Just as accounts receivable can be thought of as a temporary holding account for monies earned but not yet received, accounts payable can be thought of as a temporary holding account for monies owned but not yet paid.

Cash and Accrual Accounting

Cash accounting and *accrual accounting* are the names given to two different methods of keeping the financial books and records of a human service agency. Keeping a human service agency's accounting books and records on a cash accounting basis means that transactions are recognized (recorded) only when cash is received (when revenues are actually received) and only when cash is paid out (when expenses are actually paid).This is a simplistic, yet acceptable, way of keeping an agency's books and records, but it is not the preferred method. The preferred method is accrual accounting. *Accrual accounting* means that transactions are recognized (recorded) when revenues are earned and when expenses are incurred.

The differences between cash and accrual accounting can perhaps best be appreciated by referring back to the concepts of accounts receivable and accounts payable. Under the cash accounting method, a private nonprofit human service agency would not have any accounts receivable or accounts payable because these types of accounts would not exist. Only cash in and cash out transactions are recognized (recorded) under cash accounting. It doesn't take much imagination to understand why accrual accounting is preferable to cash accounting. Accrual accounting provides a more complete financial picture of a human service agency. Cash accounting provides only a partial picture. Under cash accounting, one never knows what revenue or expense "surprises" may be lurking about that will not be discovered until a cash in or cash out transaction occurs. For purposes of the discussions and exercises in this chapter and others, we will assume the use of accrual accounting.

Now that these definitions have been covered, we can return to the discussion of the statement of activities shown in Table 3.1.

Revenues can be classified in several ways. In the statement of activities shown in Table 3.1, revenues are divided into two classes: "operating" and "other." The idea here is to separate revenues that are earned as a result of program operations from nonoperating revenues (e.g., donations, contributions, and interest income). Using this approach, the category of "operating" revenue closely resembles the definition of revenue used in for-profit accounting.

In addition to presenting all revenues and expenses, SFAS No. 117 also requires that the statement of activities include information about changes in net assets and that revenues be separated into three categories: (1) permanently restricted, (2) temporarily restricted, and (3) unrestricted. The purpose of separating revenues into these three categories is to provide information on the extent to which funding sources and donors have placed restrictions on the purposes for which revenues can be used.

Permanently Restricted

As the category names implies, *permanently restricted* means that a revenue has permanent restrictions placed on its use. For example, consider the situation where a wealthy benefactor makes a large cash donation to a private nonprofit child day care center with the stipulation that the funds be invested and that only the investment income can be spent. This type of donation is quite common and represents a situation where the revenue (the donation) is permanently restricted.

Temporarily Restricted

Temporarily restricted means that a revenue has requirements that will eventually be satisfied. For example, a corporation might make a contribution to the same child day care center for the purchase of new playground equipment. When the playground equipment is purchased and installed, the temporarily imposed restriction has been satisfied.

Unrestricted

Unrestricted means that a revenue has no funding source or donor-imposed restrictions. The category of unrestricted revenue is the default category. If no temporary or permanent restrictions apply to a revenue, than by default it is considered unrestricted. Most revenues earned from providing services under government contracts and grants as well as revenues from fee-for-service arrangements with managed care firms and insurance companies as well as revenues from full-pay and partial-pay clients are generally treated as unrestricted revenues.

Returning to Table 3.1, we see that the statement of activities for Phoenix STS provides a comprehensive overview of the agency's revenues and expenses for the fiscal year. The agency had $645,000 in total revenues consisting of $565,000 in operating revenues and $80,000 in other, nonoperating revenues. Revenues in the amount of $535,000 were unrestricted. Revenues of $100,000 are temporarily restricted for purposes of purchasing new vehicles. And revenues in the amount of $10,000 are permanently restricted to provide recognition awards to volunteer drivers.

Total expenses for the fiscal year were $515,000. It should be noted that according to SFAS No. 117, all expenses are reported under the category of unrestricted. Expenses are separated into three categories: (1) program services and supportive services, which in turn is composed of two subcategories: (2) management and general and (3) fund-raising. The purpose of separating expenses into these three categories goes back to the accounting view of the purpose of nonprofit organizations: to operate programs. By separating expenses into these three categories, it becomes readily apparent what proportion of a private nonprofit human service agency's total expenses was for program services and what proportion was expended for administration (management and general) and fund-raising. For the fiscal year, Phoenix STS expenses included $378,000 for programs, $90,400 for management and general, and $46,600 for fund-raising. For the fiscal year, Phoenix STS had an excess of revenues over expenses in the amount of $130,000.

SFAS No. 117 also requires that the statement of activities include information about changes in net assets. As Table 3.1 illustrates, at the beginning of the fiscal year Phoenix STS had assets of $343,000, all of which were unrestricted. With the increase of revenues over expenses, Phoenix STS had an increase in assets of $130,000 ($20,000 in unrestricted revenues, $100,000 in temporarily restricted revenues, and $10,000 in permanently restricted revenues). The agency ended the fiscal year with net assets of $473,000 ($363,000 unrestricted, $100,000 temporarily restricted, and $10,000 permanently restricted).

The Statement of Financial Position

Table 3.2 presents the statement of financial position for Phoenix STS for the fiscal year ended December 31, 20XX. Again, FASB specifies the content but not a particular format. The *statement of financial position* (also called the *balance sheet*) is a summary statement of the assets, liabilities, and net assets of a private nonprofit human service agency on the last day of the fiscal year. It should be noted that the statement of financial position can be prepared to cover any accounting period (e.g., month, fiscal quarter). We are using the fiscal year here because this is the minimum standard under SFAS No. 117. The statement of financial position is sometimes referred to as "snapshot" because it shows assets, liabilities, and net assets for one day in the life of a human service agency (the end of the fiscal year or the end of the accounting period). The purpose of the statement of financial position is to identify all assets and all liabilities and to determine if there is anything left over (net assets). The statement of financial position answers the question, What is the overall financial position of the agency?

We again need to define a few terms (*the basic accounting formula, current assets, noncurrent assets, current liabilities, noncurrent liabilities,* and *fixed assets*) before proceeding.

The Basic Accounting Formula

The basic accounting formula (net assets = assets – liabilities) is used to determine what might be called the net worth of a private nonprofit human service agency. To make a comparison, when an individual applies for a loan (let's say a home mortgage), the bank usually requires the submission of a statement of net worth. The statement of net worth identifies everything of value that a person owns (cash, automobiles, stocks and bonds, etc.) and the value of all the person's debts (car

TABLE 3.2   **Phoenix Specialized Transportation Services**

Statement of Financial Position
(Balance Sheet)
December 31, 20XX

	Assets
Current Assets	
Cash (unrestricted)	$ 47,000
Accounts receivable	25,000 (a)
Prepaid expenses	5,000
	$ 77,000
Noncurrent Assets	
Cash (restricted)	$100,000 (b)
Investments	148,000 (c)
Vehicles	160,000 (d)
Other equipment	25,000 (d)
	$433,000
Total Assets	$510,000
Liabilities and Net Assets	
Current Liabilities	
Accounts payable	$ 37,000
Noncurrent Liabilities	$ 0
Total Liabilities	$ 37,000
Net Assets	
Unrestricted	$363,000
Temporarily restricted	100,000 (b)
Permanently restricted	10,000 (e)
Total Net Assets	$473,000
Total Liabilities and Net Assets	$510,000

Notes: (a) City of Phoenix.
(b) Urban Mass Transportation Administration grant and matching funds for new vehicles.
(c) Includes $10,000 fund for driver recognition awards.
(d) Less depreciation.
(e) Funds for driver recognition awards.

loans, personal loans, etc.). The difference is called net worth. Net worth can be either positive or negative. If the value of what a person owns (their assets) is greater than the person's debts (their liabilities), then he or she has positive net worth. If a person's debts are greater than what that person owns, then he or she has negative net worth.

Current and Noncurrent Assets and Liabilities

Assets and liabilities are frequently divided into current (short term) and noncurrent (long term). Current assets are cash, accounts receivable, prepaid expenses, and any investments (e.g., savings accounts, money market accounts) that can be readily converted into cash in less than a year. Noncurrent assets are *fixed assets* (land, buildings, and equipment) and investments that are not readily convertible to cash within one year. *Current liabilities* are debts that will become due in less than one year. *Noncurrent liabilities* are debts that will come due in more than one year.

On December 31, 20XX, the last day of the fiscal year, Phoenix STS had total assets of $510,000 comprised of $77,000 in current assets and $433,000 in noncurrent assets. Current assets ($77,000) are further divided into unrestricted cash ($47,000), accounts receivable ($25,000), and prepaid expenses ($5,000). Noncurrent assets ($433,000) are further divided into restricted cash ($100,000), investments ($148,000), vehicles ($160,000), and other equipment ($25,000).

On the last day of the fiscal year, Phoenix STS had total liabilities in the amount of $37,000, which were composed entirely of accounts payable. Finally, on the last day of the fiscal year, Phoenix STS had total net assets of $473,000 comprised of $373,000 (unrestricted), $100,000 (temporarily restricted), and $10,000 (permanently restricted) so total liabilities and net assets totaled $510,000. Note that the basic accounting formula is in balance:

$$\text{Net assets} = \text{Assets} - \text{Liabilities}$$
$$\$473,000 = \$510,000 - \$37,000$$

The Statement of Cash Flows

Table 3.3 presents a statement of cash flows for Phoenix STS for the fiscal year ended December 31, 20XX. Again, a statement of cash flows can follow various formats as FASB does not specify any one particular type.

The statement of cash flows provides (a) an accounting of the cash that came into and went out of a private nonprofit human service agency during the fiscal year or other accounting period and (b) identifies how much uncommitted cash (cash that is not restricted for specific purposes) the agency has. The purpose of the statement of cash flows is to determine if a private nonprofit human service agency is generating sufficient cash to meet its current operating expenses.

In addition to preparing a retrospective statement of cash flows at the end of the fiscal year or other accounting period, many private nonprofit human service agencies prepare a prospective statement of cash flows (called a *cash flow forecast*) on a quarterly or even monthly basis. The cash flow forecast looks ahead one or more months in an attempt to estimate if the cash that will be coming into the agency will be greater than, equal to, or less than the cash going out. In other words, the cash flow forecast seeks to answer the question, Can the agency pay its bills when they come due?

TABLE 3.3   Phoenix Specialized Transportation Services

Statement of Cash Flows
January 1, 20XX–December 31, 20XX

Cash on hand January 1		$ 25,000
Increases in Cash		$620,000
Investing	$ 6,000 (a)	
Financing	110,000 (b)	
Operating	504,000	
	$620,000	
Decreases in Cash		$598,000
Investing	$110,000 (b)	
Financing	0	
Operating	488,000	
	$598,000	
Net increase (Decrease) in Cash		$ 22,000
Cash on hand December 31		$ 47,000

Notes: (a) Interest income.
    (b) Offsetting entries to account for restricted donations of $100,000 for vehicles and $10,000 for driver recognition awards.

According to the statement of cash flows example shown in Table 3.3, Phoenix STS had $25,000 cash on hand on January 1, the beginning of the fiscal year. During the fiscal year, the agency had an inflow of cash in the amount of $620,000. SFAS Rules No. 117 and No. 95 require that both increases and decreases in cash be subdivided into three categories: (1) *investing activities*, (2) *financing activities*, and (3) *operating activities*. Operating activities is the default category; any increase or decrease in cash that is not due to investing or financing is accounted for in the category of operating activities. In terms of increases in cash, Phoenix STS had $6,000 from investing, $110,000 from financing, and $504,000 from operating. The $6,000 came from interest earned on investments. The $110,000 came in the form of restricted donations for vehicles ($100,000) and for driver recognitions awards ($10,000). The $504,000 came from program operations including various government and private contracts, donations, and contributions. During the fiscal year, Phoenix STS had decreases in cash totaling $598,000 comprised of $110,000 in investing and $488,000 in operating. It should be noted that the definition of *operating* used in the statement of cash flows is not the same as the definition of *operating* used in the statement of activities (Table 3.1).

The two $110,000 items in the statement of cash flows (see note *b* to Table 3.3) require some additional explanation. SFAS No. 117 requires that cash received with a donor restriction be treated in a special fashion. In the Phoenix STS statement of cash flows, the $100,000 in funds to be used to purchase new vehicles and the $10,000 for driver recognition awards is reported (per American Institute of Certified Public Accountants guidance), as both an increase in cash from financing activities and simultaneously as a decrease in cash from investing (AICPA, 1998:45). The net effect of this action is to subtract the $110,000 in committed cash from the final computation of Phoenix STS's cash availability. Were it not for this action, the "cash on hand as of December 31" would include the $110,000 in restricted donations. But the $110,000 does not constitute cash available to Phoenix STS for general purposes because the two donations are restricted. Therefore, the $110,000 donation is removed from the final calculation of cash on hand at the end of the fiscal year.[1]

For the fiscal year, Phoenix STS had a net overall increase in cash of $22,000. Finally, on December 31, 20XX, Phoenix STS had $47,000 cash on hand, with the caveat that this figure represents unrestricted cash. It should be noted that the $47,000 cash on hand balances with the $47,000 in unrestricted cash on the statement of financial position (Table 3.2). The statement of financial position also shows both the unrestricted cash on hand ($47,000) on December 31 as well as the restricted cash ($110,000) for vehicle purchases and driver recognition awards.

The Statement of Functional Expenses

Table 3.4 presents a statement of functional expenses for Phoenix STS for the fiscal year ended December 31, 20XX.

The statement of functional expenses is the fourth and last type of financial statement required by SFAS No. 117. A statement of functional expenses must be completed annually by all voluntary health and welfare organizations, which includes most private nonprofit human service agencies. SFAS No. 117 requires that the statement of functional expenses present an agency's total expenses for the fiscal year separated out by both functional categories (*programs, management and general,* and *fund-raising*) and by natural categories of expense (e.g., salaries, fringe benefits, and other operating costs such as rent, utilities, supplies, and telephone). When preparing the statement of functional expenses, some human service agencies will also separate out the various categories of expense by type of program.

Table 3.4 is an example of a basic statement of functional expenses. This table is essentially a detailed examination of the expenses of the Phoenix STS that was presented in the statement of activities (Table 3.1). The total expenses (column f) for Phoenix STS for the fiscal year ($515,000) are now separated out by individual programs (columns a and b), functional expense categories (columns c, d, and e), and

---

[1]When restricted funds are expended, they are shown on the statement of cash flows as increases in cash due to investing.

TABLE 3.4   **Phoenix Specialized Transportation Services**

Statement of Functional Expenses
January 1, 20XX–December 31, 20XX

	Transportation Program (a)	Escort Program (b)	Total Program (c)	Management and General (d)	Fund-Raising (e)	Total Expenses (f)
Salaries	$195,000	$20,000	$215,000	$62,000	$32,000	$309,000
Fringe benefits	31,200	3,200	34,400	9,900	5,100	49,400
Rent	15,000	2,000	17,000	3,000	2,000	22,000
Utilities	2,700	300	3,000	1,000	500	4,500
Telephone	3,000	1,000	4,000	2,000	2,000	8,000
Supplies	2,500	500	3,000	1,000	1,000	5,000
Vehicle maintenance	26,000	0	26,000	0	0	26,000
Vehicle depreciation	48,000	0	48,000	0	0	48,000
Escort reimbursement	0	5,000	5,000	0	0	5,000
Other	20,500	2,100	22,600	11,500	4,000	38,100
Total expenses	$343,900	$34,100	$378,000	$90,400	$46,600	$515,000

natural expense categories ("salaries" through "other"). As Table 3.4 illustrates, $309,000 was spent on salaries of which $195,000 was an expense to the transportation program, $20,000 was an expense to the escort program, $62,000 was an expense to management and general, and $32,000 was an expense to fundraising. The statement of functional expenses provides a similar breakdown for each line item (e.g., fringe benefits, rent, utilities). As one might imagine, a statement of functional expenses for a private nonprofit human service agency can provoke considerable discussion among agency staff, the board of directors, clients, and stakeholders about how the agency is using its resources. Note that the total expense figure ($515,00) in the statement of functional expenses (Table 3.4) balances with the total expense figure ($515,000) from the statement of activities (Table 3.1).

The Internal Revenue Service (IRS) Form 990

The last financial statement we are going to look at is the Internal Revenue (IRS) Form 990. Every 501(c)(3) private nonprofit human service agency is required to

Form **990-EZ**

Department of the Treasury
Internal Revenue Service

Short Form
Return of Organization Exempt From Income Tax

Under section 501(c) of the Internal Revenue Code (except black lung benefit trust or private foundation) or section 4947(a)(1) nonexempt charitable trust

► For organizations with gross receipts less than $100,000 and total assets less than $250,000 at the end of the year.

► *The organization may have to use a copy of this return to satisfy state reporting requirements.*

OMB No. 1545-1150

1998

This Form is Open to Public Inspection

A For the 1998 calendar year, OR tax year beginning January 1 **, 1998, and ending** December 31 **, 19**

B Check if:
☐ Change of address
☐ Initial return
☐ Final return
☐ Amended return (required also for state reporting)

Please use IRS label or print or type. See Specific Instructions.

C Name of organization
Palm City Child Day Care Center

Number and street (or P.O. box, if mail is not delivered to street address) | Room/suite
1234 Yellow Brick Road

City or town, state or country, and ZIP + 4
Palm City, Florida 12345

D Employer identification number
12 : 456789

E Telephone number
(000) 123-4567

F Check ► ☐ if exemption application is pending

H Enter four-digit group exemption number (GEN)

G Accounting method: ☐ Cash ☑ Accrual ☐ Other (specify) ►

I Type of organization— ► ☑ Exempt under section 501(c)( ) ◄ (insert number) OR ► ☐ section 4947(a)(1) nonexempt charitable trust

Note: ***Section 501(c)(3) organizations and section 4947(a)(1) nonexempt charitable trusts MUST attach a completed Schedule A (Form 990).***

J Check ► ☐ if the organization's gross receipts are normally not more than $25,000. The organization need not file a return with the IRS; but if the organization received a Form 990 Package in the mail, the organization should file a return without financial data. **Some states require a complete return.**

K Enter the organization's 1998 gross receipts **(add back lines 5b, 6b, and 7b, to line 9)** . . . . . ► $ 67,894.00
If $100,000 or more, the organization must file Form 990 instead of Form 990-EZ.

Part I — Revenue, Expenses, and Changes in Net Assets or Fund Balances (See Specific Instructions on page 30.)

Section	Line	Description	Sub-line	Sub-amount	Line	Amount
Revenue	1	Contributions, gifts, grants, and similar amounts received (attach schedule of contributors)			1	
	2	Program service revenue including government fees and contracts			2	48,926.00
	3	Membership dues and assessments			3	115.00
	4	Investment income			4	377.00
	5a	Gross amount from sale of assets other than inventory	5a			
	b	Less: cost or other basis and sales expenses	5b			
	c	Gain or (loss) from sale of assets other than inventory (line 5a less line 5b) (attach schedule)			5c	
	6	Special events and activities (attach schedule):				
	a	Gross revenue (not including $ ______ of contributions reported on line 1)	6a	18,476.00		
	b	Less: direct expenses other than fundraising expenses	6b	13,907.00		
	c	Net income or (loss) from special events and activities (line 6a less line 6b)			6c	4,569.00
	7a	Gross sales of inventory, less returns and allowances	7a			
	b	Less: cost of goods sold	7b			
	c	Gross profit or (loss) from sales of inventory (line 7a less line 7b)			7c	
	8	Other revenue (describe ► ______)			8	
	9	**Total revenue** (add lines 1, 2, 3, 4, 5c, 6c, 7c, and 8) ►			9	53,978.00
Expenses	10	Grants and similar amounts paid (attach schedule)			10	
	11	Benefits paid to or for members			11	
	12	Salaries, other compensation, and employee benefits			12	43,918.00
	13	Professional fees and other payments to independent contractors			13	
	14	Occupancy, rent, utilities, and maintenance			14	7,472.00
	15	Printing, publications, postage, and shipping			15	2,687.00
	16	Other expenses (describe ► ______)			16	
	17	**Total expenses** (add lines 10 through 16) ►			17	54,077.00
Net Assets	18	Excess or (deficit) for the year (line 9 less line 17)			18	(90.00)
	19	Net assets or fund balances at beginning of year (from line 27, column (A)) (must agree with end-of-year figure reported on prior year's return)			19	18,736.00
	20	Other changes in net assets or fund balances (attach explanation)			20	
	21	Net assets or fund balances at end of year (combine lines 18 through 20) ►			21	18,646.00

Part II — Balance Sheets—If Total assets on line 25, column (B) are $250,000 or more, file Form 990 instead of Form 990-EZ.

Line	(See Specific Instructions on page 34.)	(A) Beginning of year	Line	(B) End of year
22	Cash, savings, and investments	18,736.00	22	18,646.00
23	Land and buildings		23	
24	Other assets (describe ► ______)		24	
25	**Total assets**	18,736.00	25	18,646.00
26	**Total liabilities** (describe ► ______)		26	
27	**Net assets or fund balances** (line 27 of column (B) must agree with line 21)	18,736.00	27	18,646.00

FIGURE 3.2 IRS Form 990-EZ

Statement of Program Service Accomplishments (See Specific Instructions on page 34.)

Expenses
(Required for 501(c)(3) and (4) organizations and 4947(a)(1) trusts; optional for others.)

What is the organization's primary exempt purpose? **Provision of Child Day Care Services**

Describe what was achieved in carrying out the organization's exempt purposes. In a clear and concise manner, describe the services provided, the number of persons benefited, or other relevant information for each program title.

28 Provided 2,500 child care days of service

....

....

(Grants $) | **28a** | 49,325.00

29 ....

....

(Grants $) | **29a**

30 ....

....

(Grants $) | **30a**

31 Other program services (attach schedule) . . . . (Grants $) | **31a**

32 Total program service expenses (add lines 28a through 31a) . . . . ▶ | **32**

List of Officers, Directors, Trustees, and Key Employees (List each one even if not compensated. See Specific Instructions on page 34.)

(A) Name and address	(B) Title and average hours per week devoted to position	(C) Compensation (If not paid, enter -0-.)	(D) Contributions to employee benefit plans & deferred compensation	(E) Expense account and other allowances
Statement Attached				

Other Information (See Specific Instructions on page 35.)

		Yes	No
33	Did the organization engage in any activity not previously reported to the IRS? If "Yes," attach a detailed description of each activity . .		✔
34	Were any changes made to the organizing or governing documents but not reported to the IRS? If "Yes," attach a conformed copy of the changes.		✔
35	If the organization had income from business activities, such as those reported on lines 2, 6, and 7 (among others), but NOT reported on Form 990-T, attach a statement explaining your reason for not reporting the income on Form 990-T.		
a	Did the organization have unrelated business gross income of $1,000 or more or 6033(e) notice, reporting, and proxy tax requirements?		✔
b	If "Yes," has it filed a tax return on **Form 990-T** for this year?		✔
36	Was there a liquidation, dissolution, termination, or substantial contraction during the year? (If "Yes," attach a statement.)		✔
37a	Enter amount of political expenditures, direct or indirect, as described in the instructions. ▶	37a		
b	Did the organization file **Form 1120-POL** for this year?		✔
38a	Did the organization borrow from, or make any loans to, any officer, director, trustee, or key employee OR were any such loans made in a prior year and still unpaid at the start of the period covered by this return?		✔
b	If "Yes," attach the schedule specified in the line 38 instructions and enter the amount involved.	38b		
39	501(c)(7) organizations.—Enter: **a** Initiation fees and capital contributions included on line 9	39a		
b	Gross receipts, included on line 9, for public use of club facilities	39b		
40a	501(c)(3) organizations.—Enter: Amount of tax imposed on the organization during the year under: section 4911 ▶_____ ; section 4912 ▶_____ ; section 4955 ▶_____			
b	501(c)(3) and (4) organizations.—Did the organization engage in any section 4958 excess benefit transaction during the year? If "Yes," attach an explanation.			✔
c	Enter: Amount of tax imposed on the organization managers or disqualified persons during the year under sections 4912, 4955, and 4958 . . . . ▶ _____			
d	Enter: Amount of tax on line 40c, above, reimbursed by the organization . . . . ▶ _____			

41 List the states with which a copy of this return is filed. ▶ **Florida**

42 The books are in care of ▶ **Palm City Child Day Care Services**   Telephone no. ▶ (**000**) **123-4567**

Located at ▶ **1234 Yellow Brick Road** . . . . ZIP + 4 ▶ **12345**

43 Section 4947(a)(1) nonexempt charitable trusts filing Form 990-EZ in lieu of **Form 1041**—Check here ▶ ☐ and enter the amount of tax-exempt interest received or accrued during the tax year . . . ▶ | 43 |

Please Sign Here

Under penalties of perjury, I declare that I have examined this return, including accompanying schedules and statements, and to the best of my knowledge and belief, it is true, correct, and complete. Declaration of preparer (other than officer) is based on all information of which preparer has any knowledge. (See General Instruction U, page 12.)

▶		
Signature of officer	Date	▶ Type or print name and title.

Paid Preparer's Use Only

Preparer's signature ▶		Date	Check if self-employed ▶ ☐	Preparer's SSN
Firm's name (or yours if self-employed) and address ▶			EIN ▶	
			ZIP + 4 ▶	

file this form annually covering its activities for the fiscal year. The IRS Form 990 is simply too long to be displayed here. A copy of the two-page IRS Form 990-EZ is shown instead (see Figure 3.2). The IRS Form 990-EZ can only be used by 501(c)(3) private nonprofit organizations that have less than $100,000 in net assets and had revenues during the fiscal year of less than $25,000.

An examination of the IRS Form 990-EZ reveals that it contains essentially the same information that would be found in an agency's statement of financial activities (profit and loss summary) and statement of financial position (balance sheet). Revenues, expenses, assets, liabilities, and net assets are all shown.

Both the IRS Form 990 and the IRS Form 990-EZ are designed to provide stakeholders with an overview of the fiscal year financial operations of a private nonprofit human service agency. IRS regulations require that all 501(c)(3) nonprofit organizations, including human service agencies, provide copies of their latest IRS Form 990 to anyone who requests one. No charge for the copy,other than for reasonable duplicating expenses, may be made. This public access requirement exists because the Internal Revenue Service does not have the organizational capacity to monitor and evaluate every 501(c)(3) private nonprofit organization, so it hopes to enlist the assistance of stakeholders in providing this oversight function.

Summary

This chapter provided a considerable amount of information regarding the purposes, contents, and formats of financial statements. It also introduced numerous accounting terms. The reader may feel somewhat overwhelmed at this point—not all of the information presented may be clear. In the next chapter, we will discuss the basics of accounting and double entry bookkeeping. As part of this discussion, we will see how an accountant might go about maintaining a human service agency's financial books and records and preparing the financial statements. By taking a second look at the same information, a better understanding of the material will hopefully be achieved.

4 The Basics of Accounting

In the previous chapter we looked at the purposes and content of financial statements. Financial statements are prepared from the accounting books and records maintained by a human service agency. In this chapter, we will discuss the topics of accounting and double entry booking. As part of this discussion, several additional accounting terms will have to be introduced and defined. Through the use of a case study, "The Portland After School Program," we will see how accountants enter various transactions in the journal and the general ledger, how a trial balance is computed, and how a human service agency's financial statements are prepared. With the general availability of relatively low cost computer hardware and software today, the financial books and records of most human service agencies are maintained in electronic format.

Some Basic Accounting Terms

Before beginning our discussion of how a human service agency actually goes about maintaining its financial books and records, a few new accounting terms need to be introduced and defined.

Accounting itself can be defined as the art of recording, classifying, and summarizing the financial transactions of a human service agency (Lohmann, 1980:24).

A *transaction* is any financial activity that causes a change (either an increase or a decrease) in the assets, liabilities, or net assets of a human service agency. A transaction is the basic unit of analysis in accounting.

A *t-account* is an individual financial account maintained by a human service agency. Individual accounts are called t-accounts because they are separated into a debit side and credit side which gives the account the appearance of the letter *T*. Figure 4.1 is an example of a cash t-account that would be used to account for cash coming into and going out of a human service agency.

FIGURE 4.1   The Structure of a t-Account

The Cash t-Account	
(Debit)	(Credit)

Generally, there are five major classes or categories of accounts: assets, liabilities, net assets, revenues, and expenses. Already we can begin to see the relationship between the financial accounts maintained by a human service agency and the preparation of its financial statements. Revenue and expense accounts are used to prepare the statement of activities, while asset, liability, and net asset accounts are used to prepare the statement of financial position (or balance sheet). The cash t-account is used to prepare the statement of cash flows.

The *general ledger* is the name given to the aggregate of all the t-accounts maintained by a human service agency.

The *chart of accounts* is a listing of all the t-accounts in the general ledger. The chart of accounts can be thought of as a sort of table of contents to the general ledger.

A *debit* is any entry made to the left side of any t-account. A *credit* is any entry made to the right side of any t-account. Nonaccountants tend to think that a debit always means something bad, while a credit always means something good. This is not the case. A debit simply means an entry on the left side of any t-account, while a credit simply means an entry on the right side of any t-account, nothing more. A debit always has an offsetting credit and a credit always has an offsetting debit. From this dual nature of debits and credits, we derive the name *double entry bookkeeping*. As Figure 4.2 illustrates, certain general rules apply when you debit or credit an individual t-account.

A debit is used to increase an asset t-account, while a credit is used to decrease it. Liability and net assets accounts are just the reverse. A credit is used to increase liabilities and net assets, while a debit is used to decrease them. In the same vein, a credit increases a revenue account while a debit decreases it and (again just the reverse) a debit increases an expense account, while a credit decreases it.

The *account balance* is the sum of all debits and credits in an individual t-account. Certain general rules also govern the type of balance (debit or credit) that certain accounts maintain. Again referring to Figure 4.2, asset accounts gener-

FIGURE 4.2   General Rules Governing t-Accounts

Account	To Increase	To Decrease	Normal Balance
Asset	Debit	Credit	Debit
Liability	Credit	Debit	Credit
Net assets	Credit	Debit	Credit
Revenue	Credit	Debit	Credit
Expense	Debit	Credit	Debit

Note how the structure of debits and credits helps keep the basic accounting formula in balance (Net assets = Assets − Liabilities).

ally have a debit balance, while liability and net assets accounts generally have a credit balance. In this manner, the double entry booking system is able to maintain the basic accounting formula (net assets = assets – liabilities).

The *trial balance* is the totaling of all the debits and credits in the general ledger accounts at the end of an accounting period. The purpose of the trial balance is to ensure that the totals of all account balances are in balance. Given that every transaction has both a debit and credit, and given that the debit and credit entries for each transaction are equal, therefore the sum of all accounts with debit balances should equal the sum of all accounts with credit balances.

The *journal* is a chronological listing of all transactions. The journal is similar to a diary that some people keep. The journal can be thought of as the financial diary of a human service agency. The journal keeps track of all transactions. The journal identifies the reason for the transaction (e.g., to pay for supplies received, to account for a donation check) and the accounts in the general ledger that were debited and credited as a result of the transaction. Although introduced last, the journal is the first of a human service agency's financial books and records to be affected by a transaction. The journal entry is made first; then the appropriate debits and credits are *posted* to their appropriate t-accounts. One might well ask, Why not just skip the journal and simply post a transaction's debit and credit to the appropriate t-accounts? The response is that the journal helps to minimize posting errors (posting a debit or credit to the wrong t-account). And when posting errors do occur, the journal provides the necessary information to help track down the mistakes and correct them.

With this bit of introduction, we are now ready to see how accountants and bookkeepers actually go about maintaining the financial books and records of a human service agency. To aid us in this exploration, we are going to view a series of transactions from an accountant's perspective. The transactions involve the first six months of operation of a new human service agency called The Portland After School Program. The program is designed as a latch-key program to provide children between the ages of ten and sixteen with a place to go after school to engage in various recreational activities.

The Portland After School Program

The downtown Portland, Oregon, area had been without any type of latch-key program for several years. A boys club did exist several years ago, but the club moved to the suburbs. Budget cutbacks at the Portland Unified School District precluded any funding for an after-school program. However, the school district did say that if the operating funds for a latch-key program could be generated by the community, the district would allow the use of the gymnasium at one of its centrally located elementary schools to serve as the program site. The school district would not charge for the space, but the program would have to pay for the costs of utilities and would also need to have an insurance policy covering the program as well as the school district as an additional co-insured.

The downtown business community, the city government, and the local United Way all said they would support the program financially. A private nonprofit corporation was created under the laws of the State of Oregon. Designation as a 501(c)(3) nonprofit organization was secured from the Internal Revenue Service. An executive director was hired and the center began operations on January 1, 20XX.

On January 1, the executive director hands the agency's accountant, a volunteer certified public accountant (CPA), three unrestricted donation checks: $50,000 from the Downtown Portland Chamber of Commerce, $25,000 from the Portland United Way, and $25,000 from the City of Portland. The accountant makes three entries—(a), (b), and (c) —in the journal (see Table 4.1) and then posts the debits and credits to their appropriate t-accounts (see Table 4.2). For all three transactions, the cash account is debited and the revenue account is credited. The cash account is debited because cash is coming into the agency and because a debit increases the cash account. The revenue account is credited because the donations, or cash, increase the agency's net assets.

The executive director purchases a $1,000,000 fire-and-accident insurance policy covering the program and the school district at a semiannual cost of $9,000. The accountant makes an entry (d) in the journal (Table 4.1) and posts the debit and credit to their appropriate t-accounts (Table 4.2). The cash account is credited $9,000 because cash is going out of the agency, and the prepaid insurance account is debited because the agency now has six months of insurance. The payment of the $9,000 is an example of an expenditure that is not an expense. Both the cash account and the prepaid insurance account are asset accounts. The asset cash in the amount of $9,000 is not used up; it is simply swapped for another type of asset, prepaid insurance. If the $9,000 payment had been an expense (if the assets had been used up), the expense account would be debited rather than the prepaid insurance account.

Next the executive director purchases $2,500 (e) worth of recreational equipment (e.g., basketballs, baseballs, gloves, bats, footballs, volleyballs, and numerous games) and $2,500 (f) worth of arts and crafts supplies. The accountant has to pause and think for a moment about these transactions. Equipment and supplies are also usually treated as an asset swap. The asset cash in swapped for other types of assets: equipment and supplies. Equipment is usually depreciated over its useful life and supplies are usually carried in inventory and expensed when they are used up. However, the recreation equipment consists of multiple items of minor cost that do not meet the definition of fixed assets (e.g., land and equipment with a useful life of more than one year). The accountant decides to treat the purchase of recreation equipment as an expense and the purchase of supplies as an expenditure. Consequently, the accountant records the two transactions (e) and (f) in the journal (Table 4.1) and posts the debits and credits to their appropriate t-accounts (Table 4.2). For the equipment transaction, the cash account is credited in the amount of $2,500 because the agency's cash is reduced and the expense account is debited in the amount of $2,500 because the resource cash is considered used up. In the case of the supplies transaction, the cash account is again credited in the amount of $2,500, but this time the supplies account is debited in the amount of $2,500 because the supplies are not considered used up.

TABLE 4.1   Journal of the Portland After School Program

January 1, 20XX–June 30, 20XX

(a) January 1, 20XX—Received unrestricted donation check in the amount of $50,000 from the Downtown Portland Chamber of Commerce.

  Debited *Cash* $50,000
  Credited *Revenue* $50,000

(b) January 1, 20XX—Received unrestricted donation check in the amount of $25,000 from the Portland United Way.

  Debited *Cash* $25,000
  Credited *Revenue* $25,000

(c) January 1, 20XX—Received unrestricted donation check in the amount of $25,000 from the City of Portland.

  Debited *Cash* $25,000
  Credited *Revenue* $25,000

(d) January 10, 20XX—Paid Great Northwest Insurance Company $9,000 for six months of fire and liability insurance coverage.

  Debited *Prepaid Insurance* $ 9,000
  Credited *Cash* $ 9,000

(e) January 15, 20XX—Paid Oregon Sporting Goods $2,500 for recreational equipment.

  Debited *Expense* $ 2,500
  Credited *Cash* $ 2,500

(f) January 15, 20XX—Paid Portland Arts & Crafts Company $2,500 for craft and art supplies.

  Debited *Arts & Crafts Supplies* $ 2,500
  Credited *Cash* $ 2,500

(g) June 30, 20XX—Received fees from parents in the amount of $35,000.

  Debited *Cash* $35,000
  Credited *Revenue* $35,000

(h) June 30, 20XX—To account for $1,750 in fees earned, but not yet collected.

  Debited *Accounts Receivable* $ 1,750
  Credited *Revenue* $ 1,750

(i) June 30, 20XX—Received from Mr. Anonymous a temporarily restricted donation check in the amount of $10,000.

  Debited *Cash* $10,000
  Credited *Revenue* $10,000

(j) June 30, 20XX—Transferred temporarily restricted donation in the amount of $10,000 to investments.

  Debited *Investments* $10,000
  Credited *Cash* $10,000

(continued)

TABLE 4.1   Continued

(k) June 30, 20XX—Paid Portland Gas & Electric Company $6,000 for utilities.

    Debited *Expense* $ 6,000

    Credited *Cash* $ 6,000

(l) June 30, 20XX—Paid salaries and employee-related expenses in the amount of $50,000.

    Debited *Expense* $50,000

    Credited *Cash* $50,000

(m) June 30, 20XX—Paid Pacific Bell Telephone Company $500 for telephone services.

    Debited *Expense* $ 500

    Credited *Cash* $ 500

(n) June 30, 20XX—To account for monies owed, but not yet paid, to John's Deli.

    Debited *Expense* $ 1,500

    Credited *Accounts Payable* $ 1,500

(o) June 30, 20XX—To expense prepaid insurance in the amount of $9,000.

    Debited *Expense* $ 9,000

    Credited *Prepaid Insurance* $ 9,000

(p) June 30, 20XX—To expense arts and crafts supplies in the amount of $2,000.

    Debited *Expense* $ 2,000

    Credited *Arts and Crafts Supplies* $ 2,000

Now we are going to fudge a bit and jump ahead to the end of the first six months of operation of the Portland After School Program. Let's look at some summary transactions. It is important to note that each of these transactions would actually comprise several smaller transactions that would properly be accounted for when they occurred. We are dealing with these transactions in the aggregate here simply for the sake of convenience and simplicity. By the end of the first six months of operation, the agency has collected a total of $35,000 (g) in fees from the parents of children who participate in the program. Note that the $35,000 figure represents full-fee–paying parents as well as some partial-fee–paying clients. Additionally, some children from low-income and poor families also attend the program at no cost. The agency is also owed an additional $1,750 (h) in fees by parents. Just before the end of the first six months of operation, the agency is also awarded a $10,000 (i) (j) grant from a local foundation. The purpose of the grant is to purchase additional arts and crafts supplies when they are needed.

By the end of the first six months of operation, the agency has also paid the following bills: $6,000 (k) for utilities, $50,000 (l) in salaries and employee-related expenses for the executive director and the center's part-time recreation and arts/ crafts aides, and $500 (m) for telephone expenses. Additionally, the agency owes $1,500 (n) to a food service company that supplies drinks and snacks to the pro-

TABLE 4.2   Portland After School Program General Ledger (Posting)

Cash		Net Assets
(a) $50,000 (d) $ 9,000		
(b) 25,000 (e) 2,500		
(c) 25,000 (f) 2,500		
(g) 35,000 (j) 10,000		
(i) 10,000 (k) 6,000		
(l) 50,000		
(m) 500		

Prepaid Insurance
(d) $ 9,000   (o) $ 9,000

Arts and Crafts Supplies		Investments
(f) $ 2,500 (p) $ 2,000		(j) $10,000

Accounts Receivable		Accounts Payable
(h) $ 1,750		(n) $1,500

Revenue		Expense
(a) $50,000		(e) $ 2,500
(b) 25,000		(k) 6,000
(c) 25,000		(l) 50,000
(g) 35,000		(m) 500
(h) 1,750		(n) 1,500
(i) 10,000		(o) 9,000
		(p) 2,000

gram. Finally, adjustments need to be made to both the prepaid insurance account (o) and to the supplies account (p).

The accountant now has to deal with each of these transactions. A journal entry (g) is made concerning the $35,000 fees collected (Table 4.1) and the debit and credit posted to their appropriate t-accounts (Table 4.2). The cash account is debited $35,000 because cash is coming into the agency; the revenue account is credited $35,000 because these funds represent an increase in the agency's assets. To account for the $1,700 in fees earned but not yet collected, a journal entry (h) is made (Table 4.1). The accounts receivable account (Table 4.2) is debited in the amount of $1,750 and the revenue account is credited in the amount of $1,700 because all revenues (those collected as well as those not yet collected) must be accounted for in the period in which they are earned.

Accounting for the $10,000 restricted donation requires two transactions (i and j). First, the accountant makes an entry (i) in the journal (Table 4.1) identifying the donation. The cash account is then debited (Table 4.2) because cash is coming into the agency and the revenue account is credited because the cash represents an increase in the agency's assets. Second, the accountant makes an additional entry (j) in the journal (Table 4.1), transferring the $10,000 donation to the investment account. The cash account is then credited (Table 4.2) because the $10,000 is taken out and the investment account is debited because the $10,000 is now placed in this account. The purpose of this second transaction is to take the temporarily restricted $10,000 donation out of the cash account (per the requirements of SFAS No. 117 as explained in Chapter 3) so that temporarily restricted and permanently restricted cash are not commingled with unrestricted cash.

To account for the series of bills that have to be paid, the accountant makes the appropriate journal entries (Table 4.1) and posts the debits and credits to their appropriate t-accounts (Table 4.2). For the utilities transaction (k), the cash account is credited $6,000 because cash is paid out; the offsetting debit goes to the expense account because the $6,000 resource is now consumed (used up). For the salaries and employee-related expenses transaction (l), the cash account is again credited in the amount of $50,000 because cash is being paid out again and the expense account is again debited in the amount of $50,000 because the resources represented by the $50,000 are again consumed (used up). In the same vein, for the telephone transaction (m), the cash account is again credited ($500) because cash is paid out and the expense account is again debited ($500) because the resource is consumed (used up).

The $1,500 owed to the food service supplier (n) represents an accounts payable situation. The money is owed, but not yet paid. The accountant makes the journal entry (Table 4.1) and posts the debits and credits to the appropriate t-accounts (Table 4.2). The expense account is debited $1,500 because the expense must be recognized in the accounting period in which it is incurred even though the actual cash has not yet been paid out. The offsetting credit in the amount of $1,500 goes to the accounts payable account.

The final two transactions are designed to update the prepaid insurance account and the arts and crafts supplies account. The agency had prepaid insurance in the amount of $9,000 for a period of six months, but the six months have now passed. The resource prepaid insurance is now consumed (used up). The accountant makes an entry (o) in the journal (Table 4.1) and posts the debit and credit to their appropriate t-accounts (Table 4.2). The expense account is debited $9,000 because the resource prepaid insurance is now consumed (used up) and the prepaid insurance account is credited in the amount of $9,000. Note that the prepaid insurance account now has zero balance, because the original $9,000 debit is now offset by a $9,000 credit. An inventory is taken and the executive director discovers that only about $500 worth of arts and crafts supplies are still left. The accountant must adjust the arts and crafts supplies account accordingly. A journal entry (p) is made (Table 4.1) and the debit and credit are posted to their appropriate t-accounts (Table 4.2). The arts and crafts supplies account is credited $2,000 and the expense account is debited in the amount of $2,000. The $2,000 credit to the arts and crafts supplies account has the net effect of reducing the amount in this asset account to $500. The reason why the offsetting debit goes to the expense account is that $2,000 of arts and crafts supplies are now considered used up and thus net assets are reduced. Under the accrual accounting concept, all expenses must be accounted for during the term in which they are incurred.

Computing the Trial Balance

Now that all the transactions have been recorded in the journal and the general ledger, the accountant can compute a trial balance. The purpose of the trial balance is to determine if the sums of all account balances are themselves in balance. Since every debit has an offsetting credit and vice versa, if you sum all the accounts with debit balances and all the accounts with credit balances, then the results should be the same. If the sums do not balance, then clearly a journal or posting error has been made. However, even if the sums do balance, journal or posting errors could still exist. We will leave the finer aspects of this point to the care of the accountants and auditors.

The first task the accountant performs is to derive the *account balance* for each account. This task is accomplished by summing the debits and credits in each account and then subtracting one side (the side with the lower amount) from the other side. Let's look at the cash account (Table 4.3). The cash account has five debit entries totaling $145,000 and seven credit entries totaling $80,500. The lower side (the credit side) is subtracted from the higher side (the debit side). The result is that the cash account has a debit balance of $64,500. The balances for all accounts are derived (Table 4.3) and the totals transferred to the trial balance (see Table 4.4). As Table 4.4 points out, the trail balance does in fact balance. The total of all accounts with debit balances is $148,250 and the total of all accounts with credit balances is $148,250.

Closing the Revenue and Expense Accounts

Unlike the other accounts in the general ledger, the revenue and expense accounts do not have balances that carry over from one fiscal year or accounting period to the next fiscal year or accounting period. This procedure helps ensure that revenues and expenses are accounted for only one time. At the end of each fiscal year or accounting period, the revenue and expense accounts are closed and the balances transferred to the net assets account (see Table 4.5).

Remembering our definitions of revenue (an increase in net assets) and expense (a decrease in net assets), if the balances in the revenue and expense accounts are closed out and transferred to the net assets account, then the net assets at the end of the fiscal year or accounting period can be derived. Referring to Table 4.5, the revenue account is debited $146,750 and the net assets account is credited $146,750. We remember that every debit must have an offsetting credit and vice versa. The balance in the revenue account is now zero. Likewise, the expense

TABLE 4.3   Portland After School Program General Ledger (Account Balances)

Cash		Net Assets
(a) $ 50,000	(d) $ 9,000	
(b) 25,000	(e) 2,500	
(c) 25,000	(f) 2,500	
(g) 35,000	(j) 10,000	
(i) 10,000	(k) 6,000	
	(l) 50,000	
	(m) 500	
$145,000	$ 80,500	
80,500	80,500	
$ 64,500		

Prepaid Insurance	
(d) $ 9,000	(o) $ 9,000
9,000	9,000
0	

Arts and Crafts Supplies		Investments	
$ 2,500	(p) $ 2,000	(j) $10,000	
2,000	2,000		
$ 500			

Accounts Receivable		Accounts Payable	
(h) $ 1,750			(m) $1,500

Revenue		Expense	
	(a) $ 50,000	(e) $ 2,500	
	(b) 25,000	(k) 6,000	
	(c) 25,000	(l) 50,000	
	(g) 35,000	(m) 500	
	(h) 1,750	(n) 1,500	
	(i) 10,000	(o) 9,000	
		(p) 2,000	
	$146,750	$71,500	

TABLE 4.4   Portland After School Program

Trial Balance
June 30, 20XX

	Debits*	Credits**
Cash	$ 64,500	
Arts and crafts supplies	500	
Accounts receivable	1,750	
Revenue		$146,750
Investments	10,000	
Accounts payable		1,500
Expenses	71,500	
	$148,250	$148,250

*Accounts with debit balances.
**Accounts with credit balances.

account is credited in the amount of $71,500 and the net assets account is debited $71,500. The balance in the expense account is now zero. The account balance for the net assets account is now computed. Subtracting the lower side from the higher side, $71,500 is subtracted from both the debit and credit sides of the net assets account, resulting in a new balance of $75,250. Now the financial statements can be prepared.

Preparing the Financial Statements

Using the various transactions in each account as well as the final account balances, the accountant can now prepare the financial statements covering the first six months of operations of the Portland After School Program.

Statement of Cash Flows.   Using the transactions as well as the account balance in the cash account from Table 4.5, the accountant prepares the statement of cash flows (see Table 4.6). At the beginning of the fiscal year, the agency had no cash on hand. During the first six months of operation, the agency had increases in cash in the amount of $145,000 and decreases in cash in the amount of $80,500. The increases in cash are reported by the three required categories: investing ($0.00), financing ($10,000), and operating ($135,000). The decreases in cash are also accounted for using the three required categories: investing ($10,000 transferred to the investment account), financing ($0.00), and operating ($70,500). The net increase in cash of $64,500 means that on June 30, 20XX, the end of the first six months of operation, the Portland After School Program has cash on hand of $64,500.

TABLE 4.5   Portland After School Program

Closing the Revenue and Expense Accounts to Net Assets

Cash				Net Assets	
(a) $ 50,000	(d) $ 9,000			$71,500	$146,750
(b) 25,000	(e) 2,500			71,500	71,500
(c) 25,000	(f) 2,500				$ 75,520
(g) 35,000	(j) 10,000				
(i) 10,000	(k) 6,000				
	(l) 50,000				
	(m) 500				
$145,000	$ 80,500				
80,500	80,500				
$ 64,500					

Prepaid Insurance	
(d) $ 9,000	(o) $ 9,000
9,000	9,000
0	

Arts and Crafts Supplies				Investments	
(f) $ 2,500	(p) $ 2,000				(j) $ 10,000
2,000	2,000				
$ 500					

Accounts Receivable				Accounts Payable	
(h) $ 1,750				(m) $ 1,500	

Revenue				Expense	
	(a) $ 50,000		(e) $ 2,500		
	(b) 25,000		(k) 6,000		
	(c) 25,000		(l) 50,000		
	(g) 35,000		(m) 500		
	(h) 1,750		(n) 1,500		
	(i) 10,000		(o) 9,000		
$146,750	$146,750		$71,500	$ 71,500	
	0		0		

TABLE 4.6   Portland After School Program

Statement of Cash Flows
January 1, 20XX–June 30, 20XX

Cash on hand January 1		$ 0
Increases in cash		$145,000
Investing	$ 0	
Financing	10,000[a]	
Operating	135,000	
	$145,000	
Decreases in cash		$ 80,500
Investing	$ 10,000[a]	
Financing	0	
Operating	70,500	
	$ 80,500	
Net increase (decrease) in cash		$ 64,500
Cash on hand June 30		$ 64,500

[a]Temporarily restricted donation.

Statement of Activities.   Using the transactions, as well as the account bal-ances, in the revenue account, the expense account, and the investment account, the accountant prepares the statement of activities (see Table 4.7). The agency has total revenues for the first six months of operations of $146,750 comprised of $36,750 in operating revenues and $110,000 in other revenues. Revenues in the amount of $136,750 are *unrestricted* and revenues in the amount of $10,000 are temporarily restricted for the purchase of additional arts and crafts supplies.

The agency has expenses of $71,500 for the first six months. Since we are fudg-ing a bit with this case example, we really don't know how much the agency spent in each of the three categories of expenses (program services, management and gen-eral, and fund-raising). Consequently, we will have to make up some numbers to complete this section of the statement of activities. Let's say that 85 percent of the agency expenses went for program services, 10 percent for management and gen-eral, and 5 percent for fund-raising. The subject of net assets is dealt with shortly as part of the discussion of the statement of financial position (balance sheet).

Finally, the agency has an excess of revenue over expenses of $75,250 for the first six months.

Statement of Financial Position.   Reviewing all the various financial accounts and their balances, the accountant now prepares the statement of financial position

TABLE 4.7   Portland After School Program

Statement of Activities
(Profit and Loss Summary)
January 1, 20XX–June 30, 20XX

	Total	Unrestricted	Temporarily Restricted	Permanently Restricted
Revenues				
Operating revenues				
Parent fees	$ 36,750	$ 36,750		
Subtotal	$ 36,750	$ 36,750		
Other revenues				
Portland C of C	$ 50,000	$ 50,000		
United Way	25,000	25,000		
City of Portland	25,000	25,000		
Donations	10,000		$10,000[a]	
Subtotal	$110,000	$100,000	$10,000	
Total revenues	$146,750	$136,750	$10,000	
Expenses				
Program services	$ 60,775[b]			
Supportive services				
Management and general	7,150[c]			
Fund-raising	3,575[d]			
Total expenses	$ 71,500			
Excess of revenue over expense	$ 75,250			
Net assets, beginning of year	$ 0	$ 0	$ 0	
Changes in net assets	$ 75,250	$ 65,250	$10,000	
Net assets, end of June	$ 75,250	$ 65,250	$10,000	

[a]Donation for arts and crafts supplies.
[b]Computed @ 85 percent.
[c]Computed @ 10 percent.
[d]Computed @ 5 percent.

or balance sheet (see Table 4.8). First the accountant identifies all the asset accounts. The accountant identifies four asset accounts with balances: (1) the cash account with a balance of $64,500, (2) the accounts receivable account with a balance of $1,750, (3) the arts and crafts supplies account with a balance of $500, and (4) the investment account with a balance of $10,000. The first three of these asset accounts

TABLE 4.8   **Portland After School Program**

Statement of Financial Position
(Balance Sheet)
June 30, 20XX

	Assets
Current Assets	
Cash (unrestricted)	$64,500
Accounts receivable	1,750[a]
Arts and Crafts Supplies	500[b]
	$66,750
Noncurrent Assets	
Cash (temporarily restricted)	$10,000[c]
	$10,000
Total Assets	$76,750
Liabilities and Net Assets	
Current Liabilities	
Accounts payable	$ 1,500
Noncurrent Liabilities	$ 0
Total Liabilities	$ 1,500
Net Assets	
Unrestricted	$65,250
Temporarily restricted	10,000[b]
Total Net Assets	$75,250
Total Liabilities and Net Assets	$76,750

[a]Fees due and payable from parents.
[b]Arts and crafts supplies on hand.
[c]Donations to be used for the purchase of arts and crafts supplies.

are classified as current assets because they constitute cash or assets that can be converted into cash in less than one year. The investment account is treated as a noncurrent asset account because the asset (the $10,000 donation) is temporarily restricted and because we are unsure how long it will take to satisfy the donor requirement. Total current assets are $66,450; total noncurrent assets are $10,000. Total assets are $76,750.

   The accountant identifies only one liability account, accounts payable in the amount of $1,500. This is a current liability because the agency will presumably pay the bill within the twelve months, more likely—in terms of good business practices—within the next thirty to ninety days. There are no long-term liabilities, so total liabilities are $1,500.

The basic accounting formula is

$$\text{Net assets} = \text{Assets} - \text{Liabilities}$$

Using this formula, the net assets of the Portland After School Program is computed as follows:

$$\text{Net assets} = \text{Assets} - \text{Liabilities}$$
$$\$75,250 = \$76,750 - \$1,500$$

The total net assets of $75,250 are comprised of $65,250 in unrestricted assets and $10,000 in temporarily restricted assets for the purchase of arts and crafts supplies. Note that the net assets figure ($75,250) is exactly the same as the excess of revenues over expenses ($75,250) from the statement of activities (see Table 4.7). In other words, the increase in net assets over the past six months is due to the excess of revenues over expenses during the past six months. For the next accounting period, the net assets account of the Portland After Care Program will have an account balance of $75,250.

Summary

This chapter has demonstrated how the financial books and records of a human service agency are maintained using the principles of accounting and double entry bookkeeping. The process of using information contained in an agency's financial books and records to prepare the various financial statements required of private nonprofit organizations (both human service and non–human service) was also detailed.

With the widespread availability of computers and financial accounting software, the task of maintaining an agency's financial books and records is much easier today than in the past. However, the complexity and the changing nature of accounting principles are such that every human service agency needs to have access to the services of qualified accounting professionals on staff, on retainer, or on the agency's board of directors.

In the following chapter, we will see how the information contained in financial statements can be used to assess the financial condition of human service agencies.

EXERCISES

Exercise 4.1

Table 4.9 is a list of the transactions for the Portland After School Program for the second six months of operations. Prepare the journal entries for each transaction

TABLE 4.9   Journal of the Portland After School Program

July 1, 20XX–December 31, 20XX

(a) July 1, 20XX— Received unrestricted donation check in the amount of $15,000 from the Multnomah County Department of Health and Human Services.

(b) July 19, 20XX—Paid Great Northwest Insurance Company $9,000 for six more months of fire and liability insurance coverage.

(c) July 15, 20XX—Paid Portland Arts & Crafts Company $3,000 for additional arts and crafts supplies.

(d) July 15, 20XX—Transferred temporarily restricted funds in the amount of $3,000 from investments to pay for additional arts and crafts supplies.

(e) July 30, 20XX—Paid Oregon Sporting Goods $5,000 for additional recreational equipment.

(f) December 31, 20XX—Received fees from parents in the amount of $40,000.

(g) December 31, 20XX—To account for $1,750 in fees from parents earned in the first six months of operations, but collected in the second six months.

(h) December 31, 20XX—To account for $3,000 in parent fees earned in the second six months of operations, but not yet collected.

(i) December 31, 20XX—To account for expenses (John's Deli) in the amount of $1,500 incurred during the first six months of operations, but paid in the second six months.

(j) December 31, 20XX—Paid Portland Gas & Electric Company $7,500 for utilities.

(k) December 31, 20XX—Paid salaries and employee-related expenses in the amount of $55,000.

(l) December 31, 20XX—Paid Pacific Bell Telephone Company $750 for telephone services.

(m) December 31, 20XX—To expense prepaid insurance in the amount of $9,000.

(n) December 31, 20XX—To expense arts and crafts supplies in the amount of $2,000.

including an identification of the t-accounts that will be debited and credit for each transaction.

Exercise 4.2

Using the Portland After School Program general ledger (Table 4.10), post the debits and credits for the journal entries from Exercise 4.1 to their appropriate t-accounts.

Exercise 4.3

Prepare a trial balance for the Portland After School Program for the second six months of operation following the format shown in this chapter.

TABLE 4.10   Portland After School Program

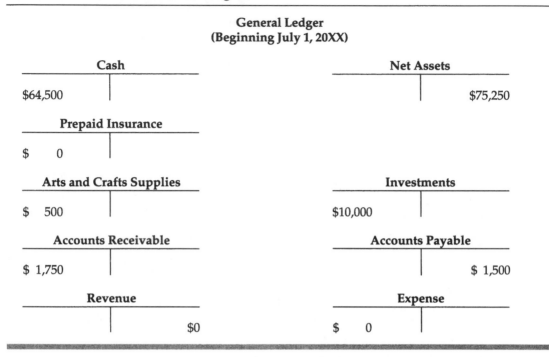

General Ledger
(Beginning July 1, 20XX)

Cash		Net Assets	
$64,500			$75,250

Prepaid Insurance	
$ 0	

Arts and Crafts Supplies		Investments	
$ 500		$10,000	

Accounts Receivable		Accounts Payable	
$ 1,750			$ 1,500

Revenue		Expense	
	$0	$ 0	

Exercise 4.4

Prepare a statement of cash flows, a statement of activities (profit and loss summary), and a statement of financial position (balance sheet) for the Portland After School Program for the second six months of operation. Follow the formats shown in Tables 4.6, 4.7, and 4.8.

CHAPTER

5   Financial Analysis

The previous two chapters provided a basic introduction to financial statements, accounting, and double entry bookkeeping. Now we are going to discuss how the information contained in financial statements can be used to assess the financial condition of human service agencies. As was the case in the past two chapters, the focus here is again on the analysis of financial statements of private nonprofit human service agencies.

Financial Analysis Ratios

Financial analysis can be defined as the process of using the information provided by financial statements to calculate financial ratios that assess the financial condition of human service agencies (Hertzlinger & Rittenhouse, 1994:133). The use of financial analysis in business has been a common practice for nearly a century (Hairston, 1985). The applicability of financial analysis to private nonprofit human service agencies has long been advocated (e.g., Hairston, 1985; Hall, 1982; Lohman, 1980). Unfortunately, financial analysis still has yet to catch on as a working concept in most private nonprofit human service agencies. This state of affairs is unfortunate because the use of financial analysis can provide insights into the financial condition of human service agencies that might not otherwise be noted. Financial analysis should not be confused with the computation of unit of service costs. Unit of service costs are different and are discussed in Chapter 7.

A multiplicity of financial ratios are available for use in assessing the financial condition of human service agencies. In a meta analysis, Kennedy (1996) identified more than twenty financial ratios advocated by one or more authoritative sources (e.g., Dalsimer, 1995; Elkin & Molitor, 1985; Hall, 1982; McMillan, 1994). From this rather large collection, seven basic financial ratios are selected that are believed to be particularly relevant for private nonprofit human service agencies: (1) the current ratio, (2) the long-term solvency ratio, (3) the contribution ratio, (4) the programs/expense ratio, (5) the general and management/expense ratio, (6) the fund-raising/expense ratio, and (7) the revenue/expense ratio.

The Current Ratio

The current ratio is developed from the statement of financial position (or the balance sheet) using the formula

$$\text{Current ratio} = \frac{\text{Current assets}}{\text{Current liabilities}}$$

The purpose of the current ratio is to assess a private nonprofit human service agency's *liquidity*. Liquidity means the extent to which the agency has cash and other assets readily convertible into cash to cover current operating expenses. As noted in Chapter 4, current (short-term) assets are generally composed of cash and accounts receivable, short-term investments, and any other asset that can be converted into cash within one year. Current (short-term) liabilities are expenses that are currently due or will come due in one year or less.

In terms of interpretation, the current ratio should be at least 1.0, but in general the higher the ratio the better. If the current ratio is less than 1.0, the human service agency may be facing liquidity problems.

The Long-Term Solvency Ratio

The long-term solvency ratio is also developed from the statement of financial position (or the balance sheet), but uses a different formula:

$$\text{Long-term solvency ratio} = \frac{\text{Total assets}}{\text{Total liabilities}}$$

The purpose of the long-term solvency ratio is to assess the ability of a private nonprofit human service agency to pay annual expenses as they come due. Another way of phrasing this is to say that the long-term solvency ratio, as its name implies, assesses the long-range financial solvency of a private nonprofit human service agency. Total assets include both current (short-term) assets and noncurrent (long-term) assets; total liabilities include both current (short-term) liabilities and noncurrent (long-term) liabilities.

In terms of interpretation, the long-term solvency ratio should be at least 1.0; but as a general rule, the higher the ratio the better. If the long-term solvency ratio of a human service agency is significantly less than 1.0, the financial viability of the organization may be in question.

The question might well be asked, Why does an agency need to compute both the current ratio and the long-term solvency ratio? Don't these two ratios say essentially the same thing?

The answer is not really. A private nonprofit human service agency can be asset rich and cash poor or cash rich and asset poor. For example, an agency could have significant current assets (as measured by a current ratio greater than 1.0), but have more total liabilities than total assets (as measured by a long-term solvency ratio of less than 1.0). Vice versa, a private nonprofit human service agency could also have more total assets than total liabilities (as measured by a long-term solvency ratio greater than 1.0), but have real liquidity problems (as measured by a current ratio of less than 1.0). In this latter case, a long-term investment (e.g., a long-term certificate of deposit) might have to be converted to cash in order to meet the cash flow needs of the agency. The combination of the current ratio and the long-term solvency ratio provide complementary short-term and long-term views of the financial condition of a private nonprofit human service agency.

The Contribution Ratio

The contribution ratio is developed from the statement of activities (or the profit and loss summary) using the formula

$$\text{Contribution ratio} = \frac{\text{Largest revenue source}}{\text{Total revenues}}$$

The purpose of the contribution ratio is to assess the agency's dependency on its major revenue source. Revenue from the agency's largest revenue source is divided by total revenues to determine the proportion of agency revenues that come from this one source.

As a general rule, the more revenue sources a private nonprofit human service agency has (the more diversified it is) the better, because the agency is not overly dependent on any one particular revenue source. Consequently, in terms of interpretation, the lower the contribution ratio the better. If the contribution ratio of a human service agency is .5 or greater, the agency is disproportionately dependent upon that one revenue source. If anything happens to that one revenue source (e.g., a government contract is canceled or a foundation grant is not renewed), the financial viability of the agency may be in serious question.

The Programs/Expense Ratio

The programs/expense ratio is developed from the statement of activities using the formula

$$\text{Programs/Expense ratio} = \frac{\text{Total program expenses}}{\text{Total expenses}}$$

The programs/expense ratio is one of several standards adopted by the National Charities Information Bureau (NCIB, 1998). The purpose of the NCIB's standards is to provide information about private nonprofit organizations that can be used by donors to make more informed decisions. The NCIB certifies nonprofit organizations as either "meeting" or "not meeting" its standards. The NCIB standard for the programs/expense ratio is a minimum ratio of .6. In terms of interpretation, the programs/expense ratio standard means that a private nonprofit human service agency should spend a minimum of 60 percent of its total expenses for programs. The NCIB adds the caveat that "greater flexibility" should be demonstrated in applying this standard to private nonprofit organizations that are less than three years old or that have total annual expenses of less than $100,000.

The General and Management/Expense Ratio

The general and management/expense ratio is also developed from the statement of activities using the formula

$$\text{General and management/Expense ratio} = \frac{\text{Total general and management expenses}}{\text{Total expenses}}$$

The purpose of the general and management/expense ratio is to determine the proportion of agency expenses that go toward the administration of a private nonprofit human service agency. Every dollar that goes for administration means that one dollar less is available for programs and to provide services to clients.

In terms of interpretation, the general and management/expense ratio can be thought of as a measure of the management efficiency of a human service agency. Borrowing on a similar ratio standard suggested by Dalsimer (1995:17), a general and management/expense ratio greater than .35 should be cause for some concern. A private nonprofit human service agency with a general and management/expense ratio greater than .35 should probably start thinking about ways of reducing administrative costs.

The Fund-Raising/Expense Ratio

The fund-raising/expense ratio is likewise developed from the statement of activities using the formula

$$\text{Fund-raising/Expense ratio} = \frac{\text{Total fund-raising expenses}}{\text{Total expenses}}$$

The purpose of the fund-raising/expense ratio is to determine the proportion of agency expenses that go toward the various fund-raising activities conducted by a private nonprofit human service agency. As is the case with general and management expenses, every dollar that goes toward fund-raising means that one dollar less is available for programs and to serve clients.

In terms of interpretation, the fund-raising/expense ratio can be thought of as a measure of the efficiency of agency fund-raising activities. Again, borrowing on a similar ratio standard suggested by Dalsimer (1995:17), a fund-raising/expense ratio greater than .15 should be cause for some concern. If the fund-raising/expense ratio is greater than .15, the human service agency might want to consider changing its approach to fund-raising. A different approach might generate more funds while also lowering fund-raising costs.

The Revenue/Expense Ratio

The revenue/expense ratio is developed from the statement of activities (or the profit and loss summary) using the formula

$$\text{Revenue/Expense ratio} = \frac{\text{Total revenues}}{\text{Total expenses}}$$

The purpose of the revenue/expense ratio is to determine if a human service agency is breaking even, making money, or losing money. The revenue/expense ratio can be thought of as the agency's "profit margin." As was discussed earlier, private nonprofit agencies are not in business to make a profit; neither, however, are they in business to lose money. A private nonprofit human service agency that loses money over several years may wind up ceasing to exist. Some financial management experts suggest that all private nonprofit organizations should strive to make a profit (to have an excess of revenue over expense) each year in order to help replace worn-out equipment, help finance expansion, and protect again unforeseen future occurrences (e.g., a decline in donations, the loss of a government contract or foundation grant) (Hertzlinger & Rittenhouse, 1994:152).

In terms of interpretation, the revenue/expense ratio should be at least 1.0, meaning that revenues and expenses are equal. If we follow the advice of Hertzlinger and Rittenhouse, the revenue/expense ratio should be greater than 1.0 in order for a human service agency to develop a contingency fund. While no exact cutoff point exists, the revenue/expense ratio should not be inordinately high. While a high revenue/expense ration means that a human service agency has been successful in putting funds aside for the future, it also means that the agency is not currently providing as much service or serving as many clients as it could.

Monitoring Ratios over Time

In addition to applying financial analysis to the financial statements of a private nonprofit human service agency for a particular fiscal year, the financial ratios themselves can be monitored over time (multiple fiscal years). By doing so, changes in the financial condition of a private nonprofit human service agency can be observed. In looking at the financial ratios over time, the objective is to discern the relative status of each individual financial ratio (is it improving, deteriorating, or staying the same?) as well as the overall financial condition of the agency (is it improving, deteriorating, or staying the same?).

Table 5.1 presents financial ratio data developed from the financial statements of the Denver Child Guidance Center for five fiscal years. Let's look at what the financial ratios can tell us about the overall financial condition of the agency.

All of the financial ratios depicted in Table 5.1 are moving in the preferred directions. Liquidity, as measured by the current ratio (current assets/current liabilities) has steadily improved. In FY00 the current ratio is .9, meaning that the

TABLE 5.1   Denver Child Guidance Center

	Comparative Financial Ratios Fiscal Years (FY) 2000–2004				
	FY00	**FY01**	**FY02**	**FY03**	**FY04**
Current ratio	.90	1.00	1.10	1.15	1.20
Long-term solvency ratio	1.20	1.24	1.28	1.30	1.31
Contribution ratio	.70	.60	.50	.47	.45
Programs/ expense ratio	.50	.55	.59	.62	.65
General and management/ expense ratio	.30	.27	.26	.24	.22
Fund-raising/ expense ratio	.20	.18	.15	.14	.13
Revenue/ expense ratio	1.05	1.02	1.10	.95	1.05

agency has more current liabilities than current assets. Fortunately in FY00, the agency has sufficient other assets to handle its liquidity problems (i.e., the long-term solvency ratio for FY00 is 1.20). The long-term solvency ratio is greater than 1.0 in all years and has steadily increased to a healthy 1.31 in FY04. The contribution ratio (revenues from the largest funding source/total revenues) is .70 is FY00, meaning that the agency is overly dependent on one particular funding source. The contribution ratio, however, declines over the five-year period, which indicates that agency management is taking positive steps to diversify its revenue base.

The programs/expense ratio is low in FY00 at .50 and violates the minimum standard of .6 set by the National Charities Information Bureau. Agency management, however, is taking aggressive steps to improve the situation so the programs/expense ratio increases to an acceptable level of .62 in FY03 and rises still further to .65 in FY04. Since the sum of the programs/expense ratio, the general and management/expense ratio, and the fund-raising/expense ratio for any given year equals 1.0, an increase in the programs/expense ratio means that one or both of the other two ratios are declining. In FY00, both the general and management/expense ratio and the fund-raising/expense ratio are high; the later ratio (.20) being greater than the standard of .15. Again, however, agency management is taking aggressive steps to bring their administrative costs and fund-raising costs under control as evidenced by the gradual decline in the general and managment/expense ratio to .22 in FY04 and a commensurate decline in the fund-raising/expense ratio to .13 in FY04.

The revenue/expense ratio jumps around somewhat as might be expected. In FY00, FY01, FY02, and FY04 the revenue/expense ratio is greater than 1.0, meaning the agency made a "profit." However, in FY03, the ratio is .95, which means that the agency had more expenses than income and might indicate that some of the preceding years' profit had to be put back into current operations.

The Denver Child Guidance Center represents a situation in which a private nonprofit human service agency has serious financial problems that are highlighted by financial analysis. Because the agency's financial problems are highlighted, agency management was able to take corrective action.

Summary

In this chapter, we looked at the use of financial analysis as a tool in the assessment of the financial condition of private nonprofit human service agencies. Seven different ratios were introduced and discussed. The suggestion was made that the use of these seven ratios provides a good basic overview of a human services agency's financial condition. The suggestion was also made that the monitoring of these seven ratios over time provides a method of assessing the direction and degree of change in the financial condition of private nonprofit human service agencies.

EXERCISES

Exercise 5.1

Table 5.2 is a summary of financial ratios computed for the Richmond, Virginia, Senior Center for fiscal years (FYS) 01, 02, and 03. Comment on each of the financial ratios (current ratio, long-term solvency ratio, contribution ratio, programs/ expense ratio, general and management/expense ratio, fund-raising/expense ratio, and revenue/expense ratio) for FY01. What can you say about the financial ratios in FY01? Do they seem appropriate, high, or low? Why? Do any of the financial ratios for FY01 violate any of the standards suggested in this chapter? Which ones? Why? Overall, how would you assess the financial condition of the Richmond, Virginia, Senior Center in FY01?

Comment on each of the same financial ratios for FY03. What can you say about the ratios in FY03? Have they changed for the better? Why? How? Do any of the financial ratios for FY03 violate any of the standards suggested in this chapter? Which ones? Why? Overall, how would you assess the financial condition of the Richmond, Virginia, Senior Center in FY03?

Exercise 5.2

Review the financial statements (statement of activity or profit and loss summary, statement of functional expenses, statement of financial position or balance sheet, and statement of cash flows) for the Phoenix Specialized Transportation Services

TABLE 5.2   **Richmond, Virginia, Senior Center**

Comparative Ratios
Fiscal Years FY01, FY02, and FY03

	FY01	**FY02**	**FY03**
Current ratio	.97	.95	.93
Long-term solvency ratio	1.10	1.08	1.05
Contribution ratio	.35	.37	.40
Programs/ expense ratio	.60	.55	.50
General and management/ expense ratio	.25	.27	.30
Fund-raising/ expense ratio	.15	.18	.20
Revenue/ expense ratio	.95	.96	.98

program (Chapter 3). Using these financial statements, compute the current ratio, the long-term solvency ratio, the contribution ratio (for the largest single funding source), the three expense ratios (programs/expense ratios; general and management/expense ratio, fund-raising/expense ratio) and the revenue/expense ratio.

Comment on each of these ratios. Do the ratios appear high or low? Are the ratios in keeping with the standards discussed in this chapter? Overall, how would you describe the financial condition of Phoenix STS?

Exercise 5.3

The following two financial statements—a statement of activities (profit and loss summary) and a statement of financial position (balance sheet)—are for the Council on Social Work Education for fiscal year 1998. (See Tables 5.3 and 5.4.) Review these two financial statements and compute the following ratios: current ratio, long-term solvency ratio, contribution ratio, programs/expense ratio, and revenue/expense ratio.

Comment on each of these ratios. Do the ratios appear high or low? Are the ratios in keeping with the standards discussed in this chapter? Overall, how would you describe the financial condition of the Council on Social Work Education? Why can't a management and general/expense ratio and fund-raising/expense ratio be computed?

TABLE 5.3   Council on Social Work Education

Statement of Activities
Year Ended June 30, 1998

	Unrestricted	Temporarily Restricted	Total
Revenue			
Membership fees and dues	$1,613,192		$1,613,192
Contributions and grants	887,385	$16,486	903,871
Annual program meeting	535,907		535,907
Accreditation fees and services	316,505		316,505
Publication sales	73,491		73,491
Investment income	159,653		159,653
Advertising	26,587		26,587
Other	35,765		35,765
Total revenue	$3,648,485	$16,486	$3,664,971
Expense			
Program services:			
Accreditation	$1,236,060		$1,236,060
Annual program meeting	446,313		446,313
Minority Fellowship			
Program—research	447,385		447,385
Minority Fellowship			
Program—clinical	207,065		207,065
Publications	348,028		348,028
Social work education and			
public human services	—		—
Annie E. Casey program	80,439		80,439
Managed care	23,602		23,602
	$2,788,892		$2,788,892
Supporting services:			
Membership services	$ 265,507		$ 265,507
Administration	319,997		319,997
	585,504		585,504
Total expenses	3,374,396		3,374,396
Change in Net Assets	$ 274,089	$16,486	$ 290,575
Net assets, beginning of year	1,063,898	46,230	1,110,128
Net Assets, End of Year	$1,337,987	$62,716	$1,400,703

Reprinted from the *Social Work Education Reporter,* Vol. 47, No. 1 (Winter, 1999):23, with permission from the Council on Social Work Education.

TABLE 5.4   Council on Social Work Education

Statement of Financial Position
June 30, 1998

Assets	Unrestricted	Temporarily Restricted	Total
Current Assets			
Cash and cash equivalents	$ 611,506		$ 611,506
Marketable securities, at market value	1,370,238		1,370,238
Accounts receivable, net of allowance for doubtful accounts of $38,414	160,133		160,133
Grants receivable	129,982		129,982
Due from (to) other funds	(62,716)	$62,716	—
Inventory	20,007		20,007
Prepaid expenses	19,709		19,709
Total current assets	$2,248,859	$62,716	$2,311,575
Furniture and Equipment, at cost	471,624		471,624
Less accumulated depreciation	(342,535)		(342,535)
	129,089	—	129,089
Total assets	$2,377,948	$62,716	$2,440,664
Liabilities and Net Assets			
Current Liabilities			
Accounts payable and accrued expenses	$ 136,873		$ 136,873
Accrued vacation	82,214		82,214
Due to IASSW	61,285		61,285
Current maturities of notes payable	9,860		9,860
Deferred rent, current portion	109,891		109,891
Deferred fees and dues	583,322		583,322
Total current liabilities	$ 983,445		$ 983,445
Deferred rent, less current portion	$ 56,516		$ 56,516
Net Assets			
Unrestricted:			
Operating	$1,184,776		$1,184,776
Plant	129,089		129,089
Board designated	24,122		24,122
Temporarily restricted	—	62,716	62,716
	$2,377,948	$62,716	$2,440,664

6 Performance Measures

A chapter on performance measures in a text on financial management may seem out of place. The development and use of performance measures are usually seen more in programmatic terms than in financial management terms. Performance measures, performance measurement, and, in particular, outcome performance measures are more likely to be thought of as a form of program assessment or evaluation than as an aspect of financial management. In reality, what can be called the performance measurement movement was initially started, and is still being championed, by a desire on the part of the accounting profession to improve government financial management and reporting.

Just as programs, program structures, and responsibility centers are basic building blocks of sound financial management practices in human service agencies, so too are performance measures. Performance measures must exist before human service administrators can use more sophisticated financial management techniques such as performance and program budgeting (Chapter 7), cost analysis (Chapter 8), forecasting (Chapter 9), and break-even analysis (Chapter 10). The existence and use of a particular type of performance measure (an output or unit of service) is also necessary for the development of fee schedules (Chapter 11). Additionally, many state, city, and county governments that engage in contract service delivery with private nonprofit human service agencies (Chapter 12) are converting to performance contracting. Performance contracting involves the linking or tying of performance measures and their accomplishment to contractor compensation and to contract extensions and renewals.

This chapter is designed as a basic introduction to the topic of performance measurement and performance measures. Performance measurement is first defined using the systems model as a conceptual framework. Next, some of the major initiatives promoting performance measurement and the development and use of performance measures are identified and discussed. The various types of performance measures (output, quality, and outcome) are then introduced and discussed. Finally, the characteristics of good performance measures are identified based on an analysis of the normative and empirical literature in the field.

Performance Measurement Defined

Performance measurement can be defined as the regular collection and reporting of information about the efficiency, quality, and effectiveness of government programs (Martin & Kettner, 1996). Four aspects of this definition warrant further elaboration.

First, performance measures can be developed for a human service program, for a human service agency, and in some instances (such as in the states of Florida, Minnesota, and Oregon) for an entire community or state. From a financial management perspective, we are primarily concerned with the development, use, and reporting of program performance measures. This perspective is in keeping with the accounting profession's use of the program as its basic unit of analysis.

Second, performance measurement is concerned with what can be called the right side of the systems model. Figure 6.1 illustrates the basic systems model, which is composed of inputs, process (a human service program), outputs, quality, outcomes, and feedback. Performance measurement is concerned only with the results or accomplishments of human service programs (process) and specifically with outputs, quality, and outcomes. The three feedback loops indicate that performance measurement data and information are used to make program (process) changes

FIGURE 6.1   The Systems Model

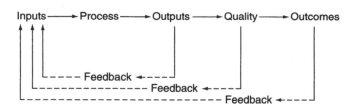

- *Inputs* are the resources (e.g., funding, staff, equipment, clients, client problems) that go into a human service program.
- *Process* refers to the way in which a human service program produces a product or provides a service.
- *Outputs* (or units of service) are the amount of product produced or service provided by a human service program.
- *Quality* means the amount (#) or the proportion (%) of the product produced or the service provided by a human service program that meets a specified quality standard.
- *Outcomes* are the quality of life changes in clients achieved, at least partially, as a result of their participation in a human service program.
- *Feedback* is a built-in form of assessment that provides information on how a human service program is performing in terms of efficiency (outputs), quality, and effectiveness (outputs), and efficiency and effectiveness ratios.

designed to improve ongoing operations. From a financial management perspective, the major reason for the development and use of performance measures is to be able to determine the cost of a human service program's outputs, quality, and outcomes. These data provide insights into the programmatic and financial operations of a human service program that cannot be determined by other means.

Third, the performance measurement movement is directed at government in general, not just at the human services and human service programs. Consequently, the approach as well as the vocabulary of performance measurement was not specifically designed with the human services in mind. The performance measurement movement is a broad-based collection of coordinated efforts to make government more transparent. *Transparency* means the desire to have governments become more open and more forthcoming with information about the programs they provide, the results and accomplishments of those programs, and their attendant costs.

Fourth, although developed with government purposes in mind, performance measurement also indirectly affects private nonprofit human service agencies. Because of the widespread use of contracting service delivery by state and local government human service agencies today, whatever directly affects them indirectly affects their contractors.

The Major Performance Measurement Initiatives

As Figure 6.2 indicates, the performance measurement movement is actually a collection of different initiatives created by a broad collection of organizations. These various initiatives share a common focus on output, quality, and outcome performance measures. A few initiatives, such as that of the U.S. Department of Health and Human Services, also include non–performance-type measures (inputs and process). The use of these non–performance-type measures is intended to be a temporary expedient until such time as all department programs have developed suitable output, quality, and outcome performance measures.

To truly appreciate the importance of what can be called the performance measurement movement, it is necessary to briefly mention The Government Performance and Results Act of 1993 (GPRA), the service efforts and accomplishments (SEA) reporting initiative of the Governmental Accounting Standards Board (GASB), and government auditing standards as established by the U.S. General Accounting Office.

The Government Performance and Results Act (GPRA)

The GPRA requires that all federal departments, agencies, commissions, and so on prepare and submit to the U.S. Congress an annual performance report to include performance measurement data and information covering all federal programs. The first annual reports were submitted to the Congress in fiscal year 2000. As part

FIGURE 6.2   Major Performance Measurement Initiatives

Initiative	Efficiency (Outputs)	Quality	Effectiveness (Outcomes)	Other
Government Performance and Results Act (GPRA)	X	X	X	
U.S. Department of Health and Human Services	X	X	X	Inputs Process
State performance measurement initiatives	X	X	X	Inputs Processes Outputs Quality Outcomes Efficiency ratios Effectiveness ratios
Governmental Accounting Standards Board (GASB)	X	X	X	Efficiency ratios Effectiveness ratios
Managed Care	X	X	X	
United Way		X	X	
General Accounting Office (GAO)	X	X	X	

X = Focus on.

of their annual performance reports, federal departments (such as the Department of Health and Human Services, the Department of Labor, and the Department of Housing and Urban Development) must report performance measures for all the programs they administer.

The period between the passage of GPRA in 1993 and the first performance reports was one of planning and experimentation. Today, most federal programs have identified performance measures including output, quality, and outcome. The effects of GPRA have also trickled down to state governments, local governments, and even to private nonprofit human service agencies. Since many federal programs such as the Social Services Block Grant, "welfare-to work," and the Older Americans Act are actually administered by state and local governments as well as by private nonprofit human service agencies, these organizations are required to also routinely report performance measurement data and other information that trickle up to the federal government.

Service Efforts and Accomplishments (SEA) Reporting

In terms of financial management, the Governmental Accounting Standards Board's (GASB's) service efforts and accomplishments (SEA) reporting may be the most important of the major performance measurement initiatives. As was noted in Chapter 3, GASB is the organization that establishes generally accepted accounting principles for state and local governments, including state and local government human service agencies.

GASB has maintained for some time that state and local governments do not provide their citizens with sufficient information about the programs they provide, the results and accomplishments achieved, and the costs involved, with emphasis on cost. GASB has issued draft regulations that would require all state and local governments to annually collect and report both programmatic and performance financial data for all their programs using the SEA reporting approach. Under SEA reporting, each government program would be required to report on (a) service efforts including total funding, the number of full-time equivalent (FTE) positions that work on each program, and the number of staff hours devoted to each program, (b) service accomplishments including the outputs, quality, and outcomes produced by each program, and (c) various efficiency and effectiveness ratios such as cost per output, cost per quality output, cost per outcome, outputs per FTE, quality outputs per FTE, and outcomes per FTE.

SEA reporting is the most sophisticated and most financially oriented of the major performance measurement initiatives. SEA reporting directly affects all state and local government human service agencies. Of the initiatives listed in Figure 6.2, state performance measurement initiatives and SEA reporting are the only two that include efficiency and effectiveness ratios, which attests to the influence of GASB and SEA reporting on the thinking and behavior of states. SEA reporting also indirectly affects most private nonprofit human service agencies because of the widespread use of contracting. The only way that state and local government human service agencies can comply with the SEA reporting requirements is to require that their contractors also report SEA data.

At the time of this writing, SEA reporting has not been mandated by GASB. Nevertheless, GASB had made clear its intention that SEA reporting will be mandated after an appropriate period of time has elapsed during which state and local governments can plan and experiment with performance measurement data collection and reporting. In anticipation of an eventual SEA mandate, most state and many local governments are already actively involved in implementing and refining performance measures and performance measurement systems.

Because SEA reporting is the most sophisticated and the most financially demanding of the major performance measurement initiatives, it represents a sort of fail safe position for government and private nonprofit human service agencies. Human service agencies with performance measurement systems modeled on SEA requirements will most likely be able to generate any performance measurement data and information that might be required of them in the future.

U.S. General Accounting Office (GAO)

The U.S. General Accounting Office (GAO) establishes what are referred to as generally accepted auditing principles for "government organizations, programs, activities and functions, and for government assistance received by contractors, nonprofit organizations, and other non-governmental organizations" (GAO, 1994:6). Any organization that receives federal funds (including any private nonprofit human service agency that receives federal funds that pass through a state or local government via a contract or grant) is directly affected by GAO auditing standards (see Chapter 15).

The GAO auditing standards are published in a book entitled *Government Auditing Standards* (GAO, 1994), frequently referred to as the "Yellow Book" because of the color of its cover. In the section of the Yellow Book dealing with "performance auditing" (pp. 62–102) appears a set of definitions of output, quality, and outcome performance that mirror those adopted by both GPRA and SEA reporting. The consistency in the use of performance measurement definitions across the various performance measurement initiatives attests to both the power and the determination of the accounting profession to make government more transparent.

Any human service agency or program that receives federal funds is a potential candidate to undergo a performance audit. Any performance audit conducted must follow the guidelines and use the performance measurement definitions spelled out in the GAO Yellow Book. Performance measures and performance measurement systems that do not adhere to the guidelines and definitions contained in the Yellow Book (which are the same as those used by GPRA and by SEA reporting) will not meet generally accepted government auditing standards. Consequently, the advisable action is for human service administrators to ensure that they develop and use performance measures for their programs that are in keeping with the GAO, GPRA, and GASB SEA definitions.

Output, Quality, and Outcome Performance Measures

Figure 6.3 provides definitions of output, quality, and outcome performance measures for human service programs and provides examples of each. The definitions are in keeping with those used by GPRA, SEA reporting, and GAO auditing standards.

Output Performance Measures

An *output*, or *unit of service*, performance measure is a measure of service product or volume and answers the question of how much product or service the program provides. The focus of an output, or unit of service, performance measure is on the service. There are three types of output, or unit of service, performance measures:

- *A material unit*—one meal, one prescription, one food basket, one voucher, and so on
- *An episode unit*—one visit, one ride, one session, one interview, and so on
- *A time unit*—one hour, one day, one week, one month, and so on

FIGURE 6.3   Output, Quality, and Outcome Performance Measures

Output

Definition: a measure of product or service volume (also known as a "unit of service")

Focus: Service

Types and Examples:

Material: "one meal" for a home-delivered meals program

Episode: "one person transported one-way one time" for a specialized transportation program

Time: "one hour" for a homemaker or home health aid program

Quality Output

Definition: an output (or units of service) that meets a stated quality standard

Focus: Service

Types and Examples:

Material: "one meal delivered hot" (at least 160 degrees) for a home-delivered meals program

Episode: "one person picked up on time" (within plus or minus five minutes of scheduled time) for a specialized transportation program

Time: "one hour of service" (with no valid client complaints) for a homemaker or home health aid program

Outcome

Definition: the results or accomplishments that are attributable, at least partially, to a human service program

Focus: Client

Examples:

1. "One client whose nutrition is maintained" (for a home-delivered meals program)
2. "One client maintained in his own home" (for homemaker or home health aid program)
3. "One client able to access needed medical, social, or other support services" (for a specialized transportation program)

Time is generally the default category; when a material or episode output, or unit of service, performance measure cannot be developed for a particular human service program, a time unit is generally adopted.

Quality Performance Measures

There are two basic types of quality performance measures: an output with a quality dimension and client satisfaction. The focus of quality performance measures is again on the service.

An *output with a quality dimension* is a unit of service with a quality dimension attached. Quality performance is usually expressed as the proportion of service provided that meets a stated quality standard. For example, a common output (or unit of service) performance measure for a home-delivered meals program is "one meal." The quality performance measure might be how many (#) or what proportion (%) of the home-delivered meals satisfy a stated quality standard (e.g., one meal delivered hot). In the same vein, a frequently used output (unit of service) performance measure for a specialized transportation program is "one-person trip" defined as one person transported one-way one time. The quality performance measure might be how many (#) or what proportion (%) of the person trips meet the stated quality standard of the client being picked up within five minutes of the scheduled time.

The use of client satisfaction as a quality performance measure usually involves the tabulation of data from client satisfaction surveys or client complaints.

Outcome Performance Measures

Outcome performance measures focus on clients. What results or accomplishments did the program achieve in terms of improving the lives of clients? For example, because elderly and disabled clients receive homemaker and home health aid services, they may be able to continue living independently in their own homes. The outcome measure, the quality of life measure of the benefit received from the program, could be defined as the number of clients maintained in an independent living situation. The point should be stressed that the GPRA and SEA reporting use the same definition of an outcome performance measure: "the results or accomplishments that are attributable, *at least partially*, to a program"(emphasis added). The use of a particular outcome performance measure for an individual program does not necessarily mean that the outcome is 100 percent attributable to the program. The ability of elderly or disabled clients to remain in their own homes would probably be affected by many factors in addition to the receipt of homemaker and home health aid services. Nevertheless, this outcome can be at least partially attributable to the receipt of homemaker and home health aid services.

Characteristics of Good Performance Measures

Based on their review of the theoretical and empirical literature on performance measurement, Martin and Kettner (1996) suggest that good performance measures should be evaluated according to five criteria (Figure 6.4): utility, precision, feasibility, unit cost reporting, and consensus.

The selection of performance measures for human service programs frequently involves trade-offs between these criteria. For example, generally the more precise the measure, the more expensive it is to collect and report the data; thus

FIGURE 6.4   Characteristics of Good Performance Measures

---

1. Usefulness

Performance measures should provide data and information that will be useful to human service administrators in managing their programs.

2. Precision

Performance measure should be precise. As a general rule, the more precise (specific) the performance measure, the better. Precision is particularly important from a financial management perspective.

3. Feasibility

Data on performance measures should be relatively easy to collect. The more time and effort needed to collect the performance measurement data, the more expensive the task.

4. Unit Cost Reporting

Performance measures should lend themselves to costing: cost per output (or units or service), cost per outcome, and so on.

5. Consensus

Performance measures should make sense to stakeholders. It makes little sense to use performance measures that stakeholders do not recognize as legitimate and useful.

Source: Adapted from Lawrence L. Martin and Peter M. Kettner (1996). *Measuring the Performance of Human Service Programs.* Thousand Oaks, CA: Sage Publications.

precision is accomplished at the expense of feasibility and vice versa. Trade-offs also frequently occur between precision and consensus. From a precision perspective, an excellent output (or unit of service) performance measure for a specialized transportation program is "one mile." Counting the miles that a vehicle covers is a precise measure and also lends itself well to unit-of-service cost considerations. But "one mile" says nothing about how much service is provided and would probably not generate consensus among stakeholders as an optimum output measure. "One-person trip" is an output (or unit of service) performance measure more routinely encountered in specialized transportation programs; it is less precise than "one mile," but it is generally more acceptable to stakeholders (consensus) because it says something about how much service is provided.

Not to be overlooked is the relationship between utility and unit cost reporting. Unfortunately, many program performance measures are frequently adopted without consideration of their utility for unit cost reporting. Any performance measure that cannot be costed out (cost per output, cost per quality output, cost per outcome) will not satisfy GASB's SEA reporting; thus, its utility is low.

The Use of Performance Measures in Financial Management

The real value of performance measures from a financial management perspective is that they enable human service administrators to relate service costs to service levels. Using GASB's SEA reporting initiative as the basis, we can use performance measurement data and budgetary data to determine for a fiscal year or some other time period.

1. The amount of service provided by a human service program measured in outputs or units of service
2. The amount or proportion of a human service program's outputs that achieve a specified quality level
3. The number of outcomes achieved by a human service program
4. Various efficiency, quality, and effectiveness ratios such as
   a. Cost per output (or unit of service)
   b. Cost per quality output
   c. Cost per outcome

The Houston Home Care Agency

The use of performance measures in conjunction with budgetary data constitutes the major focus of Chapters 7 and 8 to follow. A detailed case example, "The Houston Home Care Agency," is a central feature of both chapters. In order to relate performance measurement data and information to budgetary data and information, one first needs to develop the performance measures. In order to simplify the discussion, only output (or unit of service) and outcome performance will be used; quality performance measures will be excluded from the analysis. The following performance measures will be used throughout the case study:

1. **Visiting nurse program**
   - Output (unit of service) performance measure: "one visit"
   - Outcome performance measure: "one client able to remain in his/her own home"

2. **Homemaker program**
   - Output (unit of service) performance measure: "one hour of service"
   - Outcome performance measure: "one client able to remain in his/her own home"

3. **Home-delivered meals program**
   - Output (unit of service) performance measure: "one meal"
   - Outcome performance measure: "one client able to remain in his/her own home"

4.   **Specialized transportation program**
     ■ Output (unit of service) performance measure: "one-person trip" (one person transported one-way one time)
     ■ Outcome performance measure: "one client able to remain in his/her own home"

All four programs contribute to helping elderly and disabled clients remain in independent living arrangements. Consequently, the four programs can be said to share a common outcome performance measure. However, the four programs have different output (or unit of service) performance measures.

Summary

As suggested at the outset of this chapter, program performance measurement data combined with budgetary data enable the calculation of various efficiency, quality, and effectiveness performance ratios. These ratios enable human service administrators to utilize a variety of more sophisticated financial management tools and techniques including advanced budgeting techniques, cost analysis, break-even analysis, fee setting, forecasting, and contracting. In the next two chapters, which deal with budgeting and cost analysis, we will see how performance measurement data and information can be linked to budgetary data and information.

CHAPTER

7 Budgeting and Budget Systems

Many discussions of budgeting take the position that the process should be seen as a component part of planning. For example, Lynch (1995:362) defines a budget as "a plan for the accomplishment of programs related to objectives and goals within a definite time period, including an estimate of the resources required, together with an estimate of the resources available." The use of such terms as *plan, objectives,* and *goals* are generally associated with the rational planning model.

Other discussions of budgeting take the position that the process is primarily political in nature (e.g., Wildavsky, 1974). Because budgeting involves decisions about "who gets what, when, and how," the argument is made that politics will always be an important consideration, if not the most important consideration, in the budgeting process. While not dismissing their importance, this chapter avoids a detailed discussion of both the planning perspective and the political perspective of budgeting in order to concentrate on the financial management perspective.

Seen from a financial management perspective, budgeting can be thought of as the process by which resources are allocated to a human service agency's various programs and activities. This chapter looks at three major budgeting systems: line-item budgeting systems, performance budgeting systems, and program budgeting systems. Each of these three major budgeting systems is introduced and discussed beginning with line-item budgeting systems. As part of the discussion, the purposes served by each of the three major budgeting systems are identified, their advantages and disadvantages are noted, and examples of each are provided. As a conceptual framework, the systems model is again used and each of the three major budgeting systems is related to different components of the systems model.

Major Budgeting Systems and The Systems Model

Figure 7.1 is an example of the systems model applied to budgeting. As Figure 7.1 illustrates, each of the three major budgeting systems is designed to provide a different type of financial management feedback on the operations of human service agencies and programs. More specifically, *line-item budgeting systems* relate process

**FIGURE 7.1   Major Budgeting Systems
and the Systems Model**

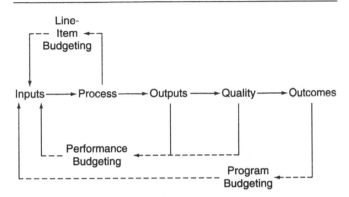

- *Line-Item budgeting systems.* Relate process to inputs and answer the question, Are agency and program expenses in keeping with approved budgets?
- *Performance budgeting systems.* Relate outputs to inputs and answer the questions, How efficient are the agency's programs?
- *Program budgeting systems.* Relate outcomes to inputs and answer the question, How effective are the agency's programs?

to inputs and provide financial management feedback on the extent to which the revenues and expenses of a human service agency or program are in keeping with its anticipated revenues and planned expenses. *Performance budgeting systems* relate outputs and quality to inputs and provide feedback on the costs to a human service program of producing outputs and quality. *Program budgeting systems* relate outcomes to inputs and provide feedback on the costs to a human service program of achieving outcomes.

When Figure 7.1 is compared with Chapter 6's Figure 6.1 dealing with the systems model and performance measures, it becomes apparent that performance measurement and the three major budgeting systems provide related feedback. A performance measurement system is designed to provide both programmatic and financial performance feedback on the extent to which a human service agency or program produces outputs, quality, and outcomes as well as their attendant costs. The three major budgeting systems (line-item, performance, and program) provide the financial performance feedback in a performance measurement system.

Even without making reference to performance measurement, financial performance feedback on the costs of producing outputs, quality, and outcomes is essential information for the financial management of human service agencies and programs today.

Line-Item Budgeting Systems

The first of the three major budgeting systems to be discussed is line-item budgeting. The line-item budgeting system is the most frequently utilized budgeting system in human service agencies and programs. A line-item budget can be prepared for a human service agency as well as for one or more individual programs. In this chapter, however, the focus will be on line-item budgeting at the agency level. Chapter 8 deals with, among other topics, line-item budgeting at the program level.

The major purpose of line-item budgeting systems is financial control. The line-item budget is an administrative tool to control spending. When developed at the agency level, a line-item budget becomes the basic agency financial plan for the fiscal year. The agency line-item budget enables the executive director, governing board members, the chief financial officer, program managers, and other staff to determine the amount of resources that will be allocated to a human service agency's various programs during a fiscal year.

Figure 7.2 presents an organization chart for the Houston Home Care Agency (HHCA). In this chapter and in Chapter 8, the HHCA will serve as a case example dealing with cost analysis. The HHCA operates three programs: a visiting nurse program, a homemaker program, and a home-delivered meals program. The agency also has a small central administrative staff. Figure 7.2 also identifies the staff assigned to each program and to the central administration.

Table 7.1 is an example of a simplified line-item budget format that might be used by a small to medium-sized human service agency like HHCA. As is usually

**FIGURE 7.2   Houston Home Care Agency
Organizational Chart**

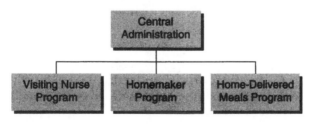

Central Administration includes an executive director, a financial manager, and three secretaries.

The Visiting Nurse Program includes a nursing coordinator and four nurses.

The Homemaker Program includes a homemaker coordinator and fifteen homemakers.

The Home-Delivered Meals Program includes a home-delivered meals coordinator and two (half-time) van drivers.

TABLE 7. 1   **The Houston Home Care Agency**

(January 1, 20X1–December 31, 20X1)

Revenues

1. Contributions (general) $ _____
2. Special events $ _____
3. United Way allocation $ _____
4. Government contracts and grants $ _____
5. Membership dues $ _____
6. Third-party payments $ _____
7. Program income $ _____
8. Investment income $ _____
9. Miscellaneous $ _____

            Total revenues $ _____

Expenses

1. Salaries and wages $ _____
2. Employee-related expenses (ERE) $ _____
3. Rent $ _____
4. Utilities $ _____
5. Supplies $ _____
6. Telephone $ _____
7. Equipment $ _____
8. Postage and shipping $ _____
9. Printing and publications $ _____
10. Travel $ _____
11. Conferences $ _____
12. Miscellaneous $ _____

            Total expenses $ _____

the case, the line-item budget covers one fiscal year and is divided into two sections: (1) a revenue section and (2) an expense section. One purpose of a line-item budget is to identify the sources of all anticipated funding (revenues) for a human service agency and the application of that funding (expenses) for a fiscal year. For example, the upper half of the line-item budget in Table 7.1 shows the sources and amounts of the various revenues anticipated to be received by the Houston Home Care Agency during fiscal year 20XX. The bottom half of the line-item budget shows all proposed (planned) expenses for the same period of time. The items in the lower half of the line-item budget illustrate various categories of proposed expenses (e.g., salaries and wages, employee-related expenses (ERE), travel, supplies). These categories are frequently referred to as *line items,* hence the name of this budgeting system: line-item budgeting. A line-item budget is also sometimes referred to as an *operating budget* because it is the basic budget that a human service agency operates under during a fiscal year.

Developing a Line-Item Budget

Prior to the beginning of each fiscal year, the staff of a human service agency (executive director, program managers, the chief financial officer, governing board members, and others) determine the amount of staff, equipment, facilities, travel, supplies, and so on that will be required to operate the agency and its various programs during the coming fiscal year.

A human service agency usually strives to have its line-item budget in place and approved by its governing authority (e.g., board of directors, governor, city council, mayor, county commission) prior to the beginning of each new fiscal year. Without an approved line-item budget in place prior to the beginning of a new fiscal year, a human service agency finds itself without a basic financial plan and, consequently, in the awkward position of incurring expenses without knowing for sure that sufficient revenues exist to cover them.

In order to have an approved line-item budget in place prior to the beginning of a new fiscal year, a human service agency may have to begin the budget process several weeks, if not months, in advance of the start date of its next fiscal year. In government human service agencies, the budget process is usually part of a larger budget process and can begin six months or more prior to the beginning of the next fiscal year.

During the budget preparation stage, program managers and other staff of a human service agency including the executive director and the chief financial officer estimate both the revenues the agency anticipates receiving and the expenses the agency proposes to incur during the fiscal year. Frequently these estimates are arrived at based primarily on what might be called educated guessing. Other times, more sophisticated forecasting techniques are employed (see Chapter 9).

Program managers have an advocacy role to play during the budget preparation process; they must strive and sometimes even fight to ensure that the best interests of their programs and clients are furthered. This advocacy role frequently entails requesting additional needed funding for more staff in order to serve more clients. Frequently the combined funding requests of program managers are greater than the estimated revenues to be received by a human service agency. At this point, a human service agency finds itself with an unbalanced line-item budget; a budget with proposed expenses greater than anticipated revenues.

Balancing an Unbalanced Line-Item Budget

A line-item budget should be balanced; anticipated revenues should be equal to or greater than proposed expenses. One way to think about a line-item budgeting system is that it is a mechanism to control agency expenses. When a human service agency's line-item budget is not balanced, it is essentially out of control.

Balancing an unbalanced budget in a human service agency can be a difficult task. As a general rule, agency resources are seldom sufficient to provide services to all the clients in need. In dealing with an unbalanced budget, social workers and other human service professionals frequently find themselves torn between what might be called programmatic concerns and financial management concerns. Allowing programmatic concerns to override financial management concerns is how human service agencies get themselves into financial difficulties. Over the years, many well-intentioned human service agencies and administrators have found themselves in deep financial trouble because they attempted to provide more services to more clients than was financially feasible. Sound financial management requires balancing programmatic concerns with fiscal reality.

Three basic ways exist to balance an unbalanced line-item budget: (1) utilize agency reserve funds, (2) increase anticipated revenues, and (3) reduce proposed expenses.

Many human service agencies set aside funds in a special account, frequently referred to as a reserve fund, for emergencies and other special needs. The utilization of a human service agency's reserve fund to balance an unbalanced line-item budget should be viewed as the solution of last resort. The reason is that dipping into a reserve fund avoids the necessity of making the more difficult choice of reducing proposed expenses or finding ways to increase revenues. Additionally, an opportunity cost arises when a reserve fund is used to balance an unbalanced budget; the funds once used are no longer available for other special needs or emergencies. Unless one-time-only expenses are involved (e.g., a one-time purchase of a piece of critical equipment), the utilization of reserve funds to balance an unbalanced budget simply delays the decision to reduce expenses or increase revenues.

The second way to balance an unbalanced line-item budget is to find additional sources of revenue. A temptation sometimes exists to balance an unbalanced budget by simply increasing revenues when no real expectation exists that the revenues will be forthcoming. On its face, this approach makes little sense. Nevertheless, human service administrators can be tempted to take this easy way out rather than reduce proposed expenses. Including revenues in an agency line-item budget when there is no real expectation of receiving them is not a sound financial management practice.

The last of the three approaches to balancing an unbalanced budget is to reduce proposed expenses. This approach can be a painful exercise in that it may entail cutting back on proposed agency travel, supplies, equipment, and so on and may even necessitate reducing agency staff. Nevertheless, an unbalanced budget must eventually be balanced. In the end, it is easier to make reductions and cuts in an agency's proposed expenses before the fiscal year begins than after. For each month that passes in a fiscal year, a human service agency has less and less flexibility in making cuts and reductions in its line-item budget.

Table 7.2 presents a balanced fiscal year line-item budget for the Houston Heath Care Agency based on the model shown in Table 7.1.

TABLE 7.2 Houston Home Care Agency Line-Item Budget

(January 1, 20X1–December 31, 20X1)

Revenues

Contributions		$ 150,000
United Way		125,000
Government grants and contracts		532,100
Third-party insurance payments		400,000
Area agency on aging		125,000
Program income		125,000
	Total revenues	$1,457,100

Expenses

Salaries and wages

Executive director		$ 100,000
Financial manager		75,000
3 secretaries @ $25,000		75,000
Nursing coordinator		65,000
4 nurses @ $50,000		200,000
Homemaker coordinator		45,000
15 homemakers @ $25,000		375,000
Home-delivered meals coordinator		40,000
2 (half-time) van drivers @ $15,000		30,000
	Total salaries and wages	$1,005,000

Employee-related expenses (@ 22% of salaries and wages)		$ 221,100

Other operating expenses

Rent		$ 35,000
Utilities		12,000
Telephone		5,000
Medical supplies		25,000
Cleaning supplies		15,000
Office supplies		10,000
Purchased meals		60,000
Equipment		5,000
Printing and duplicating		5,000
Employee travel		22,000
Postage and shipping		3,000
Van rental (2 vans)		9,000
Insurance (building)		17,000
Miscellaneous		8,000
	Total other operating expenses	$ 231,000
	Total expenses	$1,457,100

Major Advantages and Disadvantages of Line-Item Budgeting Systems

As Table 7.2 demonstrates, the major advantage of line-item budgeting is its simplicity. Any staff member, board member, volunteer or interested citizen can pick up the line-item budget of a human service agency and see (a) the source and amount of the agency's revenues, (b) how the funds will be used in terms of staff, equipment, facilities, travel, and so on, and (c) if the budget is balanced.

The major disadvantages of line-item budgeting systems are twofold. First, line-item budgets say nothing about how much service a human service agency provides, the cost of that service, the number of outcomes the agency accomplished, or their attendant costs. The first major disadvantage of line-item budgeting leads directly to the second. Resource allocation discussions and decisions tend to be framed by the line-items themselves because no other information is available. For example, during the budget process, discussions and decisions tend to take the form of deciding to increase or decrease particular line-items (e.g., salaries, employee-related expenses, travel). Such issues as the amount of service provided (efficiency considerations) and the outcomes achieved (effectiveness considerations) by a human service agency's various programs are not taken into consideration because the information is not made a part of the budget process. It is precisely because of the inability of line-item budgeting systems to deal with the issues of efficiency and effectiveness that performance budgeting systems and program budgeting systems were developed.

Monitoring a Line-Item Budget

As already mentioned, a line-item budget is essentially a financial plan. A financial plan, like many plans, may require changes from time to time. For example, during a fiscal year actual revenues received may fall behind anticipated revenues or actual expenses may exceed proposed expenses. Because things change, a line-item budget needs to be monitored during the fiscal year. The monitoring of a human service agency's line-item budget usually takes the form of monthly or quarterly financial reports that compare actual revenues received and actual expenses incurred to anticipated revenues and proposed expenses.

A simplified monthly financial report for the Houston Home Care Agency is illustrated in Table 7.3. The financial report covers the first three months, or the first quarter, of HHCA's fiscal year. Note that a similar monthly report for each of the agency's three programs could also be prepared. In the first column of the monthly financial report is HHCA's approved line-item budget for the fiscal year including both anticipated revenues and proposed expenses. The second column shows the revenues received and the expenses incurred during the past month of operations (the third month of the fiscal year). The third column shows the cumulative totals (revenues and expenses) year-to-date. And the last column shows the variance (over or under) between anticipated and actual revenues and between actual and proposed expenses.

TABLE 7.3   Houston Home Care Agency Monthly Financial Report

	Budgeted	This Month	Year-to-Date	Variance
Revenues				
Contributions	$ 150,000	$ 15,000	$ 40,000	+
United Way	125,000	12,000	36,000	+
Government grants and contracts	532,100	45,000	140,000	+
Third-party insurance payments	400,000	30,000	100,000	0
Area agency on aging	125,000	15,000	50,000	+
Program income	125,000	10,000	50,000	+
Total revenues	$1,457,100	$127,000	$416,000	(+)
Expenses				
Salaries and wages	$1,005,000	$ 80,000	$240,000	−
ERE	221,100	18,000	54,000	−
Rent	35,000	3,000	9,000	+
Utilities	12,000	1,000	3,000	0
Telephone	5,000	750	1,200	−
Medical supplies	25,000	2,000	6,000	−
Cleaning supplies	15,000	1,000	3,500	−
Office supplies	10,000	900	2,000	−
Purchased meals	60,000	4,500	14,000	−
Equipment	5,000	500	1,000	−
Printing and duplicating	5,000	750	1,250	0
Employee travel	22,000	3,000	12,000	+
Postage and shipping	3,000	400	1,000	+
Van rental (2 vans)	9,000	750	2,250	0
Insurance (building)	17,000	1,500	4,200	−
Miscellaneous	8,000	750	1,900	−
Total expenses	$1,457,100	$118,800	$356,300	(−)

Perhaps the most important feature of Table 7.3 from monitoring and financial management perspectives is the variance column. For this reason, the monthly or quarterly financial report is also sometimes referred to as a *variance report*. The variance column provides a cumulative overview of the financial position of HHCA every month during the fiscal year. The executive director, the board of directors, the chief financial person, program managers, and other staff can readily see if revenues are keeping pace with expenses. The variance column also shows the condition (over or under) of each line-item in the budget, so that if expenses are exceeding revenues, the problem areas can be pinpointed. A review of Table 7.3 leads to the conclusion that the Houston Health Care Agency is in relatively good financial condition three months into its fiscal year. Revenues are exceeding expenses and only one line-item, "travel," shows an overage (+), an excess of actual expenses over proposed expenses.

The question might well be asked, Where does the agency get the financial data to complete the monthly (or quarterly) financial or variance report? The answer is that actual expense data are compiled from the agency's financial books and records. Deriving the data for anticipated revenues and proposed expenses is somewhat less precise. Frequently, the total revenue and total expense figures from the approved line-item budget for a fiscal year are simply divided by twelve months and the assumption is made that, everything else being equal, the agency should receive one-twelfth of its revenues each month and expend one-twelfth of its budget each month. This approach is obviously overly simplistic because the receipt of revenues and the incurrence of expenses are not so predictable. Nevertheless, this approach does have the benefit of being readily understandable and variances in revenues and expenses can be discussed and explained at staff and board of directors meetings.

Performance Budgeting Systems

Unlike line-item budgeting, which can be done at the agency level or the program level, both performance budgeting systems and program budgeting systems, (which are discussed next) are accomplished only at the program level.

    The purpose of a performance budgeting system is to relate agency expenses to programs by determining (a) a program output (or unit of service) performance measure, (b) the total program cost, and (c) the cost per output or cost per unit of service. Procedurally, the development of a performance budget for a human service program requires determining the total program cost for a fiscal year and then dividing the total cost by the number of outputs (units of service) to be achieved during the fiscal year to determine a cost per output or cost per unit of service. This process is graphically illustrated in Table 7.4.

    Performance budgeting provides insights into the productivity of a human service program. Referring back to Figure 7.1, performance budgeting relates outputs (how much service a program provides) and quality to inputs (the total cost of the program). The ratio of outputs to inputs is the classic definition of efficiency or productivity. Consequently, performance budgeting can be thought of as efficiency budgeting or productivity budgeting.

TABLE 7.4   **Determining a Human Service Program's Cost per Output and Cost per Outcome**

Cost per Output	Cost per Outcome
$\dfrac{\text{Total program cost}}{\text{Total outputs}} = \text{Cost per Output}$	$\dfrac{\text{Total program cost}}{\text{Total outcomes}} = \text{Cost per outcome}$

An example of a performance budget is illustrated in Table 7.5. The format of a performance budget is decidedly different from the format of a line-item budget. In a line-item budget, the emphasis is on how the agency resources are to be spent by line-item. In a performance budgeting, the emphasis is on the volume of service provided by a program, the total cost of the program, and the cost per output or unit of service.

Advantages and Disadvantages of Performance Budgeting Systems

The major advantages of performance budgeting systems are that (a) they provide information on the amount of service provided by a human service program and the attendant costs including determination of the cost per output or per unit of service and (b) they raise the level of debate from line-items to programs, program services, program costs, and program efficiency.

TABLE 7.5   Houston Health Care Agency

Performance Budget
January 1, 20X1–December 31, 20X1

Visiting Nurse Program

1. Total program cost $_____

2. Output (unit of service)
   performance measure   One visit

3. Total outputs (units of service)   #_____

4. Cost per output (unit of service) $_____

Homemaker Program

1. Total program cost $_____

2. Output (unit of service)
   performance measure   One hour of service

3. Total outputs (units of service)   #_____

4. Cost per output (unit of service) $_____

Home-Delivered Meals Program

1. Total program cost $_____

2. Output (unit of service)
   performance measure   One meal

3. Total outputs (units of service)   #_____

4. Cost per output (unit of service) $_____

From a financial management perspective being able to determine the cost per output (or unit of service) for a human service agency's various programs is extremely important today for a variety of reasons:

- Knowing a human service program's cost per output (unit of service) means that a human service agency can translate increases and decreases in funding to increases and decreases in its service delivery capability.
- Monitoring a human service program's cost per output (unit of service) over time enables human service administrators to better understand and control costs.
- A human service program's cost per output (unit of service) can be benchmarked (compared) to similar programs provided by similar human service agencies.
- Many government human service agencies now contract with private nonprofits on the basis of outputs or units of service (see Chapter 12). Private nonprofit human service agency contractors are paid a fixed price or fee per output (unit of service). Under this type of contractual arrangement, a private nonprofit human service must know its true unit cost or it may underprice its services.

In terms of raising the level of debate, performance budgeting systems are a considerable improvement over line-item budgeting systems. In line-item budgeting systems, the debate is over what line items will be allocated what resources. In performance budgeting systems, efficiency considerations such as the amount of service provided by a program and its costs can be compared to other programs operated by a human service agency. Thus, the level of debate is raised from line items to programs and program efficiency.

The major disadvantage of performance budgeting systems and program budgeting systems as well is that human service agencies must employ sophisticated cost analysis techniques (see Chapter 8) in order to determine the full cost of a program and to derive accurate unit costs. While describing this aspect of performance budgeting as a major disadvantage, the point should also be made that being able to fully cost one's programs and derive accurate unit costs is nevertheless an essential component of the financial management of human service agencies today.

Program Budgeting Systems

The idea behind program budgeting systems is to relate agency expenses to programs, measures of program outcomes, and the cost to the program of achieving outcomes. Procedurally, a program budgeting system requires computing a human service program's total cost for a fiscal year and dividing that cost by the number of outcomes to be achieved in order to derive a cost per outcome (see Table 7.4).

Performance budgeting provides insights into the effectiveness of a human service program. Referring back to Figure 7.1, performance budgeting relates outcomes to inputs. The ratio of outcomes to inputs is a contemporary definition of effectiveness in the language of performance measurement. Consequently, program budgeting can also be thought of as effectiveness budgeting.

An example of a program budget is illustrated in Table 7.6. The format of a program budget looks much like that of a performance budget, except that in the case of a program budget format the focus is on outcomes, not outputs or units of service. In Table 7.6, only one outcome performance measure is shown: "one client maintained in his/her own home." The reason is that all three HHCA programs share this outcome. The Visiting Nurse Program, the Homemaker Program, and the Home-Delivered Meals Program represent a combination of programs designed to help elderly and physically disabled persons remain in independent living arrangements.

Advantages and Disadvantages of Program Budgeting Systems

The major advantages of program budgeting systems are that (a) they provide information on the amount of (client) outcomes achieved by a human service program and the attendant costs, including determination of cost per outcome, and (b) they raise the level of debate from service and efficiency concerns to clients and effectiveness concerns.

Being able to determine a program's cost per outcome is also extremely important for the financial management of human service agencies today because

- Knowing a human service program's cost per client outcome means that a human service agency can translate increases and decreases in funding to increases and decreases in its ability to impact upon the lives of clients.
- Monitoring a human service program's cost per client outcome over time enables human service administrators to better understand and control costs.

TABLE 7.6   Houston Health Care Agency

Program Budget
January 1, 20X1–December 31, 20X1
Visiting Nurse Program, Homemaker Program, and Home-Delivered Meals Program

1. Total program costs	$_____
2. Outcome performance measure	One client able to remain in his/her own home
3. Total outcomes	#_____
4. Cost per outcome	$_____

- A human service program's cost per client outcome can be benchmarked (compared) to similar programs provided by similar human service agencies.
- A few government human service agencies today are experimenting with contracting with private nonprofits exclusively for the achievement of client outcomes (see Chapter 12). Private nonprofit human service agency contractors are paid solely on the basis of the outcomes they achieve with clients. Consequently, private nonprofit human service agencies must know their true cost per client outcome in order to ensure that they do not underprice their services.

A major disadvantage of program budgeting systems is that good outcome performance measures are frequently hard to develop. Many human service programs still do not have generally accepted outcome measures because no agreement exists among stakeholders.

In terms of raising the level of debate, program budgeting systems are an improvement over both line-item budgeting systems and performance budgeting systems. With program budgeting systems, the debate is on effectiveness concerns (what happens to clients in terms of outcomes), not on line-items or efficiency considerations. Program budgeting systems represent one way of operationalizing that most elusive of all human service and social work goals: maintaining a client focus.

Monitoring Performance and Program Budgeting Systems

Just as line-item budgets need to be monitored during the fiscal year, so too do performance and program budgets. Table 7.7 is an example of what a monthly "Performance and Program Budget Report" might look like for the Houston Home Care Agency. The report is similar to HHCA's Monthly Financial Report (Table 7.3), but rather than the focus being on line items, the focus is on actual outputs or units of service, outcomes, and their costs compared to planned outputs or units of service, outcomes, and their costs.

An analysis of Table 7.7 indicates that all three programs operated by HHCA are performing well for the first quarter of the fiscal year. Actual outputs (units of service), outcomes, total program costs, cost per output (unit of service), and cost per outcome are in keeping with projections made during the budget process. As was the case with the "Monthly Financial Report" for HHCA, the monthly planned figures included in Table 7.7 are computed by dividing the planned figures by 12.

A Comprehensive Budgeting System

By now it should be apparent to the reader that an optimum approach to budgeting in a human service agency would be to utilize all three major budgeting systems:

TABLE 7.7   Houston Home Care Agency Monthly

Performance and Program Budgeting Report
(January 1, 20X1–March 31,20X1

	Planned	This Month	Year-to-Date	Variance
Visiting Nurse Service Program				
1. Total outputs (units of service)	7,000	600	1,800	+
2. Total program cost	$ 492,678	$ 41,056	$123,000	−
3. Cost per output (unit of service)	$ 70.38	$ 68.43	$ 68.33	−
Homemaker Program				
1. Total outputs (units of service)	32,500 (hours)	2,700	8,150	+
2. Total program cost	$ 746,019	$ 62,000	$186,000	0
3. Cost per output (unit of service)	$ 22.95	$ 22.96	$ 22.82	−
Home-Delivered Meals Program				
1. Total outputs (units of service)	32,500 (meals)	2,700	8,150	+
2. Total program cost	$ 218,403	$ 18,000	$ 54,000	−
4. Cost per output (unit of service)	$ 6.72	$ 6.67	$ 6.63	−
Program Outcomes				
1. Total outcomes	125	125	125	0
2. Total programs costs	$1,457,100	$118,800	$356,300	−
3. Cost per outcome	$ 11,656	$ 11,275	$ 11,250	−

Note: All three programs share the same outcome performance measure: to maintain 125 clients in their own homes during the fiscal year.

line-item, performance, and program. These three major budgeting systems can actually be viewed as component parts of one comprehensive budgeting system designed to provide data and information from a variety of financial management perspectives: a financial control perspective (line-item budgeting system), an efficiency or productivity perspective (performance budgeting system), and an effectiveness perspective (program budgeting system). Additionally, in order for a human service program to satisfy the requirement of the Government Performance and Results Act (GPRA) and the service efforts and accomplishments (SEA) reporting initiative of the Governmental Accounting Standards Board (GASB), all three major budgeting systems need to be utilized.

Summary

This chapter examined the purposes of line-item, performance, and program budgeting systems and provided examples of each. The chapter also looked at how a human service agency might go about monitoring these three major budgeting systems. Left unanswered at this point is exactly how human service administrators can determine the total cost of a program and how to determine a cost per output (unit of service) and a cost per outcome. Chapter 8 provides the answers to these questions including where the information comes from to complete Tables 7.5 and 7.6.

CHAPTER

8 Cost Analysis

In the previous chapter, the benefits of performance budgeting and program budgeting were discussed. Among the benefits identified were the use of performance budgeting and program budgeting to determine the full cost of a human service program, the cost per output (unit of service), and the cost per outcome. This chapter deals with the actual processes involved in implementing performance budgeting and program budgeting and in determining a program's total cost, cost per output (unit of service), and cost per outcome.

Cost analysis or *cost determination* are the names historically given to the actual process involved in determining a program's total cost (Kelly, 1984; Horngren, Foster, & Datar, 1997). For purposes of this chapter we will use the term, *cost analysis*. Working from a human service agency's line-item budget, cost analysis will be used to compute the full cost of a human service program and to develop both a performance budget and a program budget. Once the full cost of a human service program is determined, a cost per output (unit of service) and a cost per outcome can be derived.

Prerequisites for Using Cost Analysis

In order to conduct a cost analysis, a human service agency must already have in place a program structure, output and outcome performance measures for each program, and a line-item budget. Throughout this chapter, the Houston Home Care Agency (HHCA) will continue to serve as an ongoing case study. The HHCA satisfies all three requirements. HHCA operates three programs (a visiting nurse program, a homemaker program, and a home-delivered meals program). The three programs have identified output and outcome performance measures (Figure 8.1). And the HHCA has an approved line-item budget in place (Table 8.1).

The Cost Analysis Process

The primary financial management tool used in cost analysis is called a cost allocation plan. A cost allocation plan is essentially a spread sheet. An example of a cost allocation plan for the HHCA is shown in Table 8.2. The first column of the cost allocation plan contains the line-items from HHCA's approved line-item budget.

FIGURE 8.1   Houston Home Care Agency

Program Performance Measures

1. **Visiting Nurse Program**
   A. Output (unit of service) performance measure: "one visit."
   B. Outcome performance measure: "one client able to remain in his/her own home."

2. **Homemaker Program**
   A. Output (unit of service) performance measure: "one hour of service."
   B. Outcome performance measure: "one client able to remain in his/her own home."

3. **Home-Delivered Meals Program**
   A. Output (unit of service) performance measure: "one meal."
   B. Outcome performance measure: "one client able to remain in his/her own home."

Note: The three programs share the same outcome performance measure. It is the combination of the three services that enables a client to remain in his or her own home.

The second, third, and fourth columns identify each of the three programs operated by HHCA and the fifth column is labeled the "indirect cost pool." A cost allocation plan involves only the "expenses" section of a human service agency's line-item budget, the "revenues" section is excluded.

Using the cost allocation plan, the process of cost analysis involves (a) identifying direct and indirect costs, (b) assigning direct costs to programs and indirect costs to the indirect cost pool, (c) allocating the indirect cost pool to programs, (d) determining the total cost of each program, and (e) computing a cost per output (unit of service) and a cost per outcome for each program.

Identifying Direct and Indirect Costs

The total cost, or full cost, of any human service program is the sum of its direct and indirect costs. The first step in cost analysis is to identify the items in a human service agency's line-item budget as being either direct costs or indirect costs. A *direct cost* is any item of cost in an agency's line-item budget that benefits one and only one program. An *indirect cost* is any item of cost in an agency's line-item budget that benefits two or more programs. An indirect cost is sometimes referred to as a *shared cost* or an *overhead cost* because the item of cost is shared by two or more programs. Every line item in a line-item budget can be classified as either a direct cost or an indirect cost.

In the HHCA's approved line-item budget (Table 8.1), the salaries and wages of the nursing coordinator and the four nurses are direct costs to the visiting nurse program (denoted by the letter N) because they work only for this one program; they do not split their time between the visiting nurse program and either the homemaker program or the home-delivered meals program. If the nursing supervisor and the four nurses did split their time between the visiting nurse program

TABLE 8.1   Houston Home Care Agency Line-Item Budget

(January 1, 20X1–December 31, 20X1)

Revenues

Contributions	$ 150,000
United Way	125,000
Government grants and contracts	532,100
Third-party insurance payments	400,000
Area agency on aging	125,000
Program income	125,000
Total Revenues	**$1,457,100**

Expenses

Salaries and Wages

Executive director	$ 100,000
Financial manager	75,000
3 secretaries @ $25,000	75,000
Nursing coordinator (N)	65,000
4 nurses @ $50,000 (N)	200,000
Homemaker coordinator (H)	45,000
15 homemakers @ $25,000 (H)	375,000
Home-delivered meals coordinator (M)	40,000
2 (half-time) van drivers @ $15,000 (M)	30,000
Total Salaries and Wages	**$1,005,000**

Employee-Related Expenses
(@ 22% of Salaries and Wages) $ 221,100

Other Operating Expenses

Rent	$ 35,000
Utilities	12,000
Telephone	5,000
Medical supplies (N)	25,000
Cleaning supplies (H)	15,000
Office supplies	10,000
Purchased meals (M)	60,000
Equipment	5,000
Printing and duplicating	5,000
Employee travel	22,000
Postage and shipping	3,000
Van rental (2 vans) (M)	9,000
Insurance (building)	17,000
Miscellaneous	8,000
Total Other Operating	**$ 231,000**
Total Expenses	**$1,457,100**

Notes: N = Visiting nurse program
         H = Homemaker program   M = Home-delivered meals program

TABLE 8.2   Houston Home Care Agency Cost Allocation Plan Format

Budget Line Items	Visiting Nurse Program	Homemaker Program	Home-Delivered Meals Program	Indirect Cost Pool
Salaries and Wages				
Executive director				
Financial manager				
3 secretaries				
Nursing coordinator (N)				
4 nurses (N)				
Homemaker coordinator (H)				
15 homemakers (H)				
Home-delivered meals Coordinator (M)				
2 (half-time) van drivers (M)				
Salaries and Wages (Total)				
Employee-Related Expenses (@ 22% of salaries & wages)				
Other Operating Expenses				
Rent				
Utilities				
Telephone				
Medical supplies (N)				
Cleaning supplies (H)				
Office supplies				
Purchased meals (M)				
Equipment				
Printing and duplicating				
Employee travel				
Postage and shipping				
Van Rental (2 vans) (M)				
Insurance (building)				
Miscellaneous				
SUBTOTALS				
ALLOCATE INDIRECT COST POOL				
TOTAL PROGRAM COSTS				

and one or both of the other agency programs, then their salaries and wages would be treated as indirect costs. In the same vein, the homemaker coordinator and the 15 homemakers are direct costs to the homemaker program (denoted by the letter *H*) because they work only for this program. Finally, the salaries and wages of the home-delivered meals coordinator and the two half-time van drivers are direct costs to the home-delivered meals program (denoted by the letter *M*) because they work only for the home-delivered meals program. Note that line-item budgets usually do not contain little hints such as the letters *N, H,* and *M* in Table 8.1. These little hints have been added to make clear which items of cost in the line-item budget are to be treated as direct costs and which are to be treated as indirect costs. In Table 8.1 any line item without one of the little hints is treated as an indirect cost.

The executive director is an indirect cost because the work of the executive director benefits all agency programs. The executive director might spend a defined period of time working on only one program (e.g., writing a grant proposal for the visiting nurse program), but overall the work of the executive director benefits all the agency's programs. For the same reason, the financial manager is also an indirect cost. The financial manager has responsibility for all of the agency programs. The three secretaries are also indirect costs because they perform work that benefits all three programs in addition to performing work for the executive director and the finance manager.

A few line items under "other operating " are direct costs, but most are indirect costs. Medical supplies are direct costs because they are used only by the visiting nurse program. Cleaning supplies are direct costs because they are used only by the homemaker program. And purchased meals and van rental are direct costs because they are used only by the home-delivered meals program. All the other costs under "other operating" are indirect costs because they benefit two or more programs. For example, rent is an indirect cost because all three programs share the same facility. Utilities, telephone, office supplies, equipment, printing and duplicating, employee travel, postage and shipping, insurance on the building, and miscellaneous are all shared costs and are consequently treated as indirect costs.

Assigning Direct Costs to Programs and Indirect Costs to the Indirect Cost Pool

Once all items in a human service agency's line-item budget have been identified as being either direct costs or indirect costs, the next step in cost analysis is to assign the direct costs to their respective programs using the cost allocation plan. This process is illustrated in Table 8.3.

The total direct costs of the three programs are visiting nurse program ($348,300), homemaker ($527,400), and home-delivered meals ($154,400). All indirect costs ($427,000) are assigned to the indirect cost pool. The indirect cost pool serves as a temporary holding pool.

TABLE 8.3   Houston Home Care Agency Cost Allocation Plan

	(Assignment of Direct and Indirect Costs)			
Budget Line Items	**Visiting Nurse Program**	**Homemaker Program**	**Home-Delivered Meals Program**	**Indirect Cost Pool**
Salaries and Wages				
Executive director				$100,000
Financial manager				75,000
3 secretaries				75,000
Nursing coordinator (N)	$ 65,000			
4 nurses (N)	200,000			
Homemaker coordinator (H)		$ 45,000		
15 homemakers (H)		375,000		
Home-delivered meals				
Coordinator (M)			$ 40,000	
2 (half-time) van drivers (M)			30,000	
Salaries and Wages (Totals)	$265,000	$420,000	$ 70,000	$250,000
Employee-Related Expenses (@ 22% of salaries and wages)	$ 58,300	$ 92,400	$ 15,400	$ 55,000
Other Operating Expenses				
Rent				$ 35,000
Utilities				12,000
Telephone				5,000
Medical supplies (N)	$ 25,000			
Cleaning supplies (H)		$ 15,000		
Office supplies				10,000
Purchased meals (M)			$ 60,000	
Equipment				5,000
Printing and duplicating				5,000
Employee travel				22,000
Postage and shipping				3,000
Van Rental (2 vans) (M)			9,000	
Insurance (building)				17,000
Miscellaneous				8,000
SUBTOTALS	$348,300	$527,400	$154,400	$427,000
ALLOCATE INDIRECT COST POOL				
TOTAL PROGRAM COSTS				

Two explanatory points should be made here. First, the employee-related expenses (ERE) in Table 8.3 follow the salaries and wages they relate to. For this reason, some ERE are treated as a direct cost, some as an indirect cost. For example, the salaries and wages ($265,000) of the nursing coordinator and the four nurses are direct costs to the visiting nurse program. Consequently, the ERE ($58,300) that goes with these costs are also treated as a direct cost to the visiting nurse program. Likewise, the salaries and wages ($250,000) contained in the indirect cost pool also have associated ERE costs ($55,000) that are treated as indirect costs. Second, working across the row entitled "subtotals," the total of the direct costs of the three programs plus the costs in the indirect cost pool equal the total line-item budget shown in Table 8.1:

Visiting nurse program	$ 348,300
Homemaker program	527,400
Home-delivered meals program	154,400
Indirect cost pool	427,000
Total	$1,457,100

Allocating Indirect Costs To Programs

The indirect costs ($427,000) in the indirect cost pool must be allocated (assigned) to the three programs in order to determine each program's total cost or full cost. The process of assigning indirect costs to programs is called *cost allocation*. The basic principle of cost allocation is that indirect costs should be allocated to programs in relationship to the benefits each program receives. What this means is that indirect costs cannot be arbitrarily allocated to programs; some logical and defensible method, also referred to as a *base*, must be used that relates indirect costs to programs. A multitude of cost allocation methods or bases exist. Some of the more common ones (arranged from the simplistic to the complex) are direct charging, total direct costs, salaries and wages, direct labor hours, step-down method, job order costing, process costing, and activity-based costing (Martin & Menefee, 2000).

The three most common cost allocation methods, or bases, used in the human services are (1) total direct costs, (2) salaries and wages, and (3) direct labor hours. These three methodologies will be used to allocate the indirect costs in Table 8.3.

Cost Allocation Using Total Direct Costs

Cost allocation using total direct costs means that a ratio of indirect costs to direct costs is determined and used as the basis for allocating indirect costs to programs. The premise underlining this methodology is that individual programs should be allocated indirect costs in proportion to their relative proportion of total direct costs. The process of using total direct costs as the cost allocation methodology is illustrated in Table 8.4.

TABLE 8.4   **Cost Allocation Using Total Direct Costs as the Base**

$$\frac{\text{Indirect costs (from indirect cost pool)}}{\text{Total direct costs (of all programs)}} = \text{Indirect cost rate (\%)}$$

The "total direct costs" of each program are multiplied by the indirect cost rate; the resulting figure is the amount of indirect costs to be allocated to that program.

Example: Houston Home Care Agency

$$\frac{\$427,000}{\$348,300 + \$527,400 + \$154,400} = \frac{\$427,000}{\$1,030,100} = 41.452\ \%$$

Visiting Nurse Program

$348,300 \times .41452 = \$144,378$ (share of indirect costs)

Homemaker Program

$527,400 \times .41452 = \$218,619$ (share of indirect costs)

Home-Delivered Meals Program

$154,400 \times .41452 = \$64,003$ (share of indirect costs)

The total indirect costs in the indirect cost pool ($427,000) are placed in the numerator and the total of the direct costs of all three of HHCA programs is placed in the denominator, or the base. The resulting percentage (41.452%) is referred to as an *indirect cost rate*. The total direct costs of each program are then multiplied by the indirect cost rate to determine the proportion of the indirect costs in the indirect cost pool that should be allocated to that program. For example, when the total direct costs of the visiting nurse program ($348,300) are multiplied by the indirect cost rate (.41452), the result is $144,378. This figure represents the visiting nurse program's proportionate share of the indirect costs in the indirect cost pool. It should be noted that the sum of the indirect costs allocated to the three programs should equal the sum of the indirect costs in the indirect cost pool:

Visiting nurse program	$144,378
Homemaker program	218,619
Home-delivered meals program	64,003
	$427,000

Determining the Total Cost of Each Program

The next step in cost analysis is to include the indirect costs under their respective programs using the cost allocation plan format and to determine the total cost, or full cost, of each program (Table 8.5). The total cost of the visiting nurse program is

TABLE 8.5   Houston Home Care Agency Cost Allocation Plan

(Using Total Direct Costs as the Base)

Budget Line Items	Visiting Nurse Program	Homemaker Program	Home-Delivered Meals Program	Indirect Cost Pool
Salaries and Wages				
Executive director				$100,000
Financial manager				75,000
3 secretaries				75,000
Nursing coordinator (N)	$ 65,000			
4 nurses (N)	200,000			
Homemaker coordinator (H)		$ 45,000		
15 homemakers (H)		375,000		
Home-delivered meals				
Coordinator (M)			$ 40,000	
2 (half-time) van drivers (M)			30,000	
Salaries and Wages (Totals)	$265,000	$420,000	$ 70,000	$250,000
Employee-Related Expenses (@ 22% of salaries and wages)	$ 58,300	$ 92,400	$ 15,400	$ 55,000
Other Operating Expenses				
Rent				$ 35,000
Utilities				12,000
Telephone				5,000
Medical supplies (N)	$ 25,000			
Cleaning supplies (H)		$ 15,000		
Office supplies				10,000
Purchased meals (M)			$ 60,000	
Equipment				5,000
Printing and duplicating				5,000
Employee travel				22,000
Postage and shipping				3,000
Van rental (2 vans) (M)			9,000	
Insurance (building)				17,000
Miscellaneous				8,000
SUBTOTALS	$348,300	$527,400	$154,400	$427,000
ALLOCATE INDIRECT COST POOL	$144,378	$218,619	$ 64,003	
TOTAL PROGRAM COSTS	$492,678	$746,019	$218,403	

$492,678. The total cost of the homemaker program is $746,019. The total cost of the home-delivered meals program is $218,403. And the combined total cost of all three programs is $1,457,100, the total of the HHCA's line-item budget in Table 8.1.

Computing Cost Per Output
(Unit of Service) and Cost Per Outcome

The final step in cost analysis is the determination of a program's cost per output (unit of service) and cost per outcome. As Table 8.6 and Table 8.7 demonstrate, the procedures are relatively straightforward. For example, to compute a cost per output (unit of service) for the visiting nurse program (Table 8.6), the total cost of the program ($492,678) is placed in the numerator and the total outputs, or units of service (7,000 visits), to be provided during the fiscal year is placed in the denominator. The result is a cost per output (unit of service) of $70.38 per visit. Computing a

---

TABLE 8.6 Determining a Cost per Output (or Unit of Service)

1. Visiting Nurse Program

$$\frac{\$492,678}{7,000 \text{ visits}} = \$70.38 \text{ per visit}$$

The total number of outputs (or units of service) to be provided by the visiting nurse program is 7,000, computed as follows:

(125 clients) × (4 regular visits per month) × (12 months) = 6,000 visits
Plus 1,000 emergency and callback visits during the year = 1,000 visits
                                                                   7,000 visits

2. Homemaker Program

$$\frac{\$746,019}{32,500 \text{ hours}} = \$22.95 \text{ per hour}$$

The total number of outputs (or units of service) to be provided by the homemaker program is 32,500 hours of service, computed as follows:

(125 clients) × (5 hours per week) × (52 weeks) = 32,500 hours

3. Home-Delivered Meals Program

$$\frac{\$218,403}{32,500 \text{ meals}} = \$ 6.72 \text{ per meal}$$

The total number of outputs (or units of service) to be provided by the home-delivered meals program is 32,500 meals, computed as follows:

(125 clients) × (5 meals per week) × (52 weeks) = 32,500 meals

---

TABLE 8.7   Computing a Cost per Outcome

The three HHCA programs (visiting nurse, homemaker, and home-delivered meals) share the same outcome performance measure: one client able to remain in his/her own home.

The total number of outcomes to be provided by the combined three programs is 125.

125 clients able to remain in their own homes during the fiscal year

$$\frac{\$1,457,100}{125 \text{ clients}} = \$11,656.80 \text{ per outcome}$$

cost per outcome follows the same procedure, except in the case of HHCA all three programs share the same outcome performance measure. The total cost of all three programs is placed in the numerator and the total outcomes to be achieved during the fiscal year are placed in the denominator. The result is the cost per outcome of $11,656.80.

The information is now available to develop both a performance budget and a program budget for the Houston Home Care Agency. Table 8.8 is an example of what a performance budget format for HHCA might look like; Table 8.9 is an example of what a program budget might look like.

TABLE 8.8   Houston Home Care Agency

Performance Budget

Visiting Nurse Program

1. Total program cost	=	$492,678
2. Total outputs (units of service)	=	7,000 visits
3. Cost per visit	=	$70.38

Homemaker Program

1. Total program cost	=	$746,019
2. Total outputs (units of service)	=	32,500 hours
3. Cost per hour	=	$22.95

Home-Delivered Meals Program

1. Total program cost	=	$218,403
2. Total outputs	=	32,500 meals
3. Cost per meal	=	$6.72

TABLE 8.9   Houston Home Care Agency

Program Budget

1. Programs:
    Visiting nurse program
    Homemaker program
    Home-delivered meals program

2. Total program costs   = $1,457,100

3. Total outcomes   =   125

4. Cost per outcome   = $11,656.80

Allocating Indirect Costs
Using Salaries and Wages

Another common cost allocation method, or base, used by human service agencies is salaries and wages. The rationale for the use of salaries and wages as the base is that most human service programs are labor intensive: 70 percent or more of the total cost of a program is frequently comprised of salary and wage costs. The argument is thus made that using salaries and wages as the base is a more equitable way of allocating indirect costs than is the total direct cost methodology.

Allocating indirect costs using salaries and wages necessitates computing the total salary and wage costs for a human service agency and allocating indirect costs to each program based on its relative proportionate share of salary and wage costs. The process is illustrated in Table 8.10.

The total indirect costs in the indirect cost pool ($427,000) are placed in the numerator, and the total salary and wage costs of all three HHCA programs are placed in the denominator. The resulting percentage (56.556%) is the indirect cost rate using salaries and wages as the base. The total salary and wage costs of each program are then multiplied by the indirect cost rate to determine the proportion of the indirect costs in the indirect cost pool that should be allocated to that program. For example, when the salary and wage costs of the visiting nurse program ($265,000) are multiplied by the indirect cost rate (.56556), the result is $149,874 which represents the proportionate share of the indirect costs in the indirect cost pool that should be allocated to the visiting nurse program. It should again be noted that the sum of the indirect costs allocated to the three programs should equal the sum of the indirect costs in the indirect cost pool:

Visiting nurse program	$149,874
Homemaker program	237,536
Home-delivered meals program	39,590
	$427,000

TABLE 8.10 Cost Allocation Using Salaries and Wages as the Base

$$\frac{\text{Indirect costs (from indirect cost pool)}}{\text{Total salaries and wages (of all programs)}} = \text{Indirect cost rate (\%)}$$

The "salaries and wages" of each program are then multiplied by the indirect cost rate; the resulting amount is the amount of indirect costs to be allocated to that program.

Example: Houston Home Care Agency

$$\frac{\$427,000}{\$265,000 + \$420,000 + \$70,000} = \frac{\$427,000}{\$755,000} = 56.556\%$$

Visiting Nurse Program

$265,000 × .56556 = $149,874 (share of indirect costs)

Homemaker Program

$420,000 × .56556 = $237,536 (share of indirect costs)

Home-delivered Meals Program

$70,000 × .56556 = $39,590 (share of indirect costs)

When the allocation of indirect costs using the total direct costs method or base (Table 8.4) is compared with the allocation of indirect costs using salaries and wages as the method or base (Table 8.10), one can see that some shifting occurs. The visiting nurse program's proportionate share of indirect costs increases slightly (+$5,496), the homemaker program's share increases moderately (+$18,917), and the home-delivered meals program's share decreases significantly (–$24,413). The reason for the shift is, of course, due to differences in each program's salary and wage costs; the home-delivered meals program has the lowest salary and wage costs of the three programs.

The reallocation of indirect costs means that the total cost, or full cost, of each program will change as well as each program's cost per output (unit of service) and cost per outcome. The total cost of the HHCA's three programs, using salaries and wages as the base for allocating indirect costs, is shown in Table 8.11.

The total cost of the visiting nurse program is now $498,174. The total cost of the homemaker program becomes $764,936. And the total cost of the home-delivered meals program is now $193,990. The combined total cost of all three programs is still $1,457,100, corresponding to the total of the HHCA's line-item budget in Table 8.1.

The amount of outputs, or units of service, and outcomes to be provided by each program during the fiscal year remains the same. However, because indirect costs have been reallocated, each program's cost per output (unit of service) changes. The revised costs are shown in Table 8.12. Note that because all three of

TABLE 8.11   Houston Home Care Agency Cost Allocation Plan

(Using Salaries and Wages as the Base)

Budget Line Items	Visiting Nurse Program	Homemaker Program	Home-Delivered Meals Program	Indirect Cost Pool
Salaries and Wages				
Executive director				$100,000
Financial manager				75,000
3 secretaries				75,000
Nursing coordinator (N)	$ 65,000			
4 nurses (N)	200,000			
Homemaker coordinator (H)		$ 45,000		
15 homemakers (H)		375,000		
Home-delivered meals coordinator (M)			$ 40,000	
2 (half-time) van drivers (M)			30,000	
Salaries and Wages (Total)	$265,000	$420,000	$ 70,000	$250,000
Employee-Related Expenses (@ 22% of salaries & wages)	$ 58,300	$ 92,400	$ 15,400	$ 55,000
Other Operating Expenses				
Rent				$ 35,000
Utilities				12,000
Telephone				5,000
Medical supplies (N)	$ 25,000			
Cleaning supplies (H)		$ 15,000		
Office supplies				10,000
Purchased meals (M)			$ 60,000	
Equipment				5,000
Printing and duplicating				5,000
Employee travel				22,000
Postage and shipping				3,000
Van rental (2 vans) (M)			$ 9,000	
Insurance (building)				17,000
Miscellaneous				8,000
SUBTOTALS	$348,300	$527,400	$154,400	$427,000
ALLOCATE INDIRECT COST POOL	$149,874	$237,536	$ 39,590	
TOTAL PROGRAM COSTS	$498,174	$764,936	$193,990	

TABLE 8.12   Cost per Output (or Unit of Service)

1. Visiting Nurse Program

$$\frac{\$498,174}{7,000 \text{ visits}} = \$71.17 \text{ per visit}$$

The total number of outputs (or units of service) to be provided by the visiting nurse program is 7,000, computed as follows:

(125 clients) × (4 regular visits per month) × (12 months) = 6,000 visits
Plus 1,000 emergency and callback visits during the year = 1,000 visits
                                                                                                              7,000 visits

2. Homemaker Program

$$\frac{\$764,936}{32,500 \text{ hours}} = \$23.54 \text{ per hour}$$

The total number of outputs (or units of service) to be provided by the homemaker program is 32,500 hours of service, computed as follows:

(125 clients) × (5 hours per week) × (52 weeks) = 32,500 hours

3. Home-Delivered Meals Program

$$\frac{\$193,990}{32,500 \text{ meals}} = \$ 5.97 \text{ per meal}$$

The total number of outputs (or units of service) to be provided by the home-delivered meals program is 32,500 meals, computed as follows:

(125 clients) × (5 meals per week) × (52 weeks) = 32,500 meals

HHCA's programs share the same outcome measure, the cost per outcome does not change (Table 8.13).

Finally, the amount shown on HHCA's performance budget also changes, but not the figures on its program budget. The revised HHCA performance budget is shown in Table 8.14.

TABLE 8.13   Computing a Cost per Outcome

The three HHCA programs (visiting nurse, homemaker, and home-delivered meals) share the same outcome performance measure: one client able to remain in his/her own home.

The total number of outcomes to be provided by the combined three programs is 125.

125 clients able to remain in their own homes during the fiscal year

$$\frac{\$1,457,100}{125 \text{ clients}} = \$11,656.80 \text{ per outcome}$$

TABLE 8.14   Houston Home Care Agency

Performance Budget

Visiting Nurse Program

1. Total program cost	=	$498,174
2. Total outputs (units of service)	=	7,000 visits
3. Cost per visit	=	$71.17

Homemaker Program

1. Total program cost	=	$764,936
2. Total outputs (units of service)	=	32,500 hours
3. Cost per hour	=	$23.54

Home-Delivered Meals Program

1. Total program cost	=	$193,990
2. Total outputs	=	32,500 meals
3. Cost per meal	=	$5.97

Allocating Indirect Costs Using Direct Labor Hours

The third of the most common cost allocation methods, or bases, used by human service agencies is direct labor hours. *Direct labor hours* refers to those positions in a line-item budget that are designated as direct costs to one of a human service agency's programs. The rationale for the use of direct labor hours is that every full-time person works the same amount of time for a human service agency or program, while salaries and wages vary significantly depending on education, experience, prevailing wage scales, and length of service. The argument is thus made that direct labor hours is a more equitable way of allocating indirect costs than either the total direct cost methodology or the salaries and wages methodology.

Allocating indirect costs using salaries and wages necessitates computing the total direct labor hours for a human service agency and allocating indirect costs to each program based on its relative proportionate share of direct labor hours. For computational purposes, 2080 hours is the standard number of hours worked in one fiscal year by a full-time equivalent (FTE) position. For example, in the Houston Health Care Agency, the staff of the visiting nurse program who are direct costs consist of one nursing coordinator and four nurses. In the absence of any information to the contrary, any position listed in a line-item budget is assumed to be an FTE position. The visiting nurse program then has five full-time equivalent positions (five FTEs). Each FTE position works 2,080 hours; the total direct labor hours for the visiting nurse program are 10,400 (2,080 × 5). The staff of the homemaker program who are direct costs consist of one homemaker program coordinator and fifteen homemakers. The homemaker program has sixteen full-time equivalent positions (sixteen FTEs). Each FTE position works 2,080 hours; the total direct labor hours for the homemaker program are 33,280 (2,080 × 16).

The situation with the home-delivered meals program is a little different. The staff of the home-delivered meals program who are direct cost consist of one home-delivered meals program coordinator and two half-time van drivers. The two half-time van drivers constitute one FTE. Thus, the home-delivered meals program has only two FTE positions. Each FTE position works 2,080 hours; the total direct labor hours for the homemaker program are 4160 (2,080 × 2).

The process of allocating indirect costs to programs using direct labor hours as the method, or base, is illustrated in Table 8.15.

The total indirect costs in the indirect cost pool ($427,000) are placed in the numerator and the total of the total direct labor hours of all three HHCA programs is placed in the denominator, or base. The resulting figure is a cost per direct labor hour ($8.92). The direct labor hours of each program are then multiplied by the cost per direct labor hour to determine the proportion of the indirect costs in the indirect cost pool that should be allocated to that program. For example, when the direct labor hours (10,400) of the visiting nurse program are multiplied by the cost per direct labor hour ($8.92), the result is $92,768, which represents the proportionate share of the indirect costs in the indirect cost pool that should be allocated to the visiting nurse program. This time, note that the sum of the indirect costs allo-

---

TABLE 8.15   Cost Allocation Direct Labor Hours as the Base

$$\frac{\text{Indirect costs (from indirect cost pool)}}{\text{Total direct labor hours (of all programs)}} = \text{Cost per Direct Labor Hour}$$

The "direct labor hours" of each program are multiplied by the cost per direct labor hour; the resulting figure is the amount of indirect costs to be allocated to that program.

Example: Houston Home Care Agency

$$\frac{\$427,000}{10,400 + 33,280 + 4,160} = \frac{\$427,000}{47,840} = \$8.92$$

Visiting Nurse Program

10,400 × $8.92 = $92,768 (share of indirect costs)

Homemaker Program

33,280 × $8.92 = $296,858 (share of indirect costs)

Home-Delivered Meals Program

4,160 × $8.92 = $37,107 (share of indirect costs)

cated to the three programs does not exactly equal the sum of the indirect costs in the indirect cost pool because of rounding problems.

Visiting nurse program	$ 92,768
Homemaker program	296,858
Home-delivered meals program	37,107
	$426,733

When the allocation of indirect costs using direct labor hours as the method or base (Table 8.15) is compared with the allocation of indirect costs using salaries and wages as the base (Table 8.10), some major shifts occur. The visiting nurse program's proportionate share of indirect costs decreases significantly (–$57,106), the homemaker program's share increases significantly (+$59,322), and the home-delivered meals program's share decreases slightly (–$2,483). The reason for the shift is, of course, differences in each program's direct labor hours. The home-delivered meals program and the visiting nurse program have significantly fewer staff than the homemaker program. The total costs of the HHCA's three programs, using direct labor costs as the method, or base, for allocating indirect costs, are shown in Table 8.16.

The total cost of the visiting nurse program is now $441,068. The total cost of the homemaker program becomes $824,258. And the total cost of the home-delivered meals program is now $191,507. The combined total cost of all three programs is just a little under the $1,457,100 figure for HHCA's line-item budget in Table 8.1; the difference is due to rounding problems.

The amounts of outputs (units of service) and outcomes to be provided by each program during the fiscal year remain the same. However, because indirect costs have again been reallocated, each program's cost per output (unit of service) changes. The revised costs per outputs are shown in Table 8.17. Because all three of HHCA's programs share the same outcome measure, the cost per outcome does not change (Table 8.18).

Finally, the amounts shown on HHCA's performance budget (Table 8.19) also change, but not the figures on its program budget.

Which Cost Allocation Method Is Best?

Which cost allocation method is best for an individual human service agency is a decision best made after consultation with the agency's accountants, auditors, and funding sources. Different government funding sources (federal, state, and local) sometimes have differing views on which cost allocation method they want their contractors and grantees to use in allocating indirect costs. However, once a human service agency selects a cost allocation method and uses it to allocate indirect costs to programs, it should not change to a different method without first securing approval from its funding sources. As the three examples in this chapter demonstrated, the indirect costs allocated to programs can vary significantly depending

TABLE 8.16   Houston Home Care Agency Cost Allocation Plan

	(Using Direct Labor Hours as the Base)			
Budget Line Items	Visiting Nurse Program	Homemaker Program	Home-Delivered Meals Program	Indirect Cost Pool
Salaries and Wages				
Executive director				$100,000
Financial manager				75,000
3 secretaries				75,000
Nursing coordinator (N)	$ 65,000			
4 nurses (N)	200,000			
Homemaker coordinator (H)		$ 45,000		
15 homemakers (H)		375,000		
Home-delivered meals coordinator (M)			$ 40,000	
2 (half-time) van drivers (M)			30,000	
Salaries and Wages (Totals)	$265,000	$420,000	$ 70,000	$250,000
Employee-Related Expenses (@ 22% of salaries and wages)	$ 58,300	$ 92,400	$ 15,400	$ 55,000
Other Operating Expenses				
Rent				$ 35,000
Utilities				12,000
Telephone				5,000
Medical supplies (N)	$ 25,000			
Cleaning supplies (H)		$ 15,000		
Office supplies				10,000
Purchased meals (M)			$ 60,000	
Equipment				5,000
Printing and duplicating				5,000
Employee travel				22,000
Postage and shipping				3,000
Van rental (2 vans) (M)			9,000	
Insurance (building)				17,000
Miscellaneous				8,000
SUBTOTALS	$348,300	$527,400	$154,400	$427,000
ALLOCATE INDIRECT COST POOL	$92,768	$296,858	$ 37,107	
TOTAL PROGRAM COSTS	$441,068	$824,258	$191,507	

TABLE 8.17   **Determining a Cost per Output (or Unit of Service)**

1. Visiting Nurse Program

$\dfrac{\$441,068}{7,000 \text{ visits}}$ = $63.01 per visit

The total number of outputs (or units of service) to be provided by the visiting nurse program is 7,000, computed as follows:

(125 clients) × (4 regular visits per month) × (12 months) = 6,000 visits
Plus 1,000 emergency and callback visits during the year = 1,000 visits
                                                                             7,000 visits

2. Homemaker Program

$\dfrac{\$824,258}{32,500 \text{ hours}}$ = $25.36 per hour

The total number of outputs (or units of service) to be provided by the homemaker program is 32,500 hours of service, computed as follows:

(125 clients) × (5 hours per week) × (52 weeks) = 32,500 hours

3. Home-Delivered Meals Program

$\dfrac{\$191,507}{32,500 \text{ meals}}$ = $ 5.89 per meal

The total number of outputs (or units of service) to be provided by the home-delivered meals program is 32,500 meals, computed as follows:

(125 clients) × (5 meals per week) × (52 weeks) = 32,500 meals

TABLE 8.18   **Computing a Cost per Outcome**

The three HHCA programs (visiting nurse, homemaker, and home-delivered meals) share the same outcome performance measure: one client able to remain in his/her own home.

The total number of outcomes to be provided by the combined three programs is 125.

125 clients able to remain in their own homes during the fiscal year

$\dfrac{\$1,457,100}{125 \text{ clients}}$ = $11,656.80 per outcome

TABLE 8.19   Houston Home Care Agency

Performance Budget

Visiting Nurse Program

1. Total program cost   = $441,068
2. Total outputs (units of service)   =   7,000 visits
3. Cost per visit   = $63.01

Homemaker Program

1. Total program cost   = $824,258
2. Total outputs (units of service)   =   32,500 hours
3. Cost per hour   = $25.36

Home-Delivered Meals Program

1. Total program cost   = $191,507
2. Total outputs   =   32,500 meals
3. Cost per meal   = $5.89

---

upon which method, or base, is used. Different methods also can significantly affect the cost per output (unit of service) and the cost per outcome of a human service program. Thus, the selection of a cost allocation method or base is an important financial management decision that should be made only after careful consideration.

Prospective Cost Analysis Versus Retrospective Cost Analysis

The three examples of cost analysis used in the chapter are what might be called proscriptive approaches in that they use budgetary data to estimate the total cost, or full cost, of human service programs. Estimated costs are not actual costs. During a fiscal year things happen that make estimates more or less accurate. Say, for example, a nurse in the HHCA's visiting nurse program resigns and it takes four weeks to hire a replacement. The actual expenses for nurses salaries in the HHCA's line-item budget will now be less than originally planned, which in turn affects the allocation of indirect costs, the total cost or full cost of the program, and the cost per output (unit of service).

Today, in government there is a movement—one that will eventually affect government human service agencies—away from prospective estimates of program costs to retrospective determination of actual program costs. The primary financial management tool used in retrospective determination of actual program costs is called activity-based costing. It will be some time, however, before all governments and all government human service agencies have the financial accounting software and human resources to implement activity-based costing. In the interim, prospective approaches to estimating program costs using budgetary data will continue to be the norm.

Program Line-Item Budgets

Chapter 7 mentioned that a line-item budget could be prepared for a human service agency as a whole or for an individual human service program. Discussion of program line-item budgets was, however, deferred until now. Table 8.20 is an example of a line-item budget operating at the program level.

Table 8.20 is actually Table 8.5 (cost allocation plan using total direct costs as the methodology or base) with the heading changed. If, for example, the visiting nurse program is designated as an HHCA expense center, then the nursing coordinator would be responsible for ensuring that the program does not exceed its line-item budget of $492,678. The visiting nurse program's line-item budget is comprised of five items of cost: the nursing coordinator's salary, the salaries of the four nurses, the associated ERE, medical supplies, and indirect costs. The largest item in the visiting nurse program's line-item budget is indirect costs ($348,300). As often as not, this will be the case with program line-item budgets.

A fact of organizational financial management life is that one of the biggest challenges that confront program managers in managing their program line-item budgets is that indirect costs are not under their control. In order for all program managers in a human service agency to live within their line-item budgets, they must jointly cooperate, monitor, and hold down shared expenses (indirect costs). This fact or organizational financial management life is much easier to acknowledge than it is to deal with.

Summary

This chapter presented a lot of financial management material and covered a lot of financial management ground. In addition to discussing three major methodologies, or bases, that are frequently used to allocate a human service agency's indirect costs to programs, the chapter also detailed

- The process involved in determining the total cost or full cost of a human service program
- The process involved and sample formats associated with developing performance budgets and program budgets
- The process involved in determining the cost per output (unit of service) and the cost per outcome of a human service program

TABLE 8.20   Houston Home Care Agency Program Line-Item Budgets

Budget Line Items	Visiting Nurse Program	Homemaker Program	Home-Delivered Meals Program	Indirect Cost Pool
Salaries and Wages				
Executive director				$100,000
Financial manager				75,000
3 secretaries				75,000
Nursing coordinator (N)	$ 65,000			
4 nurses (N)	200,000			
Homemaker coordinator (H)		$ 45,000		
15 homemakers (H)		375,000		
Home-delivered meals coordinator (M)			$ 40,000	
2 (half-time) van drivers (M)			30,000	
Salaries and Wages (Total)	$265,000	$420,000	$ 70,000	$250,000
Employee-Related Expenses (@ 22% of salaries and wages)	$ 58,300	$ 92,400	$ 15,400	$ 55,000
Other Operating Expenses				
Rent				$ 35,000
Utilities				12,000
Telephone				5,000
Medical supplies (N)	$ 25,000			
Cleaning supplies (H)		$ 15,000		
Office supplies				10,000
Purchased meals (M)			$ 60,000	
Equipment				5,000
Printing and duplicating				5,000
Employee travel				22,000
Postage and shipping				3,000
Van rental (2 vans) (M)			9,000	
Insurance (building)				17,000
Miscellaneous				8,000
SUBTOTALS	$348,300	$527,400	$154,400	$427,000
ALLOCATE INDIRECT COST POOL	$144,378	$218,619	$ 64,003	
TOTAL PROGRAM COSTS	$492,678	$746,019	$218,403	

In Chapter 9, we shall look at some methods of forecasting workload, revenues, and expenses for a human service agency or program.

EXERCISES

The Houston Home Care Agency (HHCA) has decided to add a specialized transportation program. Because the agency's two vans are only used part of the day to deliver meals, the agency executive director reasons that the vans could be used at other times to transport clients to needed medical appointments.

The HHCA decides to assign the home-delivered meals program coordinator the additional duty of coordinating the specialized transportation program with an increase in salary to $50,000 per year. The two (half-time) van driver positions will be converted to full-time positions and the new combined salary of the two full-time van drivers will be $40,000 per year. Since all three positions will now work for two programs, their salaries and wages and associated ERE become indirect costs. Also, because the two vans will now be shared between the two programs, the van rental costs also become indirect costs. However, rather than treat these costs as indirect, the HHCA decides to convert them to direct costs through the method of "direct charging."

Direct charging is yet another method of dealing with indirect costs. But unlike the other methods discussed in this chapter, cost allocation is not used. With direct charging, a method, or base, is used to convert an item of indirect cost into an item of direct cost. The method the HHCA will use is "time sheets." The three employees will each keep a weekly time sheet. When they work for either the specialized transportation program or the home-delivered meals program, they will record the total number of hours worked. Over the course of the fiscal year, the HHCA believes that the three employees' work on the two programs will come to a 50/50 split of their time. In the same vein, when the two vans are being used, the purpose (home-delivered meals program or specialized transportation program) will be recorded. Over the course of the fiscal year, the HHCA also believes that van use by the two programs will also approximate a 50/50 split.

Table 8.21 is a new cost allocation plan for HHCA. It shows the salaries and wages, associated ERE, and the van rental expenses as direct charges to the home-delivered meals program and to the specialized transportation program. The salaries of the home delivered meals program coordinator and the van drivers, their associated ERE, and the van rental expenses are the only items of cost in Table 8.21 that differ from the original HHCA line-item budget in Table 8.1

In Table 8.21, the direct costs of the four programs plus the indirect costs in the indirect cost pool are

Visiting nurse program	$ 348,300
Homemaker program	527,400
Home-delivered meals program	119,400
Specialized transportation program	59,400
Indirect cost pool	427,000
Total agency budget	$1,481,500

TABLE 8.21   Houston Home Care Agency Cost Allocation Plan Format

Budget Line Items	Visiting Nurse Program	Homemaker Program	Home-Delivered Meals Program	Special Transportation Program	Indirect Cost Pool
Salaries and Wages					
Executive director					$100,000
Financial manager					75,000
3 secretaries					75,000
Nursing coordinator (N)	$ 65,000				
4 nurses (N)	200,000				
Homemaker coordinator (H)		$ 45,000			
15 homemakers		375,000			
Home-delivered meals coordinator (M and T)			$ 25,000	$25,000	
2 van drivers (M and T)			20,000	20,000	
Salaries and Wages (Total)	$265,000	$420,000	$ 45,000	$45,000	$250,000
Employee-Related Expenses (@ 22% of salaries & wages)	$ 58,300	$ 92,400	$ 9,900	$ 9,900	$ 55,000
Other Operating Expenses					
Rent					$ 35,000
Utilities					12,000
Telephone					5,000
Medical supplies (N)	$ 25,000				
Cleaning supplies (H)		$ 15,000			
Office supplies					10,000
Purchased meals (M)			$ 60,000		
Equipment					5,000
Printing and duplicating					5,000
Employee travel					22,000
Postage and shipping					3,000
Van rental (2 vans) (M and T)			4,500	$ 4,500	
Insurance (building)					17,000
Miscellaneous					8,000
SUBTOTALS	$348,300	$527,400	$119,400	$59,400	$427,000
ALLOCATE INDIRECT COST POOL					
TOTAL PROGRAM COSTS					

Notes: N = Visiting nurse program
H = Homemaker program
M = Home-delivered meals program
T = Specialized transportation program

Exercise 8.1

Using Table 8.21, allocate the indirect costs in the indirect cost pool using total direct costs as the method or base. What is the total cost, or full cost, of each of the four programs? Assuming the total outputs (or units of service) remain the same for the visiting nurse program, the homemaker program, and the home-delivered meals program and that the specialized transportation program will make 9,000 person trips during the year, what is the cost per output (or unit of service) for each of the four programs? Assuming that all four programs share the same outcome measure and that the total number of outcomes (125) remains the same, what is the cost per outcome?

Exercise 8.2

Using Table 8.21, allocate the indirect costs in the indirect cost pool using salaries and wages as the method or base. What is the total cost, or full cost, of each of the four programs? Assuming the total outputs (or units of service) remain the same for the visiting nurse program, the homemaker program, and the home-delivered meals program and that the specialized transportation program will make 9,000 person trips during the year, what is the cost per output (or unit of service) for each of the four programs? Assuming that all four programs share the same outcome measure and that the total number of outcomes (125) remains the same, what is the cost per outcome?

Exercise 8.3

Using Table 8.21, allocate the indirect costs in the indirect cost pool using direct labor hours as the method or base. What is the total cost, or full cost, of each of the four programs? Assuming the total outputs (or units of service) remain the same for the visiting nurse program, the homemaker program, and the home-delivered meals program and assuming that the specialized transportation program will make 9,000 person trips during the year, what is the cost per output (or unit of service) for each of the four programs? Assuming that all four programs share the same outcome measure and that the total number of outcomes (125) remains the same, what is the cost per outcome?

9 Forecasting

As part of the planning and budgeting processes that precede each new fiscal year, human service agencies are confronted with a series of questions: What will the agency caseload be? Will the caseload go up, go down, or remain the same? What does the revenue situation look like? Will revenues increase, stay the same, or decline? What about expenses? In light of changes in caseload and revenues, can the current pattern of expenses be maintained? Should expenses be reduced? Without some estimate of how many clients a human service agency will serve in the coming fiscal year and what the revenue and expense picture will look like, it is difficult to prepare a realistic line-item operating budget for a human service agency.

There are essentially two ways human service administrators can estimate future case loads, revenues, and expenses: by educated guessing or by one or more of a variety of generally accepted forecasting techniques. As a general rule, the use of one or more generally recognized forecasting techniques is preferable to simply guessing. While an educated guess can sometimes turn out to be quite accurate, it is hard to defend during the budget process.

Forecasting can be defined as techniques that predict the future based on historical data (Lee & Shim, 1990:442). One of the interesting discoveries that researchers have made about forecasting is that simple techniques perform (produce estimates) that are frequently just as accurate as complex forecasting techniques (Cirincione, Gurrieri, & Van de Sande, 1999). Consequently, one doesn't have to be an expert in math or statistics to use many of the commonly recognized forecasting techniques. This chapter presents four commonly recognized time series forecasting techniques: (1) simple moving averages, (2) weighted moving averages, (3) exponential smoothing, and (4) time series regression. The first three of these forecasting techniques are relatively simple and the calculations can be done by hand. Time series regression is a more complex forecasting technique that requires the use of a computer and a basic understanding of some statistical concepts. Today, a variety of low-cost computer programs can perform not only time series forecasting, but moving averages, weighted moving averages, exponential smoothing, and assorted other techniques that are not covered in this chapter.

Before proceeding directly to the discussion of the four forecasting techniques, a few basic forecasting rules of thumb are presented.

Some Basic Forecasting Rules of Thumb

Several rules of thumb can be used as guides in conducting forecasts and interpreting the results.

Rule 1. Examine the data for the presence or absence of a trend.   Revenues and expenses and, to a lesser extent, caseload, tend to change incrementally. Consequently, either an upward or downward trend may be present in the data. Looking at Table 9.1, an upward trend is clearly evident in the caseload data. The caseload has been trending upward for the past four fiscal years. On the other hand, the donation data do not demonstrate a trend, but rather vary (increase and decrease) from year to year. In the absence of any other data or any other contextual information about the nature of the human service agency, the type of service involved, the client population, the community, the local economy, and so on, we would expect that the trend in the caseload data would continue for fiscal year 20X5. We are less sure about the forecast for donations because of the absence of a trend.

Rule 2. The farther out the forecast, the less reliable the forecast.   A forecast that looks ahead one fiscal year will generally be more reliable (more accurate) than a forecast that looks ahead three fiscal years. The reason is simple: Things change! A good example of the problem with forecasts that look too far ahead is provided by the U.S. space program. When the United States put a man on the moon in 1969, all kinds of forecasts about the future of space exploration were made based on how long it took us to reach the moon. According to many of these forecasts, we should already have a space colony on Mars. But we don't. Why? Because things change! In the case of the space program, government funding for space exploration was cut back and our space exploration policy changed from using manned spacecraft to using unmanned spacecraft.

Rule 3. Older data are less important than more recent data.   Table 9.1 could include donation data for fiscal years 1999, 1998, 1997, and so on. But we know that a problem in forecasting is that things change. So, the older the data included in a forecast, the more opportunity for things to change and, consequently, the less reliable the forecast is likely to be.

Rule 4. The last actual value of the forecast variable is the single most important piece of information.   In Table 9.1, the caseload and donation forecasts are to be made for fiscal year 20X5; the last actual value for the caseload is 1,450 and the last actual value for donations is $25,000. In the absence of any other data, the single best predictor of the future is the last value of the forecast variable. The reason is that the last actual value is the single piece of datum that is temporarily closest to the forecast. For example, if the only datum we had in Table 9.1 was the last actual value for caseload (1,450) for fiscal year 20X4, our best forecast for 20X5 would be 1,450. The last actual

TABLE 9.1   The Palmdale Human Service Agency

Fiscal Year	Caseload	Donations
20X1	1,200	$25,000
20X2	1,300	22,000
20X3	1,400	27,000
20X4	1,450	25,000
20X5	?	?

value also provides a reality check for a forecast. For any forecast, the question should be asked, Does the forecast seem reasonable given the last actual data?

Rule 5. The more one knows about the data, the better one can interpret the forecast.   One can forecast anything. The real gut issue is how to interpret the results of the forecast. In Table 9.1, any one of a number of forecasting techniques could be used to forecast the caseload for fiscal year 20X5. But the critical issue is, What are the data trying to tell us? A trend in the caseload data is clearly evident over the past four fiscal years. The caseload was 1,200 in FY 20X1 and increased 100 cases per year for fiscal year 20X2 and 20X3. But then something happened to the trend. In FY 20X4, the caseload increased by only 50. Why? What is going on? Unfortunately, we don't know anything about the Palmdale Human Service Agency, the type of service involved, the client population, the community, the local economy, and numerous other factors that could help provide us with a context in which to interpret the forecast. If we had contextual information, we would be better able to understand what the data are trying to tell us and we would be better able to interpret the forecast. Something may be occurring with the agency, the service, or the community that might explain the caseload data for fiscal year 20X4 and thus help to interpret the forecast for 20X5.

With this brief discussion of some forecasting rules of thumb completed, we can proceed to a discussion of our four forecasting techniques.

Simple Moving Averages

The forecasting technique called *simple moving averages* involves taking historical data on the forecast variable for a series of time periods and computing a simple arithmetic (mean) average. The forecaster must decide how many time periods of the forecast variable to include in the moving average. For example, in Table 9.1, we have historical values of the forecast variables of caseload and donations for four fiscal years. Rule 3 comes into play here: Older data are less important than more recent data. Following this guideline, we might decide to use only three years of historical data on the caseload and donations to make our forecasts. Table 9.2 takes this approach to forecasting caseload and donation data for fiscal year 20X5 using simple moving averages.

TABLE 9.2   **Palmdale Human Service Agency**

**Caseload and Donations Forecasts
Using Simple Moving Averages**

Fiscal Year	Caseload	Donations
20X2	1,300	$22,000
20X3	1,400	27,000
20X4	1,450	25,000
20X2–X4	4,150	74,000
20X5	$\frac{4,150}{3} = 1,383$	$\frac{74,000}{3} = \$24,667$

Using simple moving averages, the caseload forecast for fiscal year 20X5 is 1,383, whereas the donations forecast is $24,667. The caseload forecast is derived by adding the caseload data for the three time periods and dividing by the number of time periods. The same procedure is used to forecast donations. At this point we are reminded of Rule 1 relating to the presence or absence of a trend. We know that an upward trend exists in the caseload data, but that no trend appears to exist in the donations data. Thus, we should anticipate that the caseload forecast will show a continuation of the trend, whereas the donations forecast will continue to fluctuate.

Our expectations are satisfied with respect to the donations forecast, but not for the caseload forecast. The donations forecast for fiscal year 20X5 is 24,667, which is less than the last actual data for fiscal year 20X4. The donations forecast continues to jump around. Our expectation is not satisfied for the caseload forecast. The caseload forecast for fiscal year 20X5 is 1,383, which is again less than the actual data for fiscal year 20X4. But we should expect, based on the observed trend in the caseload data, a forecast that is greater than the actual caseload for fiscal year 20X4.

What is the problem with the simple moving averages forecast of caseload for fiscal year 20X5? Rules 3 and 4 provide some guidance. Rule 3 tells us that older data are less important than more recent data. All the data in the two simple moving averages forecasts are weighted the same. Actually, no weights are used, which has the effect of treating all data as though they were weighted equally. Rule 4 suggests that the last actual value of the forecast variable is more important than the other data and should perhaps be given greater weight in the forecast.

The point needs to be made that the *moving* in *simple moving averages* means that for fiscal year 20X6, the forecast would be comprised of the actual caseload and donations data for fiscal years 20X3, 20X4, and 20X5. The actual caseload and donations data for 20X5 would be added to the moving averages and the caseload and donations data for 20X2 would be deleted. This process keeps the simple moving average's base of three fiscal years.

Weighted Moving Averages

The second of our four forecasting techniques, *weighted moving averages,* attempts to improve on simple moving averages by assigning weights to the data that comprise the forecast. In keeping with Rules 3 and 4, the idea is to place more weight on the last actual value of the forecast variable and decreasing weights on the older data. For example, a common practice in weighted moving averages is to assign a weight of "1" to the oldest datum to be used in the forecast and then assign increasing weights to more recent data so that the last actual value receives the greatest weight. Following this approach, Table 9.3 shows the results of a weighted moving average forecast for caseload and donations for fiscal year 20X5.

Using weighted moving averages, the caseload forecast for fiscal year 20X5 is 1,408 and the donations forecast is $25,167. The caseload forecast is arrived at by multiplying the caseload data for each year by its weight, adding the results together, and dividing by the total number of weights. The forecast for donations is obtained using the same approach. The caseload forecast of 1,408 appears more realistic than the simple moving averages forecast of 1,383, but it is still less than the last actual caseload data of 1,450 for fiscal year 20X4. Again, we are confronted with the problem that we cannot put a lot of confidence in a forecast of 1,408 unless we have some contextual information that explains why we should accept a caseload forecast that does not demonstrate a continuation of the identified trend. The

TABLE 9.3   Palmdale Human Service Agency

Forecasts Using Weighted Moving Averages

Caseload

Fiscal Year	Caseload	Weight	Weighted Score
20X2	1,300	1	1,300
20X3	1,400	2	2,800
20X4	1,450	3	4,350
20X5	8,450/6 = 1,408	6	8,450

Donations

Fiscal Year	Donations	Weight	Weighted Score
20X2	$22,000	1	$ 22,000
20X3	27,000	2	54,000
20X4	25,000	3	75,000
20X5	$151,000/6 = $25,167	6	151,000

donations forecast of $25,167 appears reasonable given the historical way in which donations have tended to fluctuate.

Exponential Smoothing

In order to perform a forecast using either simple moving averages or weighted moving averages, the forecaster must collect and save data for several historical time periods. *Exponential smoothing* is a forecasting technique that requires only two pieces of information: (a) the last actual value of the forecast variable and (b) the last actual forecast. With these two pieces of information and the use of a simple formula, we can forecast caseload, revenues, expenses, or any other variable. One might say that exponential smoothing takes to heart Rule 4 that the last actual value of the forecast variable is the single most important piece of information. The forecasting formula used in exponential smoothing is

$$NF = LF + \alpha \, (LD - LF) \quad \text{where} \quad \begin{aligned} NF &= \text{New forecast} \\ LF &= \text{Last forecast} \\ \alpha &= 0 \text{ to } 1 \\ LD &= \text{Last data} \end{aligned}$$

The formula is relatively straightforward with the exception of the alpha (α). Alpha is a value between 1 and 0 that is selected by the forecaster. The alpha determines how much weight in the new forecast will be placed on the last data (the last value of the forecast variable) and, conversely, how much weight will be placed on the last forecast. An alpha of 1 means that 100 percent of the new forecast will be based on the last data and 0 per cent on the last forecast. An exponential smoothing forecast using an alpha of 1 would result in a number that would be exactly the same as the last actual value of the forecast variable. An alpha of zero means that 0 percent of the new forecast will be based on the last data and 100 percent on the last forecast. An exponential smoothing forecast using an alpha of 0 would result in a number that is exactly the same as the last forecast. An alpha of .5 means that 50 percent of the new forecast will be based on the last actual data and 50 percent on the last forecast.

When using exponential smoothing, the alpha selected is determined by the accuracy of the last forecast. For example, if the caseload forecast for fiscal year 20X4 was 1,700 and the actual caseload was 1,450, then the forecast was not very accurate. In such a situation, the forecaster would want to select for the next forecast (fiscal year 20X5) a high alpha (.7 to .9) that places more weight on the last data and less weight on the last forecast. If, however, the caseload forecast for fiscal year 20X4 was 1,460 and the actual caseload for fiscal year 20X4 was 1,450, then the forecast was quite accurate. In such a situation, the forecaster would want to select for the next forecast (fiscal year 20X5) a low alpha (.2 to .3) that places more weight on the last forecast and less weight on the last data. A small alpha (.2 to .4) has the same effect as if data for several time periods were included

TABLE 9.4   Palmdale Human Service Agency

**Caseload and Donations Forecasts
Using Exponential Smoothing**

Caseload

NF = LF + α(LD − LF)
   = 1,500 + .2(1,450 − 1,500)
   = 1,500 + .2(−50)
   = 1,500 + (−10)
   = 1,490

Donations

NF = LF + α (LD − LF)
   = $26,000 + .5($25,000 − $26,000)
   = $26,000 + .5(−$1,000)
   = $26,000 + (−$500)
   = $25,500

in the forecast. In other words, a small alpha "smooths" the forecast, hence the name *exponential smoothing*.

Let's assume that the caseload forecast for fiscal year 20X4 was 1,500 and that the donations forecast was $26,000. We know that the actual caseload and donations data for fiscal year 20X4 were, respectively, 1,450 and $25,000. Because the caseload forecast was quite accurate, we will select an alpha of .2 for use in our forecast of caseload for 20X5. Because the forecast for donations was somewhat less accurate, we will select a higher alpha (.5) that will place equal emphasis on both the last forecast and the last data. This information can now be entered into the exponential smoothing formula (Table 9.4) and a fiscal year 20X5 forecast can be made for both caseload and donations.

The exponential smoothing caseload forecast is 1,490 for 20X5. This forecast appears to be realistic because the upward trend evidenced over the last four fiscal years is continued and because the new forecast is greater than the actual caseload data of 1,450 for fiscal year 20X4. Similarly, the exponential smoothing forecast for donations of $25,500 for fiscal year 20X5 appears reasonable, but we are less sure of this forecast because of the tendency of the donations data to fluctuate.

Time Series Regression

Time series regression is the last of the four generally recognized forecasting techniques to be discussed in this chapter and the only one that requires the use of a computer. Time series regression is more sophisticated than the other forecasting techniques considered, but it also more powerful and provides more insights into the data and the forecast. Time series regression forecasting also yields an estimate of how much confidence one should have in the forecast. These features make it one of the most commonly used forecasting techniques (Forester, 1993). Time series regression forecasting can be performed using any computer software package that contains a simple linear regression program.

Time series regression is an application of what is called the ordinary least squares regression model. Time series regression forecasting attempts to find a linear relationship between time (the independent variable) and the forecast variable (the dependent variable). A linear relationship can be thought of as a trend. In other words, time series regression analyzes the data looking for a trend. The time series regression model looks for (a) a positive linear relationship (or trend) between time and the forecast variable, (b) a negative linear relationship (or trend) between time and the value of the forecast variable, or (c) no linear relationship (or trend). A positive linear relationship (or trend) means that over time the values of the forecast variable are increasing. A negative linear relationship (or trend) means that over time the values of the forecast variable are decreasing. If the time series regression model finds a moderate to strong positive or negative linear relationship (or trend), the computer output can be used to make a forecast using the formula

$Y = A + BX$ where Y is the forecast (an unknown quantity)
A is the base or constant
B is the unit value change in the forecast variable
X is the increment of time to be forecasted

The use of an example should help make the discussion of time series regression forecasting more understandable. Table 9.5 demonstrates how time series regression can be used to conduct a caseload forecast using the caseload data we have used in the other forecasts. In conducting a caseload forecast using time series regression, we are going to use all four years of available caseload data. Using older data here does not violate Rule 3, because (a) a time series regression forecast needs at least four (some would say five) data points to function properly and (b) the analysis is able to differentiate between changes attributable to time (the trend) and changes attributable to other factors.

The first part of Table 9.5 shows how the data for a time series regression forecast are entered into a computer program. Time is always treated as the independent variable (IV), whereas the forecast variable (e.g., caseload or donations) is always treated as the dependent variable (DV). When the data are inputted into the computer program, it is important not to reverse these variables. Time must always be the independent variable or the computer output will be meaningless. When inputting data into a time series regression, the time periods are transformed into consecutive numbers. For example, we have four years of caseload data (the time period) so fiscal year 20X1 = 1, 20X2 = 2, 20X3 = 3, and 20X4 = 4. The oldest time period is always designated 1.

TABLE 9.5   Caseload Forecast Using Time Series Regression

Computer Input

Time (IV)	Caseload (DV)
1	1,200
2	1,300
3	1,400
4	1,450

Computer Output

Coefficients

	Unstandardized Coefficients		Standardized Coefficients		
Model	B	Std. Error	BETA	t	Sig.
Constant	1125	23.717		47.434	.000
Var 1	85	8.660	.990	9.815	.010

Model Summary

Model	R	R-Square	Adjusted R-Square	Standard Error of the Estimate
1	.990	.980	.969	19.3649

The second part of Table 9.5 shows the resulting computer output, specifically the "coefficients" and the "model summary" sections. Computer programs such as Statistical Packages for the Social Sciences (SPSS) provide a lot of output that is not essential to the purposes of conducting and interpreting the results of a time series regression forecast. For forecasting purposes, one needs to know the value of R-square, the value of A (the constant), and the value of B (Var1). In SPSS, the value of R-square is usually found as part of the model summary output, while values of the A (constant) and the B (Var1) are usually found as part of the coefficients output.

The R-square tells us how much confidence we should have in the forecast. R-square can vary between 0 and 1. R-square can also be thought of as a measure of the strength of a trend (either positive or negative) in the values of the forecast variable over time. If the R-square is greater than .7, a strong trend exists. An R-square between .5 and .7 indicates a moderate trend; R-square less than .5 indicates a weak trend. Looking at the model summary portion of the computer output (Table 9.5), we can see that the R-square for the time series regression is .980, which is significantly greater than .7. In terms of interpretation, we can say that we can have a high degree of confidence in the result of a time series regression forecast. Another interpretation is that the time series regression analysis has found a strong trend in the caseload data. This strong trend can be used for forecasting purposes.

In order to perform a time series regression forecast, we must substitute the relevant values into the formula $Y = A + BX$ (Table 9.6). To the base value of A (a constant), we add B (Var1) multiplied by X (the time period to be forecasted). Since we are using four years of caseload data in the time series regression and we are performing a forecast for the next fiscal year, $X = 5$. The result is a caseload forecast of 1,550. This caseload forecast looks good because it is a continuation of the observed trend in the caseload data and because it is greater than the last actual caseload data for fiscal year 20X4.

Why does the time series caseload forecast perform so much better than the other forecasting techniques? The answer is that time series regression is particularly sensitive to, and performs best, when a strong trend is present. The three other forecasting techniques discussed in this chapter are not as sensitive to trends.

At this point it is probably advisable to pause for a moment and explain exactly what the values of the A (constant) and the B (Var1 or variable 1) mean in a time series regression. When conducting a time series regression, many computer programs provide for the optional generation of a graph of the linear relationship between time and the forecast variable. Figure 9.1 is such a graph. The independent variable (time) is shown on the x-axis and the dependent variable (caseload) is shown on the y-axis. In the middle of the graph are four data points. The first data point represents the caseload data (1,200) for fiscal year 20X1 (year 1). The second data point represents the caseload data (1,300) for fiscal year 20X2 (year 2). The third data point represents the caseload data (1,400) for fiscal year 20X3 (year 3). And finally, the fourth data point represents the caseload data (1,450) for 20X4 (year 4).

The line in the center of the graph is the *regression line.* The regression line can be thought of as "the best line" that expresses the linear relationship (the trend) between time and the forecast variable. The line begins at 1,125. This point is called A (constant) because it is the fixed point at which the regression line begins. This point is also called the *y-intercept* because it is the point at which the regression line crosses the y-axis. The slope of the regression line then goes up 85 (B or Var1) for each time period (year). In performing the actual time series regression forecast, the regression line is simply extended out to the time period being forecasted. In

TABLE 9.6 Caseload Forecast Using Time Series Regression

$$Y = A + BX$$
$$= 1125 + 85(5)$$
$$= 1125 + 425$$
$$= 1550$$

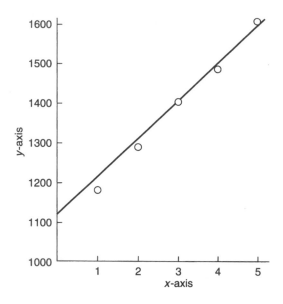

**FIGURE 9.1   Graph of Time and Caseload
with Regression Line**

this example, caseload is being forecasted for the fifth year. The mathematics of the forecast are simply to begin with the value of A (constant) and then to add the value of B (Var1) for each time period (year) up to the forecast time period (year):

$$1{,}125 + 85 \text{ (year 1)} + 85 \text{ (year 2)} + 85 \text{ (year 3)} + 85 \text{ (year 4)} + 85 \text{ (year 5)} = 1{,}550$$

Now let's do a time series regression forecast for donations. The top portion of Table 9.7 shows how the data are entered into the computer program; the lower portion shows the computer output. In the "coefficients" section of the output, we see that the value of A (constant) is 23,500 and the value of B (Var1) is 500. In the model summary section, we see that the R-square is .098. The R-square is extremely low, which means that we can have little confidence in any forecast made using time series regression. Another way of interpreting the low R-Square is that the computer could not find a trend in the data. Knowing that we can have no confidence in the results, let's go ahead anyway and do a time series regression forecast using the formula $Y = A + BX$ (see Table 9.8) The resulting forecast for donations is $27,000 in fiscal year 20X5, but we know that we can have absolutely no confidence in this forecast.

The two time series regression forecasts for caseload and for donations demonstrate the strengths and limitations of this forecasting technique. Time series regression forecasting works well when a strong (R-square = .7 or greater) trend exists, works less well when a moderate (R-square = .4 to .7) trend exist, and does not work well at all when a weak (R-square = less than .4) exists.

TABLE 9.7   Donations Using Time Series Regression

Computer Input

Time (IV)	Caseload (DV)
1	$25,000
2	22,000
3	27,000
4	25,000

Computer Output

Coefficients

	Unstandardized Coefficients		Standardized Coefficients		
Model	B	Std. Error	BETA	t	Sig.
Constant	23,500	2936.835		8.002	.015
Var 1	500	1702.381	.313	.466	.687

Model Summary

Model	R	R-Square	Adjusted R-Square	Standard Error of the Estimate
1	.313	.098	−.353	2397.9165

TABLE 9.8   Donations Using Time Series Regression

$$Y = A + BX$$
$$= \$23,500 + \$500(5)$$
$$= \$23,500 + \$2,500$$
$$= \$27,000$$

When to Use Which Forecasting Technique

The preceding discussion of the four generally recognized forecasting techniques (in particular, the discussion of time series regression) allows three more rules of thumb to be offered:

Rule 6.   When a strong trend (R-square = .7 or greater) is present in the data, use time series regression.

Rule 7.   When a moderate trend (R-square = .4 to .7) is present in the data, use moving averages or weighted moving averages.

Rule 8.   When a weak trend (R-square = less than .4) or no trend is present in the data, use exponential smoothing with the choice of alpha dependent upon the accuracy of the last forecast.

Following Rule 6, for any given forecast, a forecaster should first use time series regression and determine if a trend is present in the data and the strength of any such trend.

Summary

This chapter presented four generally recognized forecasting techniques: (1) simple moving averages, (2) weighted moving averages, (3) exponential smoothing, and (4) time series regression. The advantages and disadvantages of each forecasting technique were identified and several rules of thumb were provided to guide human services administrators in the selection of the most appropriate forecasting technique and in interpreting the results of forecasts.

EXERCISES

Exercise 9.1

The following data represent total personnel expenses for the Palmdale Human Service Agency for past four fiscal years:

20X1	$5,250,000
20X2	$5,500,000
20X3	$6,000,000
20X4	$6,750,000

Forecast personnel expenses for fiscal year 20X5 using moving averages, weighted moving averages, exponential smoothing, and time series regression. For moving averages and weighted moving averages, use only the data for the past three fiscal years. For weighted moving averages, assign a value of 1 to the data for 20X2, a value of 2 to the data for 20X3, and a value of 3 to the data for 20X4. For exponential smoothing, assume that the last forecast for fiscal year 20X4 was $6,300,000. You decide on the alpha to be used for exponential smoothing. For time series regression, use the data for all four fiscal years. Which forecast will you use? Why?

Exercise 9.2

The following data represent total "person trips" (service outputs or units of service) provided by the Palmdale Human Service Agency's specialized transportation program for the past four fiscal years:

20X1	12,000
20X2	15,000
20X3	13,500
20X4	14,250

Forecast person trips for fiscal year 20X5 using moving averages, weighted moving averages, exponential smoothing, and time series regression. For moving averages and weighted moving averages, use only the data for the past three fiscal years. For weighted moving averages, assign a value of 1 to the data for 20X2, a value of 2 to the data for 20X3, and a value of 3 to the data for 20X4. For exponential smoothing, assume that the last forecast for fiscal year 20X4 was 15,000. You decide on the alpha to be used for exponential smoothing. For time series regression, use the data for all four fiscal years. Which forecast will you use? Why?

Exercise 9.3

The following data represent total revenues (from all sources) for the Palmdale Human Service Agency for the past four fiscal years:

20X1	$15,000,000
20X2	$14,250,000
20X3	$14,000,000
20X4	$13,500,000

Forecast total revenues for fiscal year 20X5 using moving averages, weighted moving averages, exponential smoothing, and time series regression. For moving averages and weighted moving averages, use only the data for the past three fiscal years. For weighted moving averages, assign a value of 1 to the data for 20X2, a value of 2 to the data for 20X3, and a value of 3 to the data for 20X4. For exponential smoothing, assume that the last forecast for fiscal year 20X4 was $13,000,000. You decide on the alpha to be used for exponential smoothing. For time series regression, use the data for all four fiscal years. Which forecast will you use? Why?

10 Differential Cost Analysis

This chapter deals with the use of differential cost analysis in financial management decision making situations. The basic premise of differential cost analysis is that different costs are treated differently in different financial management decision situations. Hence the name *differential costs*.

Two major applications of differential cost analysis are presented. The first application is called *break-even analysis*. In break-even analysis, differential cost analysis is used to answer the question, How much service must a human service program provide during a fiscal year in order to recover its total costs? The second application can be called *decrease/discontinue* decisions. In these types of financial management decisions, differential cost analysis answers the question, What will be the effect on fixed and variable costs of a decision to reduce or discontinue a human service program?

Some Concepts and Definitions

Before proceeding to the discussion of the applications of differential cost analysis, some basic concepts and definitions need to be introduced including fixed costs, variable costs, step costs, maximum efficiency, and surplus capacity.

Fixed Costs and Variable Costs

In Chapter 8 the concepts of direct and indirect costs were introduced as part of the discussion of cost analysis. As was noted in Chapter 8, the full cost, or total cost, of a human service program is the sum of its direct costs and indirect costs. In differential cost analysis, the full cost, or total cost, of a human service program is the sum of its fixed costs and variable costs. Items of cost in the budget of a human service program can also be classified as either fixed costs or variable costs. It is the classification of costs as fixed and variable and the analysis of how these costs behave, or differ, in various financial management decision situations that constitutes the essence of differential cost analysis.

A *fixed cost* is any item of cost that does not vary with the amount of service provided. Hence the name *fixed cost*. The salary of a cook in a congregate meals program is an example of a fixed cost. Figure 10.1 provides a graphic representation of why a cook's salary is a fixed cost. The *y*-axis of the graph in the figure is the cook's monthly salary; the *x*-axis is meals per day. A meal is a commonly accepted output (or unit of service) measure for a congregate meals program because it provides a readily understandable measure of service volume. As Figure 10.1 demonstrates, the cook's monthly salary ($2,500) does not vary depending on how many meals per day the program provides. The line that expresses the relationship between the cook's monthly salary and meals per day is flat, meaning that no relationship exists. The congregate meals program can provide 25 meals per day, 100 meals per day, 150 meals per day, or any other number of meals per day between 0 and 150 and the cook's monthly salary remains fixed at $2,500. The salaries of staff working in human service programs are generally treated as fixed costs because they do not vary depending on the amount of service provided. Other types of costs that are generally considered to be fixed costs include rent, telephone, insurance, and any other cost that is not affected, or does not vary, depending on how much service a human service program provides.

A *variable cost* is any item of cost that varies with the amount of service provided. Hence the name *variable cost*. Food in a congregate meals program is an example of a variable cost. Figure 10.2 is a graphic representation of the relationship between the monthly food costs (*y*-axis) and the number of meals per day (*x*-axis). As the number of meals per day increases, so does the cost of food. Providing 100 meals per day requires more food and thus higher food costs than providing 25 meals per day. Types of costs that are generally treated as variable costs include

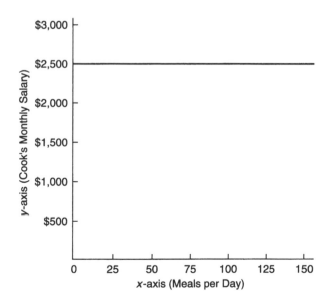

FIGURE 10.1　A Graphic Display of a Cook's Salary as a Fixed Cost

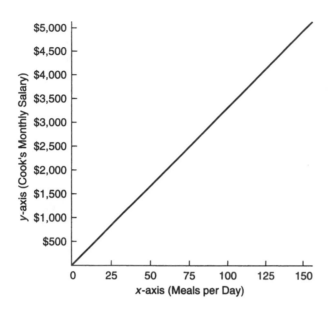

FIGURE 10.2   A Graphic Display of Food Costs as a Variable Cost

supplies in a homemaker or home health aid program (the more service that is provided, the more supplies that are used), gasoline in a specialized transportation program (the more trips that are provided, the more gasoline that is used), and any other item of cost in any other human service program that varies depending on how much service is provided.

Step Costs

A third type of cost sometimes encountered in differential cost analysis is called a *step cost*. A step cost is a fixed cost that remains fixed up to some point at which it then increases in a stepwise fashion. Hence the name *step costs*. The concept of a step cost is perhaps best explained by the use of an example. Let's assume that the cook in the congregate meals program is capable of preparing and serving up to 150 meals per day by himself. If the congregate meals program decides to provide more than 150 meals per day, a second cook will need to be hired. At 150 meals per day, the congregate meals program's fixed costs for cooks would jump, or step up, in a nonincremental fashion to a new level. This phenomenon is graphically illustrated in Figure 10.3. The cook's monthly salary ($2,500) remains fixed until the meals per day reaches 150. The exact amount of the new fixed costs will depend on the status (full-time or part-time) of the new cook as well as the salary. If the congregate meals program hires a second full-time cook at the same salary as the first cook, then monthly fixed costs for cooks would jump, or step up, from $2,500 per month to $5,000 per month.

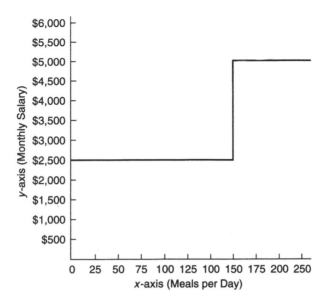

FIGURE 10.3   A Graphic Display of a New Cook's Salary as a Step Cost

Maximum Efficiency and Surplus Capacity

In the preceding congregate meals example, 150 meals per day is the maximum number that one cook can prepare and serve. At 150 meals per day, one cook is assumed to be working at maximum efficiency. If the congregate meals program served only 50 meals a day, the cook would not be maximally efficient, because an additional 100 meals per day could still be prepared and served without the congregate meals program incurring any additional fixed costs for cooks. At 50 meals per day, the congregate meals program has surplus capacity of 100 meals per day. Surplus capacity is the difference between the current service capability of a staff person, facility, or human service program and the point of maximum efficiency.

With the introduction of these concepts and definitions, the discussion can now proceed to the first application of differential cost analysis.

Break-Even Analysis

The purpose of break-even analysis is to determine how much service a human service program must provide during a fiscal year in order to generate revenues sufficient to cover expenses. Thinking back to Chapter 7 dealing with budgets and budgeting systems, one might well ask, Isn't this type of financial information readily available from a human service agency's line-item, performance, and program budgets? Well, not exactly. Budgets deal with estimation and monitoring of

FIGURE 10.4   **The Break-Even Point (BEP) Formula**

$PX = A + BX$
where P = Unit cost or price of the service
        X = Amount of service to be provided (an unknown)
        A = Fixed costs
        B = Variable costs

revenues and expenses during a fiscal year. Break-even analysis is used during the planning and budgeting processes to estimate fixed costs and variable costs and to determine the amount of service a human service program must provide in order to reach the break-even point (BEP) given different price levels. Break-even analysis is also used during the fiscal year to monitor actual service levels, actual fixed costs, and actual variable costs as well as to periodically recompute the BEP.

In break-even analysis, and for purposes of computing the break-even point, all expenses are divided into two categories (fixed costs and variable costs). Break-even analysis determines the point during the fiscal year at which a human service program will recover its fixed costs. The BEP is computed using the formula shown in Figure 10.4.

The following two case examples demonstrate the use of break-even analysis and the BEP formula. The first case example, the New River Community Council, demonstrates the use of break-even analysis at the beginning of the fiscal year as part of the planning and budgeting processes. The second case example, the Westchester Home-Delivered Meals Program, demonstrates the use of break-even analysis during the fiscal year to monitor service delivery, actual fixed costs, actual variable costs, and the BEP.

New River Community Council Case Example

The New River Community Council (NRCC) is a 501(c)(3) private nonprofit organization that engages in human services planning and advocacy and also provides financial and programmatic technical assistance to other local human service agencies. The NRCC is planning to publish a newsletter that will keep local human service agencies informed about state and community funding (contract and grant) opportunities. Within the program structure of the NRCC, the newsletter will be treated as a program and as both an expense center and a revenue center. As part of the planning and budgeting processes, NRCC wants to determine the program's fixed costs, variable costs, and BEP. NRCC plans to hire a part-time (ten hours per week) social work student to be the newsletter coordinator in charge of compiling the contract and grant information and preparing, printing, and mailing the newsletter. The salary of the newsletter coordinator (a fixed cost) will be $5,000 for the year. The newsletter coordinator's salary is a fixed cost because it does not vary depending on the number of newsletters produced. The unit cost of printing and mailing six bimonthly issues of the newsletter (the variable costs) is estimated at $4 per subscriber per year. The printing and mailing costs are variable costs because they will vary depending on how many newsletters are printed and mailed. In order to simplify this first case example, agency indirect (overhead) costs are excluded.

The tentative price of the newsletter is set at $12 per year. The executive director of NRCC uses this information and the BEP formula to compute the BEP (Table 10.1). Given the fixed costs ($5,000) and the variable costs ($4) involved and the tentative subscription price of $12, the BEP is computed at 625 subscribers.

After some discussion, the executive director of NRCC decides that the BEP is outside the *feasible range*. The feasible range is the number of potential break-even points that represent viable solutions. Feasible range issues are most frequently encountered with step costs, but they can be relevant to any type of break-even analysis. The executive director believes that a BEP of 625 is outside the feasible range because it is unreasonable to expect that the newsletter will be able to attract this number of subscribers the first year. The executive director decides to recompute the newsletter program's BEP using higher subscription rates. Table 10.2 shows the revised BEPs based on annual subscription rates of $15 (Part A) and $20 (Part B), respectively. If the subscription rate is increased to $15, the BEP will be lowered to 454 subscribers. If the subscription rate is increased to $20, the BEP will be lowered to 313 subscribers.

The executive director decides that 454 subscribers is a feasible target (a potential BEP that is within the feasible range) for the newsletter's first year; consequently, the newsletter price is set at $15. Charging $15 for the newsletter represents only a small increase ($3) in price, but results in significantly reducing the

TABLE 10.1   Computing the Break-Even Point for the New River Community Council Newsletter Program

$PX = A + BX$

$12X = 5,000 + 4X$

(Subtract $4X$ from each side.)

$8X = 5,000$

(Divide each side by 8.)

$X = 625$ (BEP)

The proof of this solution is as follows:

Revenues	Expenses	
$12(625) = $7,500	Fixed costs	= $5,000 (coordinator's salary)
	Variable costs	= $\underline{2,500}$ (variable costs)*
		$7,500

*625 members @ $4.00 = $2,500

TABLE 10.2   Revised Break-Even Points for the New River Community Council Newsletter Program

Part A. Newsletter Subscription Price of $15

$PX = A + BX$

$15X = 5,000 + 4X$

(Subtract $4X$ from each side.)

$11X = 5,000$

(Divide each side by 11.)

$X = 454$ (BEP)

Part B. Newsletter Subscription Price of $20

$PX = A + BX$

$20X = 5,000 + 4X$

(Subtract $4X$ from each side.)

$16X = 5,000$

(Divide each side by 16.)

$X = 313$ (BEP)

number (−171) of subscribers needed to reach the BEP. Collectively, Tables 10.1 and 10.2 also demonstrate how price and the BEP are inversely related. The higher the price, the lower the BEP. The lower the price, the higher the BEP.

Taking a more detailed look at Part A of Table 10.2, we can analyze exactly what the BEP formula really does. In the formula $PX = A + BX$, when $4X$ (the variable costs) is subtracted from both sides of the equation, the amount ($4) of the selling price ($15) that is needed to cover variable costs is removed from the equation. What is left ($11X$) is the amount ($11) of the selling price ($15) that is available to cover the program's fixed costs ($5,000). This amount ($11) is referred to as the *unit contribution rate*. The BEP formula then divides the fixed costs ($5,000) by the unit contribution rate ($11) with the resulting BEP being 454.

At this point in the discussion of break-even analysis, mention should be made of profitability analysis and marginal pricing.

Profitability Analysis and Marginal Pricing

How much profit will NRCC earn if 454 people subscribe to the newsletter? The answer is none. At the BEP, a human service program will earn revenues sufficient to cover its fixed and variable costs, but nothing more. How much profit will NRCC earn if 455 people subscribe to the newsletter? As Table 10.3 demonstrates, the answer is $11. Regardless of when during the fiscal year the BEP (454) is reached, total program fixed costs for the entire fiscal year will be covered. At the BEP, the *variable cost*, also called the *marginal cost*, of producing one more news-

TABLE 10.3   New River Community Council

Profitability Analysis with 455 Newsletter Subscribers

Selling price	=	$15.00
Variable costs	=	− 4.00
		$11.00 (profit)

letter is only $4. Thus, between 454 newsletters and the point at which the newsletter coordinator will be working at maximum efficiency and will need some staff assistance, the newsletter program can earn a profit of $11 on each new subscription. Given that it only costs $4 to produce each additional newsletter, when the BEP (454) is reached, the NRCC might consider offering a special trial subscription rate (50 percent off) to entice more individuals to subscribe. For example, if the NRCC were to offer a special 50 percent discounted subscription rate of $7.50, it would still earn a profit of $3.50 on each new subscription.

Pricing a product or service based on the marginal costs of production is referred to as *marginal pricing*. The concept of marginal pricing is one of the reasons that many government agencies prefer to contract with private nonprofit organizations to provide some types of human service programs rather than providing them directly. Take the case of child day care services. If a government human service agency were to directly operate a child day cay facility, its costs would include both fixed costs and variable costs. But if an already existing child day care facility operated by a private nonprofit organization has surplus capacity, then the government human service agency might be able to purchase a portion or all of the surplus capacity on a marginal cost basis. Such situations are win–win for both parties. The government human service agency does not have to pay the full cost of care (fixed costs plus variable costs), whereas the private nonprofit agency can sell its surplus capacity (for variable costs plus perhaps a small profit), thereby generating additional revenues.

Westchester Home-Delivered Meals (WHDM) Program

The Westchester Home-Delivered Meals (WHDM) program provides one hot nutritious meal five days per week to elderly clients residing in their own homes. During the planning and budgeting processes, the program director estimates that total program costs for the fiscal year will be $260,000 consisting of $95,000 in fixed costs (a cook's salary, equipment rental, and agency indirect or overhead costs) and $165,000 in variable costs (food, supplies, and disposable food containers, paper cups, and so on plus delivery costs). Note that in this case example, agency indirect costs are included.

The program director estimates that the home-delivered meals program can provide about 45,000 meals during the fiscal year. Dividing the variable costs ($165,000) by the total estimated number (45,000) of meals to be provided, the variable cost per meal is estimated at $3.66. Using the BEP formula, but solving for price rather than BEP (Table 10.4), the program director estimates the total, or full, cost per meal for the fiscal year will be $5.77. Based on this analysis, the executive director enters into a "performance contract" (see Chapter 12) with the City of Westchester to have the WHDM program provide 45,000 meals during the coming fiscal year at a unit cost of $5.77 per meal.

Four months into the fiscal year, the program director decides to conduct a break-even analysis in order to compare the estimated fixed costs, variable costs, and BEP with the actual fixed costs, variable costs, and BEP year-to-date. The program director is particularly interested in the program's variable costs because the prices of some foods (fresh fruits and vegetables) have declined slightly during the first four months of the fiscal year. A decrease in food prices may mean that the home-delivered meals program's actual BEP will be lower than the estimated BEP. Table 10.5 presents the home-delivered meals program's service and cost data for the first four months of the fiscal year.

In computing fixed costs, variable costs, and the BEP, the program director could collect the financial information from the agency's accounting records. Instead, the program director decides to the use the high–low method for computing the program's break-even point. Computing the BEP using the high–low method can be done by hand without the aid of a computer. As its name suggests, in the high–low method, the time periods with the highest and lowest amounts of service provision (service volume) are selected. In Table 10.5, July is the time period with the lowest amount of service provision (3,500 meals) and October is the time period with the highest (4,600). Using data from the high and low time periods, the program director computes fixed costs, variable costs, and the BEP using the following steps:

Step 1. The difference in service volume between the high and low time periods is computed. The resulting figure is 1,100 meals (4,600 − 3,500).

TABLE 10.4   Westchester Home-Delivered Meals Program

Computing Price Using the Break-Even Point Formula

$$PX = A + BX$$

$$P(45,000) = 95,000 + 3.66(45,000)$$

$$P(45,000) = 95,000 + 164,700$$

$$P(45,000) = 259,700$$

(Divide each side by 45,000.)

$$P = \$5.77 \text{ (price or cost per meal)}$$

TABLE 10.5   **Westchester Home-Delivered Meals Program**

Service and Cost Data (July 1, 20X1–October 31, 20X1)

Month	Meals Served	Total Costs
July	3,500	$20,500
August	4,000	22,600
September	4,200	23,350
October	4,600	24,500

Step 2.   The difference in costs between the high and low time periods is computed. The resulting figure is $4,000 ($24,500 – $20,500).

Step 3.   The variable cost per meal is computed. The cost difference ($4,000) computed in Step 2 is divided by the difference (1,100) in service volume computed in Step 1. The resulting figure is $3.64. This figure is the variable cost per unit of service (one meal). The logic here is quite simple: Since fixed costs do not vary, the only costs that can vary between the high and low time periods are the variable costs.

Step 4.   Total variable costs are computed for the low time period. However, the computations work the same for either the high or the low time period. In the low time period, the service volume (the number of meals provided) is 3,500. Service volume is multiplied by the variable costs per meal ($3.64). The resulting figure is $12,740. This figure is the amount of variable costs for the low month.

Step 5.   Total fixed costs are computed for the low time period. The total program costs in the low month are $20,500. If the variable costs ($12,740) are subtracted from the total costs ($20,500), the remainder ($7,760) is the amount of the fixed costs. Again, the logic is straightforward. Since there are only two types of costs (fixed and variable), if one knows the total costs and the variable costs, one knows the fixed costs.

Step 6.   The break-even point is computed using the BEP formula and the data generated in Steps 1 through 5 plus one additional piece of information. The additional piece of information needed to compute the BEP is the service price. The service price is $5.77, which is the contract price between the WHDM program and the City of Westchester. As Table 10.6 shows, when the computations are performed, the resulting BEP is 3,643 meals. This figure, however, is a monthly figure based on monthly data so the program director must annualize the data to get the BEP for the fiscal year:

3,643 meals per month × 12 months = 43,716 meals

TABLE 10.6   Westchester Home-Delivered Meals Program

Computing the Break-Even Point
Using the High–Low Method

$PX = A + BX$

$5.77X = 7,760 + 3.64X$

(Subtract 3.64X from each side.)

$2.13X = 7,760$

(Divide each side by 2.13.)

$X = 3,643$ (monthly BEP)

$3,643 \times 12 = 43,716$ (fiscal-year BEP)

The high–low method computes the actual BEP for the home-delivered meals program at 43,716 meals. At 43,716 meals, the home-delivered meals program will recover its fixed costs for the fiscal year. Assuming that the WHDM program completes its 45,000 meals contract with the City of Westchester, a small profit will be earned. For each meal provided above the break-even point (43,716), the home-delivered meals program will incur variable costs of $3.64 per meal, but will earn revenues of $5.77 per meal. The difference between the variable cost per meal and the revenue per meal is $2.13 per meal. The difference between contracted meals (45,000) and the BEP (43,716) is 1,284. The potential profit is $2,735 (1,284 meals × $2.13). Of course, variable costs will continue to vary during the remaining eight months of the fiscal year, so the program director will want to continue monitoring them and will also want to conduct additional break-even analyses during the fiscal year.

The preceding case examples demonstrate two principal uses of break-even analysis: (1) to estimate a human service program's fixed costs, variable costs, and BEP as part of the planning and budgeting processes and (2) to monitor a human service program's fixed costs, variable costs, and the BEP during the fiscal year. The discussion of differential cost analysis now shifts to decrease/discontinue decisions.

Decrease/Discontinue Decisions

From time to time, human service administrators are unfortunately confronted with decisions to decrease, and sometimes even to discontinue, a human service program. In these types of financial management decision situations, differential cost analysis is again used to determine the effect on a human service agency's fixed and variable costs. To demonstrate the use of differential cost analysis in decrease/discontinue decisions, the Phoenix Specialized Transportation Services (STS) case study introduced in Chapter 3 will again be used.

The Phoenix STS operates two programs: a transportation program and an escort program. In the just completed fiscal year 20XX, Phoenix STS had combined program expenses of $515,000. The Phoenix STS has three operating regions: Central Phoenix, East Valley, and West Valley. The Phoenix STS annually receives a $100,000 grant from the East Valley Coalition, a business group, to support the transportation program in the East Valley. The East Valley Coalition has just informed the program manager of Phoenix STS that this coming fiscal year may be the last time that it will be able to provide the $100,000 grant. The program manager decides that she needs to quickly compute the overall financial implications of a loss of $100,000 on the East Valley transportation operation, the transportation program as a whole, and the Phoenix STS as a whole. The program manger decides to conduct a differential cost analysis focusing on reducing, or actually discontinuing, the STS program in the East Valley. The first action the program manager takes is to review the Statement of Functional Expenses for the last fiscal year (Table 10.7).

TABLE 10.7   Phoenix Specialized Transportation Services

Statement of Functional Expenses
January 1, 20XX–December 31, 20XX

	Transportation Program	Escort Program	Total Program	Management and General	Fund-Raising	Total Expenses
Salaries	$195,000	$20,000	215,000	$62,000	32,000	309,000
Fringe benefits	31,200	3,200	34,400	9,900	5,100	49,400
Rent	15,000	2,000	17,000	3,000	2,000	22,000
Utilities	2,700	300	3,000	1,000	500	4,500
Telephone	3,000	1,000	4,000	2,000	2,000	8,000
Supplies	2,500	500	3,000	1,000	1,000	5,000
Vehicle maintenance	26,000	0	26,000	0	0	26,000
Vehicle depreciation	48,000	0	48,000	0	0	48,000
Escort reimbursement	0	5,000	5,000	0	0	5,000
Other	20,500	2,100	22,600	11,500	4,000	38,100
Total expenses	$343,900	$34,100	$378,000	$90,400	$46,600	$515,000

Note: This table also appears as Table 3.4 in Chapter 3.

Working from the financial information in Table 10.7, the program manager first computes the financial expense data for only the transportation program, excluding the escort program. Then, the program manager further separates the financial data by the three regions served by Phoenix STS. The resulting financial data are presented in Table 10.8. As Table 10.8 illustrates, during the past fiscal year, the East Valley operations had total expenses of $93,380.

Next, the program manager determines those line-item expenses of the East Valley operations that constitute fixed costs and those that constitute variable costs (Table 10.9). The $93,380 in expenses incurred in providing transportation services to the East Valley in the past fiscal year totaled $60,040 in variable costs and $33,340 in fixed costs. If the Phoenix STS discontinues its East Valley operations, $60,040 in variable costs would no longer be incurred, but the $33,340 in fixed costs (indirect, or overhead, costs) would still continue to be incurred. This latter point needs clarification. Agency indirect or overhead costs (e.g., the agency executive director's salary, rent, and utilities for the agency's offices) will not suddenly go away. Such costs will still be incurred. Perhaps over time some cutbacks or cost reductions can be made, but for purposes of differential cost analysis, indirect costs are usually treated as fixed costs.

The loss of the $100,000 grant would mean that Phoenix STS would not only have to discontinue providing all service in the East Valley, but it would also have to either (a) reduce its fixed costs by $33,340 or (b) find alternative sources of revenue in the same amount. Based on this analysis, the program manager concludes that Phoenix STS is confronted with a financial crisis. The program manager briefs

TABLE 10.8   Phoenix STS Transportation Expenses

Expense Categories	for Fiscal Year 20XX by Region West Valley	Central Phoenix	East Valley	Totals
Salaries	$39,000	$117,000	$39,000	$195,000
Fringe benefits	6,240	18,720	6,240	31,200
Rent	3,000	9,000	3,000	15,000
Utilities	540	1,620	540	2,700
Telephone	600	1,800	600	3,000
Supplies	500	1,500	500	2,500
Vehicle maintenance	5,200	15,600	5,200	26,000
Vehicle depreciation	9,600	28,800	9,600	48,000
Other	4,100	12,300	4,100	20,500
Management and general	16,200	48,600	16,200	81,000
Fund-raising	8,400	25,200	8,400	42,000
Totals	$93,380	$280,140	$93,380	$466,900

TABLE 10.9   Phoenix STS East Valley Transportation Expenses

for Fiscal Year 20XX by Fixed and Variable Costs			
Expense Categories	Total Expenses	Fixed Costs	Variable Costs
Salaries	$39,000		$39,000
Fringe benefits	6,240		6,240
Rent	3,000	$ 3,000	
Utilities	540	540	
Telephone	600	600	
Supplies	500	500	
Vehicle maintenance	5,200		5,200
Vehicle depreciation	9,600		9,600
Other	4,100	4,100	
Management and general	16,200	16,200	
Fund-raising	8,400	8,400	
Totals	$93,380	$33,340	$60,040

the executive director on the results of her analysis. The executive director calls an emergency meeting of the agency's board of directors.

The Phoenix STS case example demonstrates several points. First, when the service levels of human service programs are reduced, variable costs are also reduced. Second, when a human service program is discontinued altogether, the program's variable costs are eliminated altogether. Third, when the service levels of a human service program are reduced, or when a human service program is discontinued altogether, the program's fixed costs may or may not be reduced. Fourth, at least some portion of a program's fixed costs will consist of agency indirect costs that generally will not be reduced. Fifth, the loss of revenue associated with the reduction of a human service program's service levels, or with the discontinuance of a human service program altogether, affects not just the program but the overall agency as well.

Summary

This chapter has introduced the concepts of fixed costs, variable costs, and differential cost analysis. Two examples of differential cost analysis were demonstrated (break-even analysis and decrease/discontinue decisions) using three human service case examples. As a general rule, differential cost analysis is an appropriate financial management tool for use by human service administrators in alternative choice situations. The consideration of fixed and variable costs is also an important consideration in pricing, the topic of the next chapter.

EXERCISES

Exercise 10.1

During the sixth month of the fiscal year, the program director of the Westchester Home-Delivered Meals (WHDM) program decides to again recompute fixed costs, variable costs, and the BEP using the high–low method. Here are the number of meals served and the total costs of the program for each of the first six months:

Month	Meals Served	Total Costs
July	3,500	$20,500
August	4,000	22,600
September	4,200	23,350
October	4,600	24,500
November	4,700	25,000
December	4,900	26,000

Recompute fixed costs, variable costs, and the BEP. What are the variable costs? What are the fixed costs? How many meals will the WHDM program need to provide during the fiscal year to reach the BEP? How much profit will the program earn if it completes its 45,000-meal contract with the City of Westchester?

Exercise 10.2

It has been two years since the New River Community Council (NRCC) started its newsletter dealing with state and community funding opportunities for human service agencies. The current number of subscribers to the newsletter is 525. During the second year, the NRCC hired a new part-time newsletter coordinator (social work student). The NRCC has raised the salary of the part-time newsletter coordinator to $6,000 per year and has also hired another part-time student as an assistant for ten hours a week. The assistant is to be paid $75 per week or $3,900 per year. Together the newsletter coordinator and the part-time assistant believe they can handle up to 650 newsletter subscribers. Beyond this number, the newsletter program will require still more staff resources. In order to help cover the cost of the new part-time assistant, the executive director has also decided to increase the annual subscription price of the newsletter to $20. Additionally, the variable costs of preparing, printing, and mailing six bimonthly issues of the newsletter have risen to $4.50.

Recompute the BEP for the newsletter program. What is the new BEP? Is the new BEP a feasible solution? Why or why not? Will any slack capacity exist? If so, how much? If not, why not?

Exercise 10.3

The Mountain View Senior Adult Program (MVSAP) is interested in starting a visiting nurse program. The program would use licensed practical nurses to make home visits once a week to full-pay clients in the community. The MVSAP will treat the visiting nurse program as a profit center. If the visiting nurse program is successful and profitable, the profits will be used to expand the program to partial-pay and no-pay clients during the second year of operation. The executive director is not sure how best to implement the program. She has two major alternatives. The first alternative is to hire a small number of nurses and make them full-time employees. The second alternative is to contract with several nurses who would be interested in working part-time. To help in thinking through this financial management decision situation, the executive director decides to compute a series of BEPs based on contracting for the service and based on hiring one, two, and three full-time nurses.

The executive director makes the following assumptions about the new visiting nurse program:

- The price of the service will be set at $65 per visit.
- One full-time nurse position can provide a maximum of 120 one-hour visits per month.
- If the service is contracted, the agency plans to pay the contract nurses at the rate of $45 per visit including the cost of supplies.
- If the agency hires the nurses, the monthly salary will be $4,000 and the agency plans on spending an average of $10 per client per visit for supplies.
- Regardless of the method of service delivery (direct or contract) and regardless of the number of nurses hired, the agency plans to charge (allocate) $4,000 per month in indirect costs to the visiting nurse program.

Compute four annualized BEPs assuming the following: (1) the service is contracted, (2) one full-time nurse is hired, (3) two full-time nurses are hired, and (4) three full-time nurses are hired. What are the four BEPs? Why do these BEPs differ? Are all of these BEPs feasible solutions? If you were the executive director of the Mountain View Senior Adult Program, what method of service delivery (direct or contract) would you use? Why?

Exercise 10.4

Two years have passed since the Phoenix STS program faced the loss of funding for its East Valley operations. During the two years, Phoenix STS has attempted to broaden the funding base of the entire program, but with particular emphasis on the East Valley service area. The program manager has just received an end of the accompanying fiscal year financial report showing revenues and expenses for the three transportation service areas. The report shows that overall the transportation program made a profit (had an excess of revenues over expenses) for the fiscal year. But for its East Valley operations, the transportation program had a loss. Based upon the financial report, the program manager decides to recommend discontinuing transportation services in the East Valley service area. Is this a good financial management decision? Why? Why not?

Phoenix STS Transportation Services
Fiscal Year 20X1
Revenue and Expense Report by Region

	West Valley	Central Phoenix	East Valley	Total
Revenues	$110,000	$370,000	$90,000	$570,000
Expenses				
1. Management and general	20,000	60,000	20,000	100,000
2. Fund-raising	10,000	32,000	10,000	52,000
3. Program	75,000	250,000	75,000	400,000
Profit (or loss)	$ 5,000	$ 28,000	($15,000)	$ 18,000

CHAPTER

11 Setting Fees

Fee setting can be operationally defined as the process of determining how much an agency will charge for its products and services. Fees are usually established in one of two ways. A fee can be set on a per output (or unit-of-service) basis, or else on a per client or per participant basis. Whereas cost accounting standards and guidelines exist for the purposes of determining the full cost, or total cost, of a human service program (a major ongoing agency activity) or other agency activity (e.g., training program, workshop, seminar, special events), no comparable standards or guidelines exist for setting fees. Consequently, fee setting is as much an art as it is a science. The process of fee setting requires that human service administrators apply a variety of financial management concepts and techniques, as well as professional judgment, to determine a fee or fees that best serve the interests of clients, participants, the program or activity, and the agency.

A fee can be equal to, greater than, or less than the full cost of a human service program or other agency activity. For example, if a human service program is a revenue center, its fee might be set equal to its full cost. However, if the program is a profit center, its fee would probably be greater than the full cost. If a human service program or other agency activity uses variable fees or a sliding fee scale based on the economic circumstances of clients or participants, the fees paid by at least some clients will be less than the full cost.

This chapter discusses several major fee setting issues that human service administrators routinely consider when setting fees for programs and other agency activities. A case example (a child and family benefits seminar) is then used to demonstrate how these various fee setting issues might be dealt with. Again, the point is stressed that no hard and fast rules exist for fee setting. Rather, fees are arrived at on the basis of the financial analysis and the informed judgment of human service administrators.

Some Major Fee-Setting Issues

Figure 11.1 highlights some of the major issues that human service administrators consider when setting fees for human service programs and other agency activities. Some of these issues (direct and indirect costs, fixed and variable costs, and break-even points) have already been discussed in previous chapters. Other issues

FIGURE 11.1   Major Fee-Setting Issues

1. Direct and indirect costs
2. Depreciation and use allowance
3. Unallowable costs
4. Profit margins
5. Fixed and variable costs
6. Break-even points
7. Market prices
8. Variable fee and sliding fee schedules

are introduced here for the first time. They include depreciation and use allowance, unallowable costs, profit margins, market prices, and sliding fee schedules. Not all of these issues will apply to every fee setting situation. Nevertheless, many human service administrators ensure that they at least consider each of these issues to preclude errors of omission from occurring. In the following sections, each of these major issues is discussed in detail.

Direct and Indirect Costs

A good place to begin the discussion of fee setting is by ensuring that the full cost of any human service program or other agency activity has been identified. As discussed in Chapter 8, the full cost or total cost of a program or other agency activity is the sum of its direct costs plus a reasonable proportional (allocated) share of indirect (overhead) costs. When an agency initiates, reduces, or terminates a human service program, indirect costs are routinely reallocated. Often, however, no indirect costs are allocated to other agency activities (e.g., one-day training sessions, workshops, seminars, special events). As a general rule, all agency activities (major and minor) should usually be assigned at least some indirect costs.

One reason frequently given for why human service agencies do not include indirect costs in computing the full cost of minor agency activities is that the effort involved is not worth the return. This need not be the case. Let's assume, for example, that a human service agency has a total fiscal year operating budget of $2 million of which $1,750,000 is total direct (program) costs and $250,000 is indirect (overhead) costs. The agency's indirect cost rate (using total direct costs as the base) is 14.3 percent. The human service agency decides to conduct a one-day workshop with direct costs of $10,000. How can one quickly and simply determine what amount of indirect costs should be allocated to the proposed workshop? Why not $1,430, which is 14.3 percent of $10,000? Using this simple approach, a human service agency can ensure that it takes full advantage of all opportunities to recover indirect costs. There is, of course, the possibility that a human service agency using this approach could "overrecover" indirect costs. If such a situation occurs, the accountants and auditors can sort things out at the end of the fiscal year.

Depreciation and Use Allowance

Facility and equipment assets used in the provision of human service programs and other agency activities break, run down, wear out, and eventually have to be repaired or replaced. In order to have sufficient funds available for the rehabilitation of facilities and the repair or replacement of equipment, these assets are frequently depreciated or a use allowance is computed.

Under the concept of *depreciation,* both the cost of an asset and its useful life are computed. Dividing the cost of the asset by its useful life generates a figure (a dollar amount) that represents the depreciation of that asset for one fiscal year. A portion of the annual depreciation is then included as a cost to all human service programs and other agency activities that benefit from the use of the asset. Sometimes, however, a human service agency does not have a formal depreciation schedule on its facilities and equipment. In such instances, a use allowance can be computed in lieu of depreciation. A *use allowance* is simply some defensible cost that is charged to a human service program or other agency activity for "the use" of a facility or piece of equipment. Under the use allowance approach, the fair market rent on a comparable facility or a comparable piece of equipment is first computed. The resulting dollar amount is then apportioned between a human service agency's programs and other agency activities according to how much use each makes of the asset. For example, if the fair market rent for a photocopy machine is $600 per month and the machine is equally shared by three human service programs, then a $200 use allowance per month would be charged to each program.

If depreciation or use allowance is computed and included as part of a human service agency's cost allocation plan, it should not, of course, be added in a second time. The concepts of depreciation and use allowance are both recognized and recoverable under most federal contracts, grants, and cooperative agreements (see Chapter 12).

Unallowable Costs

Unallowable costs are any items of cost that a funding source will not pay for or reimburse. For example, some private foundations restrict the extent to which their grants funds can be used to purchase equipment. The federal government and many state and local governments also identify specific items of cost that they consider unallowable (e.g., lobbying costs) for which they will neither pay nor reimburse. Chapter 15, dealing with audits and auditing, provides a more in-depth treatment of the topic of unallowable costs and how human service administrators can identify them.

The problem with unallowable costs is that they frequently need to be excluded from the computations when determining fees for human service programs or other agency activities. If a government or a foundation is going to be charged the fee and the computational base of the fee includes unallowable costs, a human service agency or program is exposing itself to a potential audit exception. If no government or private foundation will be charged the fee, then this issue is moot.

Unallowable costs should be excluded early in the fee setting process so that they do not affect the determination of fixed and variable costs and the computations involved in determining break-even points (BEPs).

Profit Margins

Before computing break-even points, the issue of including a profit margin should be considered. For our purposes here, a *profit margin* will be operationally defined as some additional increment over and above the full cost or total cost of a human service program or other agency activity. Defined in this way, several arguments can be put forward on the advisability of including a profit margin when setting a fee for a human service program or other agency activity:

- The inclusion of a profit margin is necessary if the human service program is designated as a profit center.
- Many one-time activities, although not designated as profit centers, are actually designed to generate excess revenues to help support other agency programs. For example, training sessions and workshops frequently have two purposes: imparting valuable information to trainees and participants and generating excess revenues for the agency. If a profit margin is not included in the fee charged to trainees and workshop participants, revenues cannot exceed costs and no excess revenues can be generated.
- Flexibility in fee setting is frequently desired. This flexibility can take a variety of forms including reduced fees, sliding fee schedules, or fee waivers for certain types of individuals or groups (e.g., low-income people). In order to break even, some profit margin must be included in the fee to be charged full-pay clients and participants in order to offset the loss of revenue for clients and participants that are charged a reduced fee or no fee.
- The setting of any fee is at best an educated guess. Uncontrollable variables can work against a fee actually generating revenues sufficient to cover expenses. For example, variable costs can be underestimated or demand for the program or activity can be overestimated. The inclusion of a profit margin provides a contingency or cushion against the effects of uncontrollable variables.

What should be the size of a profit margin? No hard and fast rule exists, but a figure of 2 to 5 percent is frequently used in the private nonprofit sector. In terms of computing the profit margin, the full cost of the program or activity becomes the base. Two to 5 percent of the base is computed and the resulting amount is then added to the base.

Fixed and Variable Costs

Another major issue in fee setting is the identification of fixed costs and variable costs. Fixed and variable costs were discussed at length in Chapter 10. The focus of

Chapter 10, however, was on understanding the differences between fixed and variable costs and how they are used in break-even analysis and decrease/discontinue decisions. The identification of fixed and variable costs is also an important issue in fee setting.

As discussed in Chapter 10, the total variable costs of a human service program or other agency activity depends upon the amount of service provided (i.e., the number of outputs or units of service provided or the number of clients or participants served). For example, workshops, seminars, and special events frequently include participant workbooks and handouts and may also include coffee breaks, lunch, and so on. The total cost of these items will vary depending upon how many people participate. Consequently, fixed and variable costs must be identified and one or more BEPs computed assuming various levels of service output (or units of service), clients, or participants.

Break-Even Points

Break-even points are yet another important consideration in fee setting. Different BEPs have different associated fees. In general, lower BEPs result in higher fees, whereas higher BEPs result in lower fees. Two factors that affect BEPs are capacity issues and go/no-go decisions.

Frequently, the size of a facility, equipment availability (e.g., computer workstations), or some other "capacity" factor will determine the maximum number of outputs (or units of service) that can be provided or the maximum number of clients or participants that can be served. Capacity issues are directly related to the computation of break-even points. If an individual BEP is greater than the capacity of a facility or is greater than the availability of equipment, it represents a solution that is outside the feasible range.

Go/no-go decisions usually apply to one-time agency activities (e.g., training sessions, workshops, seminars, special events) and are concerned with establishing *cutoff points*, which are guaranteed minimum numbers of outputs (or units of service), clients, or participants without which the program or activity will be canceled. Like most of the issues involved in fee setting, no hard and fast rules exist to aid in determining a cutoff point. The establishment of a cutoff point has a lot to do with how much risk a human service agency is willing to assume and how important the activity is to clients, participants, or the community.

Frequently, a cutoff point and the break-even point are one and the same. For example, training organizations frequently set their combined go/no-go decision points and break-even points at relatively low levels. For example, take the case of a seminar that can accommodate a maximum of 40 participants. The agency conducting the seminar might set its combined go/no-go decision point and BEP at 25 participants. If fewer than 25 participants register, the seminar will be canceled because otherwise the agency would lose money. If exactly 25 participants register, the seminar will be held because it will at least break even (including possibly a 2 to 5 percent profit margin). And if more than 25 participants register, the agency will make a larger profit because fixed costs will already be covered.

Market Prices

The going market price per output (or unit of service) or per client or participant can represent a constraint on the fee that can be set for a human service program or other agency activity. For example, if the going rate for a home-delivered meal in a particular community is $5 to $6 and a human service agency proposes to set a fee at $7.50 for its home-delivered meals, it may well price itself out of the market. Governments as well as individuals and family members might not be willing to pay a $7.50 fee per home-delivered meal if they can get a comparable meal from another agency for $5 to $6. Likewise, if an agency decides to set a fee of $250 for a training session or workshop, when comparable training sessions and workshops in the community are priced between $100 and $125, no one may register.

When all the other fee setting issues just mentioned have been considered and when a proposed fee has been set for a human service program or other agency activity, the fee then needs to be compared with market prices. If the proposed fee is significantly higher than the market price in the community, then the fee may need to be adjusted downwards if possible.

Variable Fee and Sliding Fee Schedules

The final major fee setting issue to be discussed is that of variable fees and sliding fee schedules. Rather than having one fee that applies to all clients and participants regardless of economic circumstances and ability to pay, many human service agencies and programs prefer to establish variable fees or sliding fee schedules.

When considering variable fees or sliding fee schedules, it is important for human service administrators to keep in mind their effect on revenues. As an example, let's say that the full cost of a program is $150,000 and that demand for the program is estimated at 15,000 outputs or units of service. The minimum fee must be $10 in order for the program to break even (to generate revenues equal to expenses). A decision to offer a variable fee or sliding fee schedule means that revenues will not equal expenses, unless some clients and participants are charged a higher fee to offset the lower fee charged to other clients. It is a basic economic fact that in order for some clients and participants to pay a lower fee or no fee at all, other clients and participants must pay more. Of course, some additional funding source might be found to make up the loss of revenue associated with the use of variable fees or sliding fee schedules. The effect of variable fees and sliding fee schedules on revenues may seem obvious, but it is an issue that is all too frequently overlooked.

Let's now look at an example of the application of these major issues to the setting of a fee for a seminar.

Government Benefits Seminar Case Example

Advocates for Children, a 501(c)(3) private nonprofit agency, wants to conduct a one-day seminar for area social workers and volunteers on federal and state benefits available to children and families. The seminar will be a one-time activity and is designed both to provide a valuable service to the community and to generate a small profit to help support the agency. Advocates for Children is a midsize agency with a total annual operating budget of $750,000 consisting of $600,000 in direct (program) costs and $150,000 in indirect (overhead) costs. The agency's indirect cost rate (using total direct costs as the base) is 25 percent.

The agency's executive director plans to rent a conference room for the seminar. The conference room can accommodate a maximum of 60 trainees. The executive director anticipates that the seminar will be fully subscribed (all 60 seminar slots will be filled). The executive director wants to set aside 10 slots for volunteers who will be charged only 50 percent of the seminar fee. The question that now confronts the executive director is, What should be the seminar fee?

The executive director prepares a budget identifying the costs involved in conducting the seminar (Table 11.1) assuming 60 trainees attend the seminar. The budgeted costs include (1) the rental of the conference room, (2) the rental of audiovisual equipment, (3) the cost of the four seminar leaders, (4) the cost of the seminar workbook that each trainee will receive, (5) the cost of the lunch that each trainee will receive, and (6) the cost of a coffee break that each trainee will receive. The total cost of the seminar as identified in the budget is $4,360.

Having completed the budget, the executive director decides to use Figure 11.1 as a checklist in helping to determine the fees for the seminar. Following Figure 11.1, the executive director immediately realizes that the budget does not contain all the direct and indirect costs of the seminar because no agency indirect costs (overhead) are included. In order to include agency indirect (overhead) costs in the cost of the seminar, the executive director multiplies the total budget costs (direct costs) of the seminar ($4,360) by 25 percent. The resulting figure, $1,090 is then added to the budget (Table 11.2) for a revised figure of $5,450. Since the facilities and equipment are being rented, their costs are already included and no need exists to consider depreciation and use allowance. Unallowable costs will not be a problem because no governments or foundations will be directly paying the seminar fee. In

TABLE 11.1 Government Benefits Seminar

Proposed Budget

1. Conference room rental	$ 250.00
2. Audiovisual equipment rental	100.00
3. 4 presenters @ $500	2,000.00
4. 60 workbooks @ $15	900.00
5. 60 lunches @ $15	900.00
6. 60 coffees @ $3.50	210.00
Total costs	$4,360.00

TABLE 11.2   **Government Benefits Seminar**

Proposed Budget

1. Conference room rental	$ 250.00
2. Audiovisual equipment rental	100.00
3. 4 presenters @ $500	2,000.00
4. 60 workbooks @ $15	900.00
5. 60 lunches @ $15	900.00
6. 60 coffees @ $3.50	210.00
Total costs	$4,360.00
7. Indirect costs @ 25% of $4,360.00	$1,090.00
Subtotal	$5,450.00
8. Profit margin @ 5% of $5,450.00	$ 273.00
Total	$5,723.00

terms of profit, the executive director decides to factor in a margin of 5 percent. The 5 percent profit margin is applied to the revised budget figure of $5,450 (Table 11.2). The computed profit margin ($273) is then added into the budget, resulting in the figure of $5,723.

The executive director now computes fixed and variable costs and determines a tentative break-even point. As Table 11.3 demonstrates, the variable costs of the seminar include (a) workbooks at $15 each, (b) lunch at $15 per person, and (c) the coffee break at $3.50 per person. All other costs of the seminar are fixed costs.

The executive director decides to set both the break-even point and the go/no-go decision point at 45 trainees. Even though the executive director fully expects 60 trainees to attend the seminar, by setting the BEP and the go/no go decision point at 45, a margin of error is built in for uncontrollable variables (e.g., bad weather on the day of the seminar). If a minimum of 45 full-pay trainees attend the seminar, Advocates for Children will at least break even on the seminar. If more than 45 full-pay trainees attend the seminar, the agency will make an additional profit (over and above the 5 percent) because, at 45 trainees, all the seminar's fixed costs will be covered. The difference between the seminar fee and the variable cost will be pure profit. Using the BEP formula, but solving for price (or fee), the executive director determines a tentative fee for the seminar of $116 (Table 11.4).

The executive director knows that other agencies in the community charge fees of $125 to $150 for comparable one-day seminars and workshops. Consequently, the tentative fee is below community market prices. The executive director now has to factor into the tentative fee, a price differential to account for the loss

TABLE 11.3   Government Benefits Seminar

Identification of Fixed and Variable Costs

Fixed Costs

1. Conference room rental @ $200	$ 250.00
2. Audiovisual rental @ $100	100.00
3. 4 presenters @ $500	2,000.00
4. Indirect (overhead) costs @ 25%	1,090.00
5. Profit margin @ 5% of total costs	273.00
Total fixed costs	$3,713.00

Variable Costs

1. Workbooks @	$ 15.00
2. Lunches @	$ 15.00
3. Coffee @	$ 3.50
Total variable costs	$ 33.50

TABLE 11.4   Computation of the Seminar Fee

Using Forty-Five Trainees as the Break-Even Point

$XP = A + BX$

$45P = 3{,}713 + 33.50(45)$

$45P = 3{,}713 + 1{,}508$

$45P = 5{,}221$

(Divide both sides by 45.)

$P = \$116.00$

of revenue associated with the variable or sliding fee schedule involved in offering ten volunteers a half-priced fee. As Table 11.5 demonstrates, if Advocates for Children offers ten volunteers a reduced fee ($58), the revenue loss will be $580. To offset this revenue loss, the $580 is apportioned among the 50 full-pay trainees. The result is an increase of $12 in the full fee from $116 to $128. The fee of $128 is still on the low side of community market prices. Note that because of the new full fee ($128), the reduced fee ($58) is no longer exactly 50 percent less than the full fee.

TABLE 11.5   Computing the Effect of Variable Fees on Seminar Revenues

60 trainees @ $116 =	$6,960.00
50 trainees @ $116 =	$5,800.00
10 trainees @ $ 58 =	580.00

$$\text{Revenue } \$6,380.00$$

$$\text{Revenue loss on 10 half-priced fees} = \$6,960.00$$
$$6,380.00$$

$$\$\ 580.00 \text{ (revenue loss)}$$

$$\text{Increase in full fee to offset revenue loss } \frac{\$\ 580.00}{50} = \$11.60$$

$$\text{Adjusted full fee} = \$\ 128.00 (\$116 + \$12)$$

Revenue computations:

60 trainees @ $116.00 =	$6,960.00
50 trainees @ $128.00 =	$6,400.00
10 trainees @ $ 58.00 =	580.00
	$6,980.00

Summary

This chapter has looked at a number of major issues that should be considered when setting fees for human service programs and other agency activities. The major issues identified in the chapter can be used by human service administrators as a guide in thinking through the fee setting process and arriving at a fee or fees that best serve the interest of clients, participants, the program or the activity, and the agency.

In the next two chapters, the subject changes to issues of revenue generation beginning with the topic of government contracts and grants.

EXERCISES

Exercise 11.1

The child and family government benefits seminar was such a success that Advocates for Children will conduct a second seminar in an adjoining community. The executive director decides that this second seminar will attempt to maximize revenues. Consequently, no reduced fee schedule will be offered. All trainees will pay the full seminar fee. The seminar will take place in a smaller conference room than the earlier one. The room can only accommodate a maximum of 45 trainees. Here is the proposed budget for the seminar:

Proposed Seminar Budget

1. Conference room rental $175.00	$ 175.00	
2. Audiovisual equipment Rental	75.00	
3. 4 presenters @ $500	2,000.00	
4. 45 workbooks @ $15	675.00	
5. 45 lunches @ $12	540.00	
6. 45 coffees @ $3.50	158.00	
	Subtotal	$3,623.00
7. Indirect costs @ 25% of $3,675.00		$ 906.00
	Subtotal	$4,529.00
8. Profit margin @ 5% of $4,594.00		$ 227.00
	Total	$4,756.00

You are the executive director. Following the checklist in Figure 11.1, perform all the computations necessary to set a fee. What will your fee be? What is your break-even point? What is your go/no-go decision point?

Exercise 11.2

As the executive director of Advocates for Children, you have had a change of heart. You decide not to attempt to maximize revenues in this second seminar. You decide to exclude a profit margin in the fee computation, but you will include indirect costs. Additionally, the local United Way in the community hosting the seminar has guaranteed 45 participants. If fewer than 45 participants register for the seminar, the United Way will make up the difference. In exchange for this guarantee, the United Way has asked you to set the seminar fee as low as possible. Following the checklist in Figure 11.1, perform all the computations necessary to set a fee. What will your fee be?

Exercise 11.3

Advocates for Children is considering operating a residential summer camp (to be called Camp Delmar) for children between the ages of 12 and 16 who have physical and mental disabilities. The camp will be a "camp within a camp" in that another camp (Camp Oceanside) will provide transportation to and from the facility and will allow Camp Delmar to use two dormitory-type buildings (one for boys, the other for girls) for a one-week period. Camp Oceanside will charge Camp Delmar a fee $125 per camper per week. The $125 is all inclusive (lodging, food, transportation to and from the camp, etc.). Although the two dormitories can accommodate up to 20 children each, the plan is that Camp Delmar will have only 10 boys and 10 girls.

As executive director, you develop a proposed budget for Camp Delmar:

Proposed Budget for Camp Delmar

1. 3 Supervising social workers @ $750.00 per week	$2,250.00
2. 5 camp counselors @ $300 per week	1,500.00
3. 20 Camp Oceanside fees @ $125 per camper per week	2,500.00
Total costs	$6,250.00

As the executive director of Advocates for Children, you decide (with the approval of your board of directors) not to include a profit margin or indirect (overhead) costs in determining a fee for Camp Delmar. Furthermore, a wealthy member of the board of directors has agreed to donate $2,500 to Camp Delmar in order to reduce the fee charged to parents. What will your fee be? What is your break-even point?

12 Government Contracts and Grants

Federal, state, and local government funding is one of the most common and most important sources of financial support for human service agencies and programs. Consequently, human service administrators need to be knowledgeable about the ins and outs of various types of government funding and how to identify government funding opportunities. Human service administrators also need to be familiar with the differences between procurement and assistance relationships as well as the differences between the major types of government human service contracts.

This chapter looks at the topics of government contracts, grants, and the less well known cooperative agreements. The chapter also provides guidance on how to locate information about government grants, contracts, and cooperative agreements. Because state and local governments today make more use of contracts for human services than they do of grants, the chapter also describes the two major procurement approaches used to select contractors and the three major types of government human service contracts.

Contracts, Grants, and Cooperative Agreements

A good place to begin a discussion of government funding is with the Federal Grant and Cooperative Agreement Act. As Figure 12.1 illustrates, the act identifies two types of financial relationships (procurement and assistance) and three types of financial instruments (contracts, grants, and cooperative agreements).

A *procurement relationship* is said to exist when a federal department or agency expends funds to secure (purchase) goods or services for its own purposes. An *assistance relationship* is said to exist when a federal department or agency provides funds to another agency (such as a state or local government human service agency or a private nonprofit human service agency) to assist that agency in discharging its own responsibilities.

The distinction between a procurement relationship and an assistance relationship is more than just semantics. Differing sets of federal regulations apply to procurement relationships and assistance relationships. Also, different case law covers procurement and assistance relationships. For example, agencies competing for federal contracts (procurement relationships) can file complaints with the General Accounting Office (GAO) if they believe they have been treated unfairly.

FIGURE 12.1   Uses of Contracts, Grants, and Cooperative Agreements as required by the Federal Grant and Cooperative Agreement Act

Procurement ⎯⎯⎯⎯⎯⎯⎯⎯⎯⎯⎯⎯⎯⎯⎯⎯⎯⎯⎯→ Contract
                        (The government is a *purchaser.*)

Assistance ⎯⎯⎯⎯⎯⎯⎯⎯⎯⎯⎯⎯⎯⎯⎯⎯⎯⎯⎯→ Grant
                        (The government is a *patron.*)

Assistance ⎯⎯⎯⎯⎯⎯⎯⎯⎯⎯⎯⎯⎯⎯⎯⎯⎯⎯⎯→ Cooperative
                        (The government is a *partner.*)   Agreement

Purchaser
The federal department or agency is a *purchaser* of goods and services through the use of a *contract.*

Patron
The federal department or agency is a *patron* supporting the efforts of another agency through the use of a *grant.*

Partner
The federal department or agency is a *partner* sharing decision making with another agency through the use of a *cooperative agreement.*

No similar appeals process exists for grants and cooperative agreements (assistance relationships).

The difference between procurement and assistance relationships also has practical service delivery implications for human service agencies and for clients. In assistance relationships, service recipients are considered to be the clients of the human service agency receiving federal funding, not the federal department or agency. In procurement relationships, the reverse is the case; service recipients are considered to be clients of the federal government whereas the human service agency is simply a paid service provider.

The Federal Grant and Cooperative Agreement Act restricts the use of contracts to procurement relationships. The act subdivides assistance relationships into two categories: (1) those that are required to use grants and (2) those that are required to use cooperative agreements. Referring again to Figure 12.1, sometimes a federal department or agency acts much like a patron and is essentially "giving" money to support the activities of a state or local government or a private nonprofit agency human service agency. In assistance relationships of this nature, the act requires that the funding instrument be a grant. The point should be stressed that even when a federal department or agency gives money to another agency, the funds still come with strings attached, but not nearly the number of strings that come with cooperative agreements and contracts.

In some situations, a federal department or agency may wish to become a partner with a state or local government or private nonprofit human service agency in a sort of joint venture arrangement. For example, the U.S. Department of

Health and Human Service might be interested in testing a new treatment modality or program design, or in conducting some type of special evaluation, or it may simply want to be actively involved in making decisions about a particular demonstration program or activity. For assistance relationships of this type, the act requires that the funding instrument be a cooperative agreement.

The Federal Grant and Cooperative Agreement Act also requires that every federal program identify the nature of its financial relationships (procurement or assistance) and the types of financial instruments (contracts, grants, cooperative agreements) it uses. Consequently, when a state or local government or private nonprofit human service agency is considering applying for funding under a particular federal program, it can determine in advance the types of financial relationship and financial instrument that the program uses.

Unfortunately, the Federal Grant and Cooperative Agreement Act applies only to federal departments and agencies. State and local governments have their own policies concerning when a contract or a grant is the more appropriate financial instrument. In general, state and local governments tend to favor procurement relationships over assistance relationships and favor contracts over grants. Cooperative agreements are unique to the federal government; state and local governments generally do not use cooperative agreements. However, sometimes when a state or local government uses a grant, for all practical purposes it takes on the characteristics of a cooperative agreement.

Sources of Information about Government Contracts, Grants, and Cooperative Agreements

How does one locate information about government contracts, grants, and cooperative agreements, how much funding is available, and who can apply? At the federal level, two primary sources are the *Catalogue of Federal Domestic Assistance* and the *Commerce Business Daily*.

The *Catalogue of Federal Domestic Assistance* is an encyclopedic listing of all domestic (noninternational) human service and non–human service federal programs in all federal departments and agencies that provide assistance-type funding to state and local governments, Indian tribal governments, and private nonprofit agencies. The catalogue is cross referenced by type of program and by federal department and agency. A brief description of each program appears in the catalogue together with its annual funding levels as well as information about who is eligible to apply for the funding. Figure 12.2 is an abridged catalogue listing for the Social Services Block Grant (SSBG) program.

As Figure 12.2 illustrates, the SSBG provides federal funding for a variety of human service programs directed at five major objectives: (1) preventing, reducing, or eliminating dependency; (2) achieving or maintaining self-sufficiency; (3) preventing neglect, abuse, or exploitation of children or adults; (4) preventing or reducing inappropriate institutional care; and (5) securing admission or referral for institutional care when other forms are inappropriate. The U.S. Department of

FIGURE 12.2   The *Catalogue of Federal Domestic Assistance* Listing for the Social Services Block Grant (Abridged)

93.667 Social Services Block Grant

020 (Social Services)

030 FEDERAL AGENCY: ADMINISTRATION FOR CHILDREN AND FAMILIES, DEPARTMENT OF HEALTH AND HUMAN SERVICES

040 AUTHORIZATION: Social Security Act, Title XX, as amended; Omnibus Budget Reconciliation Act of 1981, as amended, Public Law 97–35; Jobs Training Bill, Public Law 98–8; Public Law 98–473; Medicaid and Medicare Patient and Program Act of 1987; Omnibus Budget Reconciliation Act of 1987, Public Law 100–203; Family Support Act of 1988, Public Law 100–485; Omnibus Budget Reconciliation Act of 1993, Public Law 103–66; 42 U.S.C. 1397 et seq.

050 OBJECTIVES: To enable each State to furnish social services best suited to the needs of the individuals residing in the State. Federal block grant funds may be used to provide services directed toward one of the following five goals specified in the law: (1) to prevent, reduce, or eliminate dependency; (2) to achieve or maintain self-sufficiency; (3) to prevent neglect, abuse, or exploitation of children and adults; (4) to prevent or reduce inappropriate institutional care; and (5) to secure admission or referral for institutional care when other forms of care are not appropriate.

060 TYPES OF ASSISTANCE: Formula Grants.

080 ELIGIBILITY REQUIREMENTS:

081 Applicant Eligibility: The 50 States, the District of Columbia, Puerto Rico, Guam, the Virgin Islands, the Commonwealth of the Northern Mariana Islands, and American Samoa.

090 APPLICATION AND AWARD PROCESS:

092 Application Procedure: Submission of a pre-expenditure report application is required.

093 Award Procedure: States are awarded funds quarterly.

120 FINANCIAL INFORMATION:

121 Account Identification: 75-1534-0-1-506.

122 Obligations: (Grants) FY 98 $2,299,000,000; FY 99 $1,909,000,000; and FY 00 est $2,380,000,000.

Health and Human Services administers the SSBG program. Only states and other select governments may apply for SSBG program funding. The amount of funding available for fiscal year 2000 is $2.38 billion and the funding instrument used is a *grant*. While the SSBG example does not provide direct funding for private nonprofit human service agencies, many other federal programs listed in the catalogue do.

An online version of *the Catalogue of Federal Domestic Assistance* can be accessed, and service statements can be downloaded, through the Internet home page of the federal Office of Management and Budget (see this book's Appendix).

The *Commerce Business Daily* is a newspaper-type publication that is published every working day and lists announcements of human service and non–human service contracts, grants, cooperative agreements, requests for proposals (RFPs), and invitations for bids (IFBs) made by various federal departments and agencies (RFPs and IFBs will be discussed shortly). The announcements state who can apply, how much funding is available, and application deadlines. Figure 12.3 is an example of an announcement for a job creation/retention program in areas impacted by the North American Free Trade Act. Up to $6 million is available. Any 501(c)(3) or 501(c)(4) nonprofit agency can apply as well as private institutions of higher education, state and local governments, and Indian tribal governments. The type of financial instrument used is a grant.

Finding out about the availability of human service contracts and grants from state and local governments is somewhat more involved. The two most common ways are to be placed on a bidders list or by reading the legal advertisements section of the daily newspaper.

The process for being placed on a state or local government's bidders list usually involves contacting the government's procurement office or human service agency. Various forms must be completed and submitted. Private nonprofit human service agencies may also be required to submit copies of their articles of

FIGURE 12.3 Listing from the *Commerce Business Daily* (Abridged)

COMMERCE BUSINESS DAILY ISSUE OF OCTOBER 19, 1999 PSA#2457

Community Adjustment and Investment Program

GRANT SOLICITATION: FOR JOB CREATION/RETENTION IN TRADE IMPACTED COMMUNITIES SINCE THE ADVENT OF NAFTA *(North American Free Trade Agreement)*

ANNOUNCEMENT 001: The North American Development Bank, on behalf of the United States Community Adjustment and Investment Program (the "CAIP"), will issue a Solicitation for Grant Applications on October 15, 1999. Up to $6 million will be available on a competitive basis to fund grants for specific projects and technical assistance designed to aid in creating and preserving private sector jobs in designated communities that have lost, or may lose, jobs due to changes in international trade patterns associated with the passage of the NAFTA. Applicants for CAIP grants may seek to combine grant funds with loan funds from the CAIP direct lending program.

ELIGIBLE APPLICANTS: 501(c)(3) and 501(c)(4) nonprofit organizations, public and private institutions of higher education, state and local political subdivisions and agencies, and Indian tribal governments. For further information or a copy of the Solicitation for Grant Applications, please contact the Project Director at (999) 123-4567.

DEADLINE: The deadline for receipt of applications is January 17, 20XX. It is expected that grant awards will be announced in March 20XX.

Source: Adapted from the *Commerce Business Daily* <http://www.ld.com/cbd/today/index> (10/19/99).

FIGURE 12.4   **Announcement of a Request for Proposals (RFP) for a Child Care Assistance Program**

The State Department of Human Services (the "Department") is soliciting proposals from qualified organizations to administer the department's child care subsidy program called the Child Care Assistance Program (CCAP).

Proposals must be received no later than 5:00 P.M. on Friday, January 31, 20XX. Late proposals will not be considered. A mandatory proposer's conference will be held on Monday, January 3, 20XX, at the department's headquarters.

To request a copy of the request for proposals (RFP), interested parties should contact the department's Office of Contract Services at (999) 123-4567.

incorporation, bylaws, and most recent annual report. As part of the application process, a human service agency generally has to identify the types of services it is interested in providing. When a human service agency is placed on a state or local government's bidders list, it is then routinely sent notices of impending requests for proposals (RFPs) or invitations for bids (IFBs) or the actual IFB or RFP package itself for the indicated services.

The other method of learning about state and local government contracting opportunities is to frequently check the legal advertisements section of the major local newspaper. The procurement laws and regulations of most state and local governments require that contracting opportunities (both human service and non–human service) be announced in a "newspaper of general circulation" within the government's service area. Figure 12.4 is an example of a request for proposals (RFP) announcement in the legal advertisements section of a newspaper. At a minimum, these legal advertisements usually state the department that is making the announcement, the type of solicitation involved (IFB or RFP), and the due date. The amount of available funding may be specified. Some state and local government departments also maintain home pages on the Internet. Announcements of IFBs and RFPs frequently appear on these home pages.

Types of Procurements

As previously mentioned, state and local governments tend to prefer the use of contracts over grants. This has not always been the case. In the early 1970s, grants were preferred to contracts for human service programs. However, with the creation of Title XX of the Social Security Act in 1975 (now the Social Services Block Grant), the federal government required states to either provide human services directly or use contracts. Other federal human service programs administered by state and local governments also began switching from grants to contracts (Kettner and Martin, 1987; Lauffer, 1997). Today, contracts are the state and local government financial instruments of choice for human service programs. Lauffer

(1997:74) forecasts that by the year 2010, over 80 percent of all government funding for human service programs will involve the use of contracts.

Procurement is the generic term for the process used by governments (federal, state, and local) to select contractors and award contracts (both human service and non–human service). The following discussion focuses on procurement at the state and local government levels, though the processes and procedures are also broadly representative of the federal government's approach.

In selecting contractors and awarding contracts, state and local governments generally use one of two procurement approaches: the request for proposals (RFP) or the invitation for bids (IFB). The request for proposals approach is also known as *competitive negotiation*. The invitation for bids approach is also called *formal advertising, competitive bidding,* and *sealed competitive bidding.* Although the names vary, the two approaches are fairly standardized across state and local government departments as well as federal departments and agencies. Both procurement approaches are competitive in nature, meaning that they are designed to solicit more than one bid or proposal. Of the two approaches, the RFP is used more frequently for human service programs, although significant use is also made of the IFB.

The Request for Proposals (RFP)

In the RFP approach, interested human service agencies (prospective contractors) prepare a proposal, usually with an accompanying operating budget, as specified in the state or local government's RFP package. In the proposal narrative section of the RFP package, a prospective contractor details how it intends to provide the service including any specific treatment modalities; identifies the education, qualifications, and experience of staff who will be involved in providing the service; and in general attempts to impress the state or local government that it would make the best contractor. In the budget section, a prospective contractor identifies all the items of cost (both direct and indirect or overhead) it estimates will be incurred in providing the service. The RFP package gives the due date for submission of completed proposals, specifies the criteria by which proposals will be evaluated, and usually states that late proposals will not be considered.

The state or local government reviews all the proposals submitted on time and selects the prospective contractor whose proposal is the most advantageous to the government, price and other factors (e.g., service quality issues) being considered. Though the criteria used in the evaluation of proposals, as well as the individual weights assigned to each criterion, vary from procurement to procurement, they also tend to be generally reflective of similar issues and concerns. Figure 12.5 is an example of a set of proposal evaluation criteria and weights for a human service RFP.

In Figure 12.5, the criteria are divided into four major categories: proposal criteria, organizational criteria, service delivery criteria, and cost criteria. As a general rule, cost is not the most important criterion in the evaluation of proposals submitted in response to a RFP. If a state or local government wants to make cost the major

FIGURE 12. 5   Representative Criteria Used to Evaluate Proposals Submitted in Response to a Request for Proposals

1. **Proposal Criterion**

    A. The proposal is properly completed, contains all attachments, exhibits, and budgets; and is signed by an authorized representative of the proposer. (10 points).

2. **Organizational Criteria**

    A. The proposer has the programmatic and financial ability to successfully provide the program or service (15 points).

    B. The proposer has a successful history of providing the program or service (10 points).

    C. The proposer has a successful history of providing the program or service under previous government contracts or grants (10 points).

3. **Service Delivery Criteria**

    A. The proposer's overall service delivery approach is both feasible and acceptable (15 points).

    B. The proposer has (or can acquire) the necessary staff, equipment, and facilities to provide the service (15 points).

4. **Cost Criterion**

    A. The proposer's costs are both allowable and reasonable (25 points).

factor in a procurement, then it will generally use the invitation for bid. As Figure 12.5 indicates, significant weight is usually placed on the proposer's programmatic and financial capabilities, its previous service delivery experience, and the feasibility and acceptability of its service delivery approach.

When all proposals have been scored, the state or local government sits down with the highest-scoring proposer and the two parties negotiate a final agreement. When all the terms and conditions of the final agreement are reduced to writing and signed by both parties, a legally binding contract comes into being (Kettner & Martin, 1987).

The Invitation for Bids (IFB)

The invitation for bids (IFB) approach is generally used only when a state or local government department knows exactly what it wants to purchase in terms of the type of service, staff qualifications, quality standards, client characteristics, and other factors. In the IFB approach, no negotiation takes place. The state or local government department specifies (sometimes in great detail) in the IFB package the service it wishes to purchase. Prospective contractors interested in providing the service simply fill in the sections of the IFB package that ask for the unit price and/or the total price they propose to charge. Like the RFP package, the IFB package usually states that bids submitted late will not be considered. The IFB package is structured in such a fashion that once a prospective contractor completes and signs the document, it becomes a firm legal offer (Kettner & Martin, 1987).

At the specified time for the opening of bids, the state or local government opens all bids submitted on time and records the bid prices. The contract is usually awarded to the responsible prospective contractor (meaning that the agency has the necessary programmatic and financial capabilities to provide the service) submitting the lowest responsive bid (meaning that the bid was properly completed and submitted on time). Because a completed IFB package constitutes a firm legal offer, the state or local government department has only to sign the IFB document and a legally binding contract comes into existence.

Because most state and local government departments want to have at least some negotiations with a prospective contractor when human service programs are involved, the RFP approach tends to be used more often than the IFB approach. Nevertheless, the procurement of at least some human services by at least some state and local governments does involve the IFB approach. As a general statement (see Figure 12.6), the RFP approach is used more frequently with *soft services* (services directed at clients), whereas the IFB approach is used more frequently with *hard services* (services directed at things). As Figure 12.6 illustrates, the difference between hard and soft services is one of degree more than an absolute distinction. Thus, on the soft services end of the continuum, one would generally find the RFP approach used for such human services as counseling and various therapies, whereas at the hard services end of the continuum, one would expect to find the IFB approach used with such human services as specialized transportation, congregate meals, and home-delivered meals.

Human service administrators need to understand the differences between the RFP approach and the IFB approach and what the differences mean in terms of the selection of contractors and the awarding of contracts. In the case of the RFP approach, cost and price information included in a submitted proposal is simply information that will be used in final contract negotiations. However, when a

FIGURE 12.6 The Relationship between Soft and Hard Human Services and the Two Major Procurement Approaches

Request for Proposals (RFP)		Invitation for Bids (IFB)	
Soft Services		Hard Services	
Adoption	Counseling	Specialized transportation	Home-delivered meals

human service agency includes a price in an IFB package, the agency must be prepared to accept a contract for that amount.

Types of Contracts

Government contracts are generally classified according to their method of compensation (Keyes, 1990). When contracting for human services, state and local governments tend to use (1) cost reimbursement contracts, (2) performance contracts, and (3) capitated (managed care) contracts.

Cost Reimbursement Contracts

Under a *cost reimbursement contract*, a contractor *is* reimbursed for actual allowable expenses incurred in the provision of the service, usually in accordance with an approved line-item operating budget that is included as part of the contract. If an expense is not actually incurred, then it is not reimbursable. Because of this principle, a "settling up" generally occurs following the completion of a cost reimbursement contract. For example, a final accounting or an audit of a $100,000 cost reimbursement contract might determine that only $95,000 in allowable expenses were actually incurred by the contractor. If the contractor received the full payment of $100,000, it would have to return the excess funding for which no offsetting allowable expenses were incurred. Though cost reimbursement contracts usually have a face dollar value, the amount is best thought of, not as a guaranteed figure, but rather as a maximum that can be claimed.

From the perspective of state and local government departments, a major deficiency of cost reimbursement contracts is that they do not relate the contractor's compensation to any performance considerations. Because of this deficiency, many state and local governments are moving away from the use of cost reimbursement contracts in favor of performance contracts or capitated (managed care) contracts.

Performance Contracts

A *performance contract* is one that focuses on the outputs and outcomes of service provision and ties either contract payments, contract extensions and renewals, or both to their achievement (Martin, 2000b). The subjects of outputs (the amount of service provided measured in units of service) and outcomes (quality of life changes in clients as a result of service provision) were discussed at length in Chapter 6 dealing with performance measures.

There is no one single way to structure a performance contract. The structure of a performance contract is limited only by the creativity of the state or local government. Figure 12.7 provides several examples of how a performance contract might be structured.

FIGURE 12.7   **Examples of Performance Contracts**

Payment (Outputs or Units of Service)

1. The contractor shall be paid at the rate of $____ per hour for each hour of counseling services provided.
2. The contractor shall be paid at the rate of $____ per meal for each home-delivered meal provided.

Payment (Outcomes)

1. The contractor shall be paid at the rate of $____ for each client who completes the job training program.
2. The contractor shall be paid at the rate of $____ for each client who completes the drug treatment program.

Payment (Mixture of Outputs and Outcomes)

1. The contractor shall be paid:
   A. 75 percent of its per client fee for each client who completes the job training program.
   B. 15 percent of its per client fee for each client who is placed in a job.
   C. 10 percent of its per client fee for each client who remains in the job for a period of at least six months.

Renewal or Extension

In order for the contract to be renewed or extended:
A. ____ percent of the families served by the contractor will have no verified reports of child abuse or neglect during the past six months (child abuse program).
B. ____ percent of persons discharged will successfully complete treatment with no documented alcohol or other drug use during the month prior to discharge (drug treatment program).
C. ____ percent of homeless persons served will receive housing and other supportive services (homeless services program).

As Figure 12.7 illustrates, a performance contract can tie a contractor's compensation to outputs (units of service), outcomes, or a combination thereof. The achievement of specific levels of outputs or outcomes can also be considerations in contract renewals and extensions. Some federal job training programs (e.g., welfare-to-work initiatives) require that state and local governments use performance contracts.

Unlike cost reimbursement contracts, the amount of compensation that a contractor receives is not determined by the amount of expense incurred, but rather by (a) the amount of outputs (units of service) provided, (b) the number of outcomes achieved, or (c) some combination thereof. If a contractor provides the mutually agreed amount of outputs (units of service) or achieves the mutually agreed number of outcomes, the revenues earned should be equal to or greater than expenses incurred. However, if a contractor's actual performance falls short of its contractually obligated performance, revenues may well be less than the actual expenses and a contractor could lose money on a contract. A performance contract involves more contractor risk than does a cost reimbursement contract. However, a performance contract is still less risky from the contractor's perspective then is a capitated (managed care) contract.

Capitated (Managed Care) Contracts

Capitated (managed care) contracts are designed to control the utilization of services and resources (Kamerman & Kahn, 1998). Under capitated contracts, a contractor usually receives a fixed payment to provide services to a client for a fixed period of time. As is the case with performance contracting, there is no one general approach to capitated contracting. Some of the more ambitious examples of capitated contracting for human services programs are found in the State of Kansas.

The Kansas Department of Social and Rehabilitative Services (Kansas SRS) has been experimenting with capitated contracting for child welfare services for several years now. Under the Kansas SRS approach, a contractor is paid a one-time fee for each child placed in its care irrespective of how long the child remains in care. For example, a contractor providing foster care services might receive a one-time payment of $15,000 for each child placed in its care. This payment is the only compensation the contractor receives no matter how long the child remains in care. Assuming that the average annual cost of foster care nationally is between $17,000 and $25,000 (Eggers,1997), if a child remains in the contractor's care for more than about nine months, the contractor will lose money. If an appropriate and timely placement is made, however, the contractor could actually make money on the contract. To ensure that financial considerations do not drive quality-of-care considerations, the capitated contracts used by the Kansas SRS contain specific performance standards. Figure 12.8 provides examples of performance standards utilized in Kansas SRS foster care capitated contracts. According to Kamerman and Kahn

FIGURE 12.8   Examples of Kansas Social and Rehabilitative Services Capitated (Managed Care) Contract Performance Standards for Residential Foster Care

1. At least 90 percent of children will not experience a confirmed incident of abuse or neglect.
2. At least 90 percent of children in care will not experience more than three placement moves subsequent to referral.
3. At least 65 percent of children will be placed with at least one sibling.
4. At least 70 percent of children will be placed within the region where they live.

Source: Adapted from Lawrence L. Martin (2000b). "Performance Contracting in the Human Services: An Analysis of Selected State Practices." *Administration in Social Work* (forthcoming).

(1998), capitated contracting could well become the wave of the future in human service contracting.

Cost reimbursement contracts, performance contracts, and capitated contracts have different objectives and create differing sets of duties and obligations on the part of human service agencies serving as contractors. Performance contracts and capitated contracts place substantially more financial risk on contractors.

Summary

This chapter looked at the topics of procurement relationships, assistance relationships, contracts, grants, and cooperative agreements. The chapter also discussed the two major types of procurements (requests for proposals and invitations for bids) and the three major types of human service contracts (cost reimbursement, performance, and capitated or managed care). The suggestion was made that human service administrators need to understand the conceptual and practical differences between procurement and assistance relationships and between the different types of financial instruments used by governments.

In the next chapter, the discussion shifts from government funding for human service programs to private sources of funding and to various other fund development techniques.

13 Fund Development

In Chapter 11, the topic of service fees was considered. Chapter 12 then covered government contracts and grants. In this chapter, several other revenue enhancement strategies used by human service agencies and programs are explored under the topic of fund development.

Attempting to cover the multifaceted topic of fund development in one chapter necessarily precludes coverage of all possible approaches. The strategy adopted here is to identify and briefly describe some of the more common as well as some of the more entrepreneurial approaches to fund development. The chapter begins with a discussion of some of the more traditional approaches (foundation grants, United Way affiliation, annual campaigns, special events, and client donations) and then moves to some of the more entrepreneurial approaches (affinity marketing, bequest programs, life income programs, commercial ventures, and for-profit corporate subsidiaries).

Foundation Grants

Foundation grants have long been a major source of funding for human service agencies and programs. Foundation grants have become even more attractive in recent years because of the bull market on Wall Street. Most foundations have at least a portion of their assets in stocks. The significant increase in stock values during the 1990s has resulted in significant increases in the assets of many foundations. Individual investors have also done well in the stock market in recent years; as a result, donations to foundations have also increased.

Some 44,000 foundations exist in the United States today. The combined assets of these foundations total some $230 billion (Council on Foundations, 1999). The ten largest foundations (Table 13.1) have combined assets of over $80 billion. The largest foundation in the United States ($17 billion in assets) is the Bill and Melinda Gates Foundation named after the chairman of the Microsoft Corporation and his wife. By law, foundations must expend an average of 5 percent of their assets each year in grants. When one considers the number of foundations (44,000) and their combined total assets ($230 billion), the potential foundation funding available each year is truly impressive. On average, foundations award some $15 billion in grants each year.

TABLE 13.1   The Ten Largest Foundations in the United States

	Assets in 1999
1. Bill and Melinda Gates Foundation	$17.1 billion
2. David and Lucille Packard Foundation	13.0 billion
3. Ford Foundation	11.4 billion
4. Lilly Foundation	11.1 billion
5. Robert Wood Johnson Foundation	8.1 billion
6. W. K. Kellogg Foundation	6.2 billion
7. Pew Charitable Trusts	4.8 billion
8. John D. and Catherine T. MacArthur Foundation	4.2 billion
9. Andrew W. Mellon Foundation	3.5 billion
10. Rockefeller Foundation	3.5 billion
	Total $82.9 billion

Source: Adapted from *The Chronicle of Philanthropy*, 11(21) (August, 1999):8.

Not all foundations exist exclusively for the purpose of funding human service agencies and programs. Foundations are created for a variety of purposes including health, education, the arts, and the environment. Nevertheless, many foundations do support human service agencies and programs. The challenge for human service administrators is accessing information about these 44,000 foundations and their funding priorities.

Types of Foundations

Foundations can be classified in many different ways. For purposes of this discussion, foundations are classified into five major categories: family foundations, corporate (business) foundations, general interest foundations, special interest foundations, and community foundations. Note that these categories are not mutually exclusive. Consequently, an individual foundation can be included in more than one category. For example, a family foundation could also be a special interest foundation, a corporate foundation could also be a general interest foundation, and so on.

Family Foundations

Family foundations are usually named after the founding family member(s) and derive their original assets from family donations. Referring again to Table 13.1, the top ten largest foundations in the United States are all family foundations. The combined assets of all family foundations in the United States exceed $100 billion. Family foundations make grants totaling some $6 billion annually (Council on Foundations, 1999).

The funding interests of family foundations are usually tied closely to the wishes of the family member(s). For example, the Bill and Melinda Gates Foundation has two primary interests: global health and learning. With respect to learning, the foundation states that it is particularly interested in closing the "digital divide" between those who have access to the Internet and those who do not.

Corporate (Business) Foundations

Many foundations are closely associated with specific American businesses. Foundations of this type were usually started by a specific business and they maintain strong ties to that business. Corporate (business) foundations usually derive their grant making funds from the profits of the business. The types of programs they fund are frequently related to the nature of the business. Examples of corporate foundations include the Sears Roebuck Foundation, Federated Department Stores Foundation, and Mutual of New York Foundation. Again, not all company-sponsored foundations have human services as a funding priority, but many do. For example, the Mutual of New York Foundation funds community-based agencies that serve people who have AIDS or are HIV-positive. Corporate foundations awarded grants totaling in excess of $8 billion in 1998 (Council on Foundations, 1999).

General Interest Foundations

General interest foundations are those that have a generic funding priority such as education, health, human services, the environment, or the arts. General interest foundations are usually willing to consider proposals for any program or activity that falls within their generic purview. A good example of a general interest foundation is the Robert Woods Johnson Foundation, whose funding interest is the broad area of health. Many human service agencies and programs with a health component have benefited over the years from funding from this important foundation.

Special Interest Foundations

As their name suggests, special interest foundations have narrowly defined (specific) funding interests. Special interest foundations exist for such purposes as addressing specific health issues (e.g., cancer), particular social problems (e.g., teenage pregnancy, literacy), or particular target groups (e.g., women, children, the elderly). Special interest foundations will usually only consider proposals for programs and activities that fall within their narrowly defined areas of interest.

Community Foundations

Yet another type of foundation is the community foundation. Although community foundations can be an important source of funding for human service agencies and programs, they are generally less well known than other types of foundations. Because they are less well known, community foundations warrant special mention.

A community foundation serves as a sort of clearinghouse for individuals, families, and businesses that desire to have their charitable activities managed by trained professionals, but who do not want to hire their own staff. Consequently, a community foundation is really a collection of grant making programs that are frequently quite diverse in terms of funding interests and priorities. For example, the New York Community Trust, a community foundation, administers some 1,300 different grant making programs.

A community foundation usually serves a defined geographic area such as a city, a county, or sometimes even a state. Some 500 community foundations exist across the United States (Council on Foundations, 1999). Most major U.S. cities as well as many medium-sized cities have a community foundation. Some community foundations are quite large in terms of assets; others are modest in size. Two of the largest community foundations are also two of the oldest. The New York Community Trust has assets of $1.7 billion; the Cleveland (Ohio) Foundation has assets of nearly $1.5 billion. More modest in size are the Vermont Community Foundation and the Waco (Texas) Foundation with assets of $13 million and $12 million, respectively (*Chronicle of Philanthropy*, 1998:8; 1999:14).

The Arizona Community Foundation is a good example of an average-size community foundation. The Arizona Community Foundation has assets of some $200 million (*Chronicle of Philanthropy*, 1999:14). As Figure 13.1 illustrates, the goal of the Arizona Community Foundation is to serve the interests of the state's various communities through the provision of grants and technical assistance to nonprofit organizations (both human service and non–human service). The Arizona Community Foundation's funding priorities include families and children, children and youth, and social justice.

FIGURE 13.1   The Arizona Community Foundation

Goal: To meet the charitable needs of Arizona's communities through grants, technical assistance, and other services to nonprofit organizations.

Areas of Special Interest:

- Families and the elderly
- Children and youth
- Education
- Scholarships
- Neighborhood and community-based economic and social development
- The environment
- Social justice

Source: Adapted from Arizona Community Foundation home page <http://www.azfoundation.com> (3/13/2000).

Finding Out about Foundations

How can human service administrators access information about foundations, their funding priorities, and who can apply? Four good sources of information are the Foundation Center, the *Chronicle of Philanthropy*, the Council on Foundations, and the Internet.

One of the largest repositories of information about foundations is the Foundation Center. Located in New York City, the Foundation Center maintains information (including funding priorities and application processes and deadlines) on the majority of U.S. foundations including old, established foundations as well as newly created ones. The Foundation Center publishes annual compendiums describing foundations by type, state, funding priorities, and so on. The Foundation Center maintains an Internet home page which serves as a gateway to its online and hard-copy resources (see Appendix).

The *Chronicle of Philanthropy*, a monthly newspaper-type subscription service, contains funding announcements made by foundations, information on how to apply, and application deadlines. The *Chronicle of Philanthropy* essentially provides the same type of information about foundation grants that the *Commerce Business Daily* provides about federal government contracts, grants, and cooperative agreements (see Chapter 12). The *Chronicle of Philanthropy* also maintains an Internet home page (see Appendix).

A nonprofit organization based in Washington, D.C., the Council on Foundations (1999), describes itself as working to "support foundations by promoting knowledge, growth and action in philanthropy." Its Internet home page provides a useful gateway to accessing information about community foundations throughout the United States (see Appendix).

Finally, more and more individual foundations today—in particular, the larger foundations—maintain their own Internet home pages that provide basic essential information on funding priorities, application processes, and submission deadlines. For example, the Pew Charitable Trusts is a well-established foundation in Philadelphia, Pennsylvania. By consulting its Internet home page, one can discover that in 1998, the foundation had assets of $4.8 billion and made 298 grants totaling $213 million to nonprofit organizations. The Pew Charitable Trusts has a specific fund directed at health and human services (The Pew Charitable Trusts, 1999).

United Way of America Membership

Another traditional source of funding for many human service agencies and programs is the United Way of America. The United Way is an affiliated fund-raising organization, which means that it conducts joint fund-raising activities on behalf of its member agencies. The national United Way of America is an umbrella organization that represents some 1,200 independent local United Ways. Local United Ways in turn represent their affiliated health and human service members. The major fund-raising activity of both the national United Way of America and local United Ways is their annual campaign, which has strong ties to the business community. In 1999, the United Way annual campaign raised $3.5 billion (United Way of America, 1999).

While member agencies do give up some individual fund-raising discretion (e.g., no independent fund-raising activities during the annual campaign), United Way membership has considerable financial benefits. Once a human service agency is accepted as a member, it is generally guaranteed to receive at least some United Way funding each year. Because United Way funds come from private sources, they have the additional benefit of satisfying the "matching" or cost sharing requirements imposed by many government and foundation grants.

Though specific criteria for United Way affiliation can vary from community to community, some consistency also exists. The requirements for membership in the local United Way of New York City are generally reflective of the criteria used by many local United Ways. To become a member of the United Way of New York City (Figure 13.2), a human service agency must meet the following criteria: provide services in one of the five city boroughs, possess an Internal Revenue Service designation as a 501(c)(3) nonprofit organization, have been incorporated for at least three years, have a full-time executive director and an active board of directors, and provide certain documents (a copy of its most recent audit and IRS 990 submission). United Ways generally exclude from membership organizations whose primary missions are religious, cultural, or educational in nature.

Information about the national United Way of America (see Appendix) as well as information about local United Ways can be accessed through the Internet. In addition to the Internet home page maintained by the national United Way of America, some 350 local United Ways now maintain their own home pages.

FIGURE 13.2   United Way of New York City

Affiliation Criteria

1. The agency must provide health and/or human services to at least one borough of the City of New York.

2. The agency must be an Internal Revenue Service (IRS) 501(c)(3) nonprofit organization.

3. The agency must be incorporated for at least three (3) years.

4. The agency must have a full-time paid executive director.

5. The agency must have a responsible and active board of directors.

6. The agency must submit a copy of its most recent financial audit conducted by a certified public accountant (CPA) and a copy of its most recent IRS 990 Form.

Source: Adapted from The United Way of New York City, home page <http://www.uwnyc.org> (3/13/2000).

Other Traditional Fund Development Approaches

Foundation grants and United Way membership are only two of several traditional fund development and fund-raising approaches. This section describes annual campaigns, special events, and client donations.

Annual Campaigns

Just as the United Way conducts an annual campaign, so do many human service agencies and programs. Annual campaigns can be defined as a once-a-year major fund-raising effort that usually involves direct mail and/or telephone solicitations to agency or program members, friends (both individuals and businesses), volunteers, and clients. Annual campaigns frequently occur in the later months of the calendar year when individuals and businesses may be looking to make a charitable contribution in order to reduce their taxable income.

When conducting annual campaigns, many human service agencies distinguish between two types of activities that have long been recognized by fund-raising professionals: donor renewal and donor acquisition (Smallwood & Levis, 1977). *Donor renewal* is the activity associated with contacting those individuals and business that have previously donated to the human service agency. *Donor acquisition* is the activity associated with identifying individuals and businesses that might donate to the agency. Many human service agencies and programs treat donor renewal and donor acquisition as two separate and distinct activities within their annual campaigns. The reason for this dual approach is that donor renewal activities are less costly and have higher success rates than donor acquisition activities. The primary goal of an annual campaign is to get previous donors to make another donation. A secondary goal is to get previous donors to increase the amount of their donation.

A problem for a relatively new human service agency or program conducting an annual campaign is, of course, that it has a small existing donor base and thus must expend more resources in donor acquisition than in donor renewal. New human service agencies and programs that conduct annual campaigns will be largely involved in expensive donor acquisition activities. Consequently, new human service agencies and programs might best think of a annual campaign as a long-range approach to fund development that may not produce significant revenues over the short term. However, after a number of annual campaigns, some of the activity will shift from donor acquisition to donor renewal. The use of board members and volunteers is one way that both new as well as established human service agencies and programs can reduce the costs of annual campaigns.

Special Events

Special events is a generic term used to describe a variety of fund-raising techniques including award dinners, auctions, raffles, "thons" (e.g., walk-a-thons, bike-a-thons, skate-a-thons), and other one-time or periodic happenings. A human service agency or program keeps the net proceeds (the excess of revenues over expenses) from the special event. Consequently, a special event seeks to maximize revenues and minimize expenses. In order to minimize expenses, a special event attempts to get individuals and businesses to donate goods and services that can be auctioned, raffled, or given away to participants.

Award dinner (e.g., "person-of-the-year") special events seek to have the facility, the decorations, the food, the drinks, the flower arrangements, the door prizes, and so on donated. The individuals and businesses providing the goods and services receive recognition and an income tax deduction for their donations.

The main attraction of an awards dinner is the honoring of some individual (frequently a celebrity, elected official, or community leader) whose name familiarity will attract interest and attendance. Individuals attending the dinner are charged a price (e.g., $150 per person). The amount charged for the awards dinner (over and above the estimated actual cost) can be taken by participants as a tax-deductible charitable contribution. Participants have a good time, help to promote a worthy human service agency or program, and also receive a tax deduction.

Auctions function in essentially the same way as award dinners, except that in the case of auctions, individuals and businesses are solicited to donate goods and services of significant market value (e.g., airline tickets, hotel accommodations, cruise ship vacations, restaurant meals) that serve as the attraction. It is not unusual for a special event to combine both a nonaward dinner and an auction. Dinners and auctions are particularly attractive special events for the winter months because they can be held indoors.

A variant of the basic auction special event is the celebrity auction. In celebrity auctions, goods and services are donated by national or local celebrities (elected officials, sports figures, actors, or television personalities). Sports memorabilia (particularly autographed items) usually attract spirited bidding as do such items as lunch with the mayor or dinner with a local TV personality.

Raffles generally involve selling a small number of raffle tickets for a particularly attractive prize. For example, luxury automobile raffles have become popular in recent years. In raffles of this nature, the donation of a luxury automobile is first secured. The vehicle might have a sticker price of $50,000. A finite number (e.g., 500) of raffle tickets are then sold for a donation of, say, $100 each. The attraction from the donor's perspective is that because only a small number of raffle tickets are sold, the donor actually has a real chance of winning. The individual or business donating the luxury automobile receives a tax deduction, the winner of the raffle gets the car, the nonwinners get a tax deduction, and the human service agency raises $50,000. A caution here is that in some communities raffles, like the one just described, are considered to be gambling. Human service agencies and programs considering raffles should seek legal advice before proceeding.

"Thons" (e.g., walk-a-thons, bike-a-thons, skate-a-thons) are particularly good springtime special events as they can be held outdoors. Thons can be relatively inexpensive special events in that participants generally receive a T-shirt (or some other small token acknowledging their participation) and refreshments, both of which can be donated by individuals and businesses. Participants solicit pledges from family members, friends, and business associates to support their walking, biking, or skating effort.

Thons frequently require securing the approval and cooperation of the local government, including both the police and fire/rescue departments. A parade permit may be required and police and fire/rescue may be necessary for crowd control and emergency purposes (e.g., participant illness or overexertion). Some municipalities charge organizations for the cost of police and fire/rescue services. In other cities, parade costs may be included as part of the government's overall operating budget. A major downside of thons is that in many communities specific types of thons have already been adopted and are already associated with particular charitable causes and particular nonprofit organizations.

Special events also represent a way to involve a human service agency's board of directors and volunteers in fund-raising activities. The responsibility for securing donated goods and services is frequently undertaken by board members and volunteers. Thons represent a way in which agency board members, staff, volunteers, clients, friends, and others can become involved in fund-raising and show their support for a human service agency or program.

Client Donations

A fund development activity that is frequently overlooked by many human service agencies and programs is client donations. Unlike client fees, which were discussed in Chapter 11, client donations are freewill offerings made to a human service agency or program by service recipients. In addition to raising revenues, a formalized donation fund-raising activity provides clients with an opportunity to contribute something (even small amounts) toward the cost of maintaining the program. For at least some client groups, being able to contribute toward the cost of a program lessens the feeling that they are receiving some sort of welfare. Programs funded under the Older Americans Act have long been required to have a donation policy in place for just this reason.

Entrepreneurial Fund Development Approaches

As competition for funding has become more intense in recent years, human service agencies and programs have become more creative in their fund development approaches. This section looks at several entrepreneurial approaches to fund development including affinity marketing, bequest programs, life income programs, commercial ventures, and for-profit corporate subsidiaries.

Affinity Marketing

Affinity marketing, also referred to as *cause-related marketing*, involves situations in which human service agencies and programs enter into joint venture promotional campaigns with businesses. These joint ventures can take several forms. Three major forms are sales promotions, credit card promotions, and charity shopping malls.

Sales promotions involve a business donating some amount of money in relation to its sales to a human service agency or program over some period of time. Frequently, these sales promotions are timed to coincide with a particular holiday or special community event. For example, a local supermarket might advertise that for every turkey sold during November, some amount of money (e.g., 50 cents per turkey) will be donated to a local homeless shelter to help provide Thanksgiving dinners.

Credit card promotions usually take the form of a donation being made to a human service agency or program each time the card is used during some specific period of time. For example, a credit card company such as MasterCard or American Express might advertise that it will make a donation to some human service agency or program every time its credit card is used during December.

Historically, credit card promotions have been a fund development strategy employed by only large multistate private nonprofit organizations. However, as competition among credit card companies and among the banks that issue them becomes more intense, credit card promotions at the state and community levels are becoming more prevalent. With respect to sales campaigns, even small human service agencies and programs operating in small communities can use this approach to fund development. All that is required is an idea and a cooperating business.

The *charity shopping mall* is a recent variation on the theme of affinity marketing. Charity shopping malls are operated and maintained by e-commerce Internet sites. Several of these e-commerce charity shopping malls have recently appeared on the scene. All are operated by for-profit businesses. Under the concept of a charity shopping mall, an individual charity (such as a private nonprofit human service agency) registers with an individual e-commerce Internet business. The Internet business pledges to donate some amount of its sales to the various charities on its registry. For example, Amazon.com typically donates 5 percent of sales to the charities on its registry (Moore & Williams, 1999:25).

The long-term fund development potential to human service agencies and programs of registering with a charity shopping mall are far from clear at the present time. E-commerce is still a relatively new concept. Nevertheless, many people predict that e-commerce will become the wave of the future. Consequently, charity shopping malls could become a significant source of revenue for human service agencies and programs in the future.

Affinity marketing, in all its various forms, represents a win–win situation for both the human service agency or program on the one hand and the participating business or credit card company on the other. The human service agency or program receives revenues it would otherwise not receive; the business receives publicity for being a good corporate citizen as well as the potential for increased sales.

Bequest Programs

Bequest programs are one variant of what is generically referred to as *planned giving*. In this form of planned giving, individuals include in their wills or estate plans a stipulation that certain funds, stocks, bonds, or property be transferred to a named private nonprofit human service agency or program upon their passing. A bequest program is a method by which individuals can thank a human service agency or program for services or kindnesses they or family members received.

Bequest programs obviously require a high degree of tact and sensitivity in their implementation. Also, they do not necessarily generate significant revenues over the short term. A bequest program is perhaps best thought of as a long-term fund development strategy. Human service agencies that provide certain types of services (e.g., specialized transportation, in-home care, hospice) or serve particular types of clients (e.g., the elderly) may be best positioned to use bequest programs as a fund development approach.

Life Income Programs

Life income programs are another form of planned giving. Two variants of life income programs are charitable remainder trusts and pooled income funds.

Charitable remainder trusts involve a donor making a contribution of cash, stock, bonds, or property to a human service agency or program. In return, the donor is able to take a personal income tax deduction up to Internal Revenue Service limits. However, the donor also receives a guaranteed income stream for life based on the value of the donated assets. Upon the passing of the donor, the remainder of the funds in the trust is transferred to the human service agency or program.

Pooled income funds involve cash donations from a donor that are pooled and invested in stocks, bonds, and so on along with other such cash donations received by the human service agency or program from other donors. Again, the donor gets a tax deduction as well as an income stream for life.

Life income approaches require either that the human service agency or program have a sophisticated fund development professional working for it or that a relationship exists with a community foundation or the trust department of a bank. A community foundation or a bank trust department can handle the legal and financial paperwork involved as well as invest and manage the funds.

Commercial Ventures

A commercial venture begins when a human service agency or program (either government or private nonprofit) essentially goes into business. For purposes of this section, a *commercial venture* is operationally defined as any situation in which a human service agency or program provides goods and services to another organization or to the general public.

Human service agencies become involved in commercial ventures more often than many people realize. Three examples illustrate this point:

- A government human service agency operates a large congregate-meals program and contracts to provide another private nonprofit human service agency with home-delivered meals.

- A private nonprofit human service agency operates a job training program for food service and custodial workers and also operates a restaurant, a catering service, and a custodial service. While undergoing training, trainees work in the restaurant, the catering service, and the custodial service.
- A self-help program operated by a small, rural, private nonprofit human service agency goes into e-commerce by creating an Internet home page and selling handicraft items made by elderly members of the community.

Most of the time, commercial ventures are perfectly legitimate entrepreneurial forms of fund development. However, the Internal Revenue Service restricts the extent to which private nonprofit human service agencies and programs can compete with private sector businesses and still maintain their IRS 501(c)(3) status. The Support Center is a San Francisco–based private nonprofit organization that provides programmatic and financial technical assistance to other private nonprofit organizations. According to the Support Center (Figure 13.3), private nonprofit human service agencies and programs engaging in commercial activities need to be aware of two major concerns. First, if a commercial venture is not directly related to the exempt purposes for which the private nonprofit organization exists, then a human service agency or program is required to pay taxes (at corporate rates) on the income earned. Second, if the size of the commercial venture becomes too large (if the tail begins to wag the dog), the agency's IRS 501(c)(3) status could be jeopardized.

Before launching a commercial venture, a human service agency or program should consult with its legal advisors and accountants. This admonition should not, however, be interpreted as discouraging the undertaking of commercial ventures.

FIGURE 13.3   Internal Revenue Service (IRS) Regulations Concerning Commercial Ventures Conducted by Private Nonprofit Organization 501(c)(3) Organizations

1. "Unrelated business income" is income generated from the operation of a commercial venture that is not substantially related to the human service agency's exempt purpose.

2. All IRS 501(c)(3) nonprofit organizations are subject to a tax (at corporate rates) on unrelated business income.

3. As a general rule, revenues derived from commercial ventures are not considered unrelated business income when all work is performed by volunteers.

4. When commercial ventures go beyond a human service agency's exempt purposes, the agency's IRS 501(c)(3) status could be jeopardized.

Source: Adapted from "What Is the Unrelated Business Income Tax?" <http://www.igc.org> (10/18/99). Copyright © 1994–97 Support Center, 706 Mission Street, 5th Floor, San Francisco, CA USA 94103-3113. (415) 541-9000. Reprinted with permission. All rights reserved.

For-Profit Corporate Subsidiaries

The creation of a for-profit corporate subsidiary avoids the problem of a private nonprofit human service agency or program placing its IRS 501(c)(3) status in jeopardy by becoming involved in a commercial venture. A for-profit corporation can usually engage in any lawful business activity that it desires.

Creating a for-profit corporate subsidiary is relatively easy. Though the procedural requirements (filing status, number of incorporators, etc.) vary from state to state, the basic premise is relatively straightforward. A for-profit corporation is created that is controlled by the private nonprofit corporation. Control can take a variety of forms. One form is to have the board of directors, or a subgroup, of the private nonprofit human service agency also serve as the board of directors of the for-profit corporation. The interlocking board of directors ensures that the activities of the for-profit corporation will not diverge from the intentions of the private nonprofit human service agency.

The profits of the for-profit corporation are taxed as would be the case with any for-profit business. The aftertax profits, minus any retained earnings needed to continue or expand the operations of the for-profit business, are donated (transferred) to the private nonprofit human service agency subject to IRS limitations. An additional benefit of creating a for-profit corporate subsidiary is that operating costs (e.g., staff, facilities, equipment) can be shared by the private nonprofit human service agency and the for-profit corporation.

Summary

This chapter has briefly explored the topic of fund development. Several traditional approaches to fund development were identified (foundation grants, United Way affiliation, special events, and client donations) as well as several entrepreneurial approaches including affinity marketing, bequest programs, life income programs, commercial ventures, and for-profit corporate subsidiaries. The fund development approaches discussed are not the only ones that exist, but they represent a good cross section. Numerous books and monographs are published each year that can be consulted to further explore the fund development approaches identified in this chapter or to learn about other fund development methods.

In the next chapter, the discussion moves from fund development to risk management. Risk management is a relatively new concept for many human service agencies and programs, but one that is rapidly gaining acceptance. The argument can be made that fund development is concerned with raising revenues for a human service agency or program, whereas risk management is concerned with holding on to those revenues.

14 Risk Management

Although the concept of risk management is an integral part of the financial management practices of most governments and private sector businesses, it is still a relatively new concept to human services administration. The fact that many human service agencies do not practice risk management is a major concern. It can take years of diligent efforts of the board of directors, the executive director, program managers, and other administrators to accumulate a small reserve fund for a human service agency. But, it takes only one accident, one lawsuit, or one fire to wipe out that reserve fund and perhaps even threaten the financial viability of the agency itself.

In addition to helping to maintain the financial viability of a human service agency, risk management has several other advantages (Johnson & Ross, 1991:356) including reducing insurance costs, making more efficient use of resources, and, in general, lowering the overall cost of providing goods and services. In terms of this last advantage, Hyman (1994) notes that a formalized risk management program is one of the few ways a human service agency can reduce service delivery costs without cutting either staff positions or operating budgets.

This chapter looks at the concept of risk management and the major activities that comprise a risk management program. The chapter makes the case that risk management should be treated as a program within the program structure of a human service agency. The chapter then discusses a wide variety of specific applications of risk management under the headings of insurance issues, governing board issues, human resource management issues, basic internal financial control issues, workplace hazard issues, volunteer liability issues, and records management issues.

What Is Risk Management?

Risk management can be defined as the identification, planned control, and reduction of risks to a human service agency. Risk management is concerned with protecting the financial, human, and other resources of a human service agency and providing products and services in a responsible fashion (Tremper & Kostin, 1993). As Figure 14.1 illustrates, risk management is comprised of five essential tasks: risk identification, risk evaluation, risk control, risk funding, and administration.

FIGURE 14.1 The Major Activities of Risk Management

1. Risk identification
2. Risk evaluation
3. Risk control
4. Risk funding
5. Administration

Source: Allen Hyman (1994). "The Principles of Risk Management."
Issues & Options 2 (10):1.

Risk identification refers to the ongoing identification of activities and situations within a human service agency that have high potential for incurring legal liability; causing personal injury to clients, staff, or others; or creating disruptions in the operations of the agency. Everyone has heard the expression, "This is an accident just waiting to happen." Risk identification involves identifying those accidents, problems, and issues that are just waiting to happen.

Risk evaluation involves the prioritization of risk. The task of risk identification may lead to the discovery of potential risks that a human service agency is only partially aware of or perhaps is not aware of at all. Risk evaluation involves placing some sort of economic value on each of the identified risks with the idea that those risks with the greatest potential economic impact will receive the greatest attention.

Risk control is the process of deciding what to do about a particular risk once it is identified and is evaluated as having major economic consequences. The essential idea of risk control is to either do away with the potential risk all together or find some way of minimizing its potential negative consequences. A simplified example is the discovery through risk identification and risk assessment that a human service agency is seriously underinsured. Risk control would involve moving as quickly as possible to find an acceptable insurance carrier with the best policy that meets the needs of the agency at the best price.

Risk funding is concerned with developing a financial plan to ensure that adequate funds are available to cover risk-related expenses. Identifying and evaluating risks is of little benefit to a human service agency without the resources to reduce or remove them. A good example was the Y2K computer problem that plagued business, government, and human service agencies at the end of the twentieth century. Many organizations, including some human service agencies, had to delay dealing with the Y2K problem until the last possible moment because they didn't have the necessary funds. Risk funding involves setting aside funds each fiscal year during the budget process to ensure that the agency has the financial ability to deal with identified risks and also to build a "rainy day fund" to handle unforeseen contingencies.

Administration is the actual conduct of a risk management program. The use of the term *risk management program* suggests that the function of risk management should be treated as a major activity (a program) within the program structure of a human service agency. As such, a risk management program should be headed by a program manager. In a large government or private nonprofit human service agency, the risk management program may be headed by a full-time program manager called a risk manager. In smaller human service agencies, the job of the risk manager may be assigned to a staff person as an additional responsibility or the executive director of the agency may assume this function. The important point is that the risk management program needs both a locus and a focus of responsibility. Unless someone in the human service agency is designated to "wear the hat of the risk manager," the risk management function may not receive the attention it deserves.

Major Risk Management Issues Areas

The following sections look at some of the major issues areas where risk management problems are traditionally found in human service agencies. In terms of the five tasks of risk management, the major issue areas identified next can be thought of a generic human services risk management template. The major issue areas to be discussed include (1) insurance issues, (2) governing board issues, (3) human resource management issues, (4) basic internal financial control issues, (5) workplace hazard issues, (6) volunteer liability issues, and (7) records management issues.

Insurance Issues

The first major issues area that most risk managers focus on is a human service agency's insurance coverage. Most human service agencies carry basic fire, theft, and liability insurance, but this may be all. Human service agencies should also consider carrying "errors-and-omissions" insurance that covers the actions of the board of directors and top management. Errors-and-omissions insurance provides coverage for management decisions (actions and failure to act) that can result in potential liability exposure and lawsuits. Human service agencies that use volunteers in their programs should also consider carrying insurance that covers their actions. More will be said about this issue in the section dealing with volunteer liability issues.

The risk manager should ensure that the human service agency is receiving the best rates for its various insurance coverages: fire, theft, liability (including errors and omissions and volunteers), automobile, employee health, and others. One simple way of helping to reduce insurance costs is to bundle various insurance coverages with one insurance carrier. Another way of reducing insurance costs is to join a risk pool. Human service agencies in many communities form groups that pool their agencies' various insurance needs. In general, the more purchasing power one has in the insurance market, the better the price one can negotiate. Yet another method of reducing insurance costs is to become self-insured. Self-insurance involves putting funds aside each year in a special account to pay for future claims against the agency. A human service agency can be partially or totally self-insured. For example, a self-insurance fund might be set up to cover small claims with an insurance policy that kicks in at some predetermined dollar (e.g., $100,000) value. Many risk pools have a self-insurance aspect to them.

One might well ask, How can a staff person assuming the position of risk manager as an additional duty be expected to know all the ins and outs of insurance? The answer is that such an expectation is unrealistic. Fortunately, insurance agents or brokers exist that do not represent any one particular insurance carrier, but rather offer their services to assist agencies in analyzing their insurance needs and in securing the best possible coverage at the best possible price. The point should also be made that outside expertise and technical assistance for many of the major risk management issue areas identified in this chapter can frequently be secured at low cost or no cost.

Governing Board Issues

The board of directors of a private nonprofit human service agency has a fiduciary responsibility to safeguard and protect the assets of the agency. To properly exercise its fiduciary role, the board of directors needs to be knowledgeable about the affairs of the agency, must be involved in the oversight of the agency and its operations, and must act with the best interests of the agency in mind at all times.

The Nonprofit Risk Management Center suggests that in order to discharge their fiduciary responsibilities, members of boards of directors should demonstrate certain characteristics (Figure 14.2).

Board members should be knowledgeable about the issues on which they are voting and should ensure that contracts and grants received by the agency or made by the agency to other organizations and individuals are within the scope of the corporation's charter and bylaws. Board members are not compensated for their

FIGURE 14.2 Preferred Characteristics of Governing Board Members

1. Board members regularly attend board meetings.
2. Board members are active, responsible, and participate.
3. Board members carefully examine all agenda items before voting.
4. Board members verify that the agency's various programs, services, and activities are in keeping with the agency's corporate charter and bylaws.
5. Board members verify the qualifications of persons with whom the agency does business—in particular, contractors and grantees.
6. Board members serve without compensation.
7. Board members have no material conflicts of interests.

Source: Adapted from Charles Tremper and Gwynne Kostin (1993). *No Surprises: Controlling Risks in Volunteer Programs.* Washington, DC: Nonprofit Risk Management Center.

work, but are frequently reimbursed for reasonable expenses incurred for attendance at board meetings and the performance of other board-related responsibilities. Board members should have no conflicts of interest; they should not be employed by the agency, serve as a paid consultant to the agency, or sell any products or services to the agency.

In an ideal world, one would expect that individual board members would also demonstrate characteristics 1 through 5 in Figure 14.2. Unfortunately, human service agencies exist in the real world. Often, a high-profile elected official, a celebrity, or a wealthy benefactor will be asked to serve on a board of directors for the cachet associated with the individual's name. In such instances, no real expectation exists that the individual will be actively involved in the affairs of the agency or will regularly attend board meetings. A small number of such individuals can be of great assistance to a human service agency, particularly in the area of fund development. However, when too many members of the board of directors of a human service agency fail to demonstrate characteristics 1 through 5, the situation poses a real threat to the corporate governance of the agency and to the board's fiduciary responsibilities. The risk manager should monitor the activities of the board of directors and call deficiencies in board governance to the attention of the executive director. While a great deal of tact may be needed by the risk manager in dealing with governing board issues, they must nevertheless be addressed.

Human Resource Management Issues

Human resource management issues deal with the complex and constantly changing nature of employment law. A host of federal, state, and local laws and regulations govern such human resource practices as hiring, firing, promotion, classification, assignment, and contracting. Additionally, certain specific rights and protections are extended to ethnic minorities, women, older workers, and persons with physical and mental disabilities. The issue of sexual harassment in the workplace also falls within the purview of human resource management issues. The number of new workplace lawsuits alleging violation of employment laws increases with each passing year. When an employee of a human service agency violates an employment law, the individual as well as the agency incurs liability exposure and the possibility of having to pay monetary damages as a result of a lawsuit. Figure 14.3 summarizes some major federal employment laws and regulations.

Most medium to large government and private nonprofit human service agencies have a human resources department or unit staffed by trained professionals knowledgeable about employment law. In such cases, the risk manager works closely with the human resources department or unit. In smaller human service agencies, the human resource function may be assigned to a staff person as an additional function or the executive director may discharge this function. Regardless of how the human resource management function is structured, the task of the risk manager is to ensure that agency staff are trained in and knowledgeable about employment laws and regulations and adhere to the agency's human resource

FIGURE 14.3 Major Federal Employment-Related Laws and Regulations

- **Civil Rights Act of 1964 (Title VII)**

  Prohibits discrimination in employment or any activities or considerations involving employment (e.g., wages, classification, promotion, training, referral, assignment) on the basis of race, color, sex, religion, or national origin.

- **Presidential Executive Order 11246 (Affirmative Action)**

  Requires employers doing business with the federal government as well as recipients of federal contracts and grants to undertake "affirmative action" with respect to the hiring of minorities and women.

- **Age Discrimination in Employment Act**

  Prohibits discrimination against so-called older workers (persons over the age of forty).

- **Equal Pay Act**

  Prohibits paying employees differently based on sex or gender for work that requires equal skill, effort, and responsibility or work that is performed under similar conditions.

- **Americans with Disabilities**

  Prohibits employers from discriminating against, and requires making "reasonable accommodation" for, persons with a physical or mental disability.

---

policies and procedures. When the agency has a human resources department or unit, the role of the risk manager is supportive. In the absence of a human resource department or unit, the role of the risk manager is more directive.

Another human resource management issue that is, or should be, of concern to a risk manager today is the increasing use of contract employees. *Contract employees* are individuals who function as employees of the agency, but who work under a contractual relationship that identifies them as consultants. The Internal Revenue Service takes a dim view of this practice. In the view of the IRS, the use of contract employees is in many instances a not so subtle method of attempting to circumvent the necessity of complying with withholding, Social Security, Medicare, and workers compensation laws and regulations. The IRS aggressively monitors the use of contract employees and has filed numerous actions against both governments and private sector (for-profit and nonprofit) businesses and agencies, seeking recovery of funds plus penalties and interest.

Figure 14.4 identifies the twenty tests that the IRS uses to determine if a consultant or contract employee should actually be classified as an agency employee. The IRS makes the disclaimer that the facts of each case must be decided on an individual basis in terms of which of the twenty tests apply and the weights that should be ascribed to each test. The job of the risk manager in this area is to monitor the use of contract employees by the agency and to bring to the attention of the agency's executive director situations that may violate the IRS tests.

FIGURE 14.4   IRS Tests for Identification of Employees

Workers are employees if they

1. Must comply with the agency's instructions about the work
2. Receive training from or at the direction of the agency
3. Provide services that are integrated into the agency
4. Provide services that must be rendered personally
5. Have a continuing working relationship with the agency
6. Hire, supervise, and pay assistants who work for the agency
7. Must follow set hours of work
8. Work full-time for the agency
9. Must perform their work on the agency's premises
10. Must perform their work in a sequence set by the agency
11. Must submit regular reports to the agency
12. Receive payments of regular amounts at set intervals
13. Receive payments for business or travel expenses
14. Rely on the agency to furnish tools and materials
15. Lack a major investment in facilities used to perform their work
16. Cannot make a profit or suffer a loss from the relationship with the agency
17. Work for only the agency
18. Do not offer their services to the general public
19. Can be fired by the agency
20. May quit work anytime without incurring liability

Source: Adapted from General Accounting Office (GAO) (1996). *Tax Administration: Issues in Classifying Workers as Employees or Independent Contractors.* Washington, DC: Author.

Basic Internal Financial Control Issues

Stories continue to appear in the press concerning the misuse of funds by executive directors and other staff of private nonprofit organizations; some of these stories unfortunately concern human service agencies. While the number of such incidents is small, they nevertheless reflect badly on all private nonprofit organizations, both human service and non–human service. Reports of the misuse of funds invariably hinder a human service agency's fund-raising. Significant misuse of funds can result in claims and lawsuits against the agency and its board of directors.

One way of minimizing the potential for the misuse of funds in a human service agency is to institute a few basic internal financial controls. *Basic internal financial controls* can be defined as actions taken by a human service agency to minimize the potential for misuse of assets, while maximizing the potential for detection if misuse occurs. The implementation and monitoring of basic financial controls should be the responsibility of the risk manager. Figure 14.5 presents some basic rules of internal financial control that have withstood the test of time (Gross, 1974; Jenkins, 1977).

FIGURE 14.5   Some Basic Internal Financial Controls for Private Nonprofit Organizations

1. Two persons should routinely open the agency's mail and make a list of all cash and noncash funds received. The two persons should be periodically rotated.
2. Numbered receipts should be issued for all donations and other monies received.
3. Cash and noncash donations and other monies should be deposited in the bank on a timely basis (at least once each week).
4. All expenses should be paid by check with supporting documentation as to the nature and reasons for the expense.
5. Two signatures should be required on all checks (e.g., the executive director and the agency finance person or accountant should sign them).
6. A staff person (other than the accountant or bookkeeper) should receive bank statements directly from the bank and reconcile them.
7. A staff person (other than the accountant or bookkeeper) should approve write-offs of accounts receivable and other assets.
8. Excess cash should not be maintained at the agency, but rather deposited in an interest-bearing bank account.
9. An inventory of the agency's fixed assets should be done annually.

Sources: Adapted from Patricia Jenkins (1977). *Guide to Accounting for Nonprofits.* Los Angeles: The Grantsmanship Center; Malvern Gross (1974). *Financial and Accounting Guide for Non-Profit Organizations.* New York: Ronald Press.

The use of numbered receipts for all donations and monies provides an audit trail. Having two people who are rotated frequently open the mail and receive and account for all cash and other donations makes this process more transparent. Depositing monies in a timely fashion prevents too much cash from accumulating in the agency. Documenting all expenses and requiring two signatures on all agency checks precludes any one person from having total control over the agency's checkbook. The receipt and review of bank statements by someone other than the agency accountant or bookkeeper provides a mechanism for quickly spotting problems and irregularities and resolving them. Having someone other than the agency accountant and bookkeeper approve write-offs of accounts receivables provides a second objective review of why such actions are being taken. Finally, conducting an annual inventory of fixed assets (e.g., equipment) is important to ensure that expensive items do not go missing; it also provides documentation for insurance claims for theft, loss, or damage.

Taken together, these basic rules of internal financial control create a system of checks and balances that should be sufficient in most cases to dissuade anyone from attempting to misuse agency resources. And, should the misuse of agency resources occur, the potential for the misuse to continue undetected for any prolonged period of time is minimized.

Workplace Hazard Issues

The identification and reduction or elimination of workplace hazards is another major issue that deserves the attention of a risk manager and a risk management program. Whenever an employee suffers a workplace injury, a human service agency incurs potential legal liability that can result in a lawsuit and a claim for damages as well as an increase in insurance premiums and workers' compensation payments. When a human service agency is aware of a workplace hazard and does not take steps to reduce or eliminate it, the agency may also face allegations of negligence.

As Figure 14.6 illustrates, a risk manager's responsibilities should include the periodic inspection of the workplace to ensure that emergency and safety equipment are up-to-date and that federal Occupational Safety and Health Administration (OSHA) standards are being met. Two major OSHA concerns today are building ventilation systems (because of "sick building syndrome") and ergonomic issues. In the case of ergonomic issues, carpal tunnel syndrome experienced by individuals whose work requires extensive computer data entry is a major cause of lost worker productivity, of use of sick leave and health benefits, and of filing workers' compensation claims.

Again, risk managers do not have to be experts in all aspects of workplace hazards. Upon request, city and county fire departments will make safety inspections of an agency's workplace and identify deficiencies and recommend changes. OSHA will do likewise. Additionally, OSHA publishes many materials on workplace standards that are available free or at minimal cost.

Volunteer Liability Issues

Volunteer organizations (human service agencies that make significant use of volunteers in the provision of their services) create yet another important risk management issue area. As a general rule, human service agencies tend not to exert the

---

FIGURE 14.6   Risk Management Workplace Hazard Inspections

- To ensure that emergency and safety information is properly posted and up-to-date (e.g., exits are clearly marked and not blocked, fire extinguishers are operational)

- To ensure compliance with Occupational Safety and Health Administration workplace standards for
  1. Lighting
  2. Ventilation
  3. Noise levels
  4. Hazardous materials
  5. Ergonomics and so on

same level of control and do not expect the same level of compliance with agency policies and procedures from volunteers as they do from paid staff. Being overly laissez faire with respect to volunteers can result in a human service agency incurring unnecessary liability exposure.

Many human service administrators believe erroneously that volunteers and the agencies that use them are immune from liability lawsuits. While all fifty states do have statutes limiting somewhat the liability of volunteers, volunteers are still liable for any harm they cause due to bad faith actions, willful and intentional actions, gross negligence, fraud, and violation of fiduciary responsibility by board members (Nonprofit Risk Management Center, 1996).

Many large government and private nonprofit human service agencies have offices of volunteers headed by a trained professional knowledgeable about recruitment, selection, training, and retention of volunteers. In such cases the agency's risk manager works closely with the volunteer director. In small human service agencies, the position of volunteer director may not exist so the function may be assigned to one or more staff persons as an additional responsibility. In either case, the task of the risk manager is to monitor the agency's volunteer program to ensure that volunteers are properly screened (particularly those who will be working with vulnerable clients), are adequately trained, and comply with agency policies and procedures.

Records Management Issues

An area that is frequently overlooked when it comes to risk management is records management. *Records management* is concerned with the maintenance and protection of a human service agency's records. Three specific risk management issue areas that should be the focus of the risk manager are ensuring that a backup system exists for critical agency records, the safeguarding of staff personnel files and client records, and adherence to the records maintenance and retention requirements of the Internal Revenue Service and state and local governments.

A situation that many human service agencies have never thought about is a catastrophic loss of agency computer files. A fire, a theft, or a natural disaster can destroy an agency's computers and computer systems. To the extent that a human service agency's records (financial and programmatic) are primarily automated, a catastrophic loss could endanger the ability of the agency to continue operations and to bill for services already provided. A common fail-safe approach used to guard against a catastrophic loss of agency records is to maintain an off-site backup capability. The agency's files (financial and nonfinancial) are periodically (e.g., weekly) backed up and stored off-site (e.g., in a bank safety deposit box). In a catastrophic loss situation, the agency is able to reconstruct its files up to the date of the last backup.

Human service agencies are generally sensitive to the need to protect staff personnel files and client files and records. But a section of the Americans with Disabilities Act (ADA) that applies to records management is not as well known. Under the ADA, it is illegal for an agency to combine staff health records with staff personnel files and records. In order to ensure that an employee's health status (e.g., HIV-positive status) does not affect personnel decisions, the ADA requires that health and personnel records be separately maintained.

Various federal, state, and local government regulations govern how long the records (financial and nonfinancial) of a human service agency must be maintained. In addition, many government contracts and grants specify record retention periods. The purpose of record retention periods is to ensure that a human service agency's financial and programmatic records will be available for follow-up reviews and audits.

Again, in large government and private nonprofit human service agencies, the records management function may be assigned to another department, unit, or staff person. The task of the risk manager is not to duplicate or interfere with the records management activities but to monitor the situation to ensure that the agency has an off-site records backup capability and that legal exposure issues related to other records management issues do not arise.

Summary

Risk management is a relatively new concept to the human services. This chapter introduced the concept of risk management, identified the essential tasks of risk management, and suggested that risk management be treated as a program with the program structure of a human service agency. The chapter also looked at seven major risk management issue areas and identified ways in which a risk manager and a risk management program can reduce a human service agency's liability exposure while also reducing agency costs.

15 Auditing

Perhaps nothing strikes more fear into the hearts of human service administrators than to hear the words "We're going to be audited." This response is unfortunate, because human service agencies and programs that maintain their financial books and records according to Generally Accepted Accounting Principles (GAAP) and whose financial management practices are conducted in a professional and ethical fashion have little to fear from an audit. An audit can actually improve the management practices of a human service agency or program by pointing out financial and programmatic issues and problems that agency staff may be unaware of. The "audit anxiety" experienced by many human service administrators may be related as much to a lack of understanding about what audits are and what auditors do than to any real concerns about the potential discovery of agency financial management problems or deficiencies. In other words, the more human service administrators know about audits and auditing, the less anxiety-producing the experience should be.

With the goal of demystifying auditing and audits, this chapter looks at the sources of auditing standards, cost policies, and other financial management requirements that frequently apply to human service agencies (both public and private nonprofit), the differences between internal and external auditors, and the major types of audits and their purposes. The chapter also briefly discusses some of the more important factors that should be taken into consideration by human service administrators (both government and private nonprofit) when selecting an auditor to conduct a financial statement audit or financially related audit of a human service agency or program.

Sources of Auditing Standards, Cost Policies, and Financial Management Requirements

As Figure 15.1 illustrates, the major sources of auditing standards, cost policies, and financial management requirements with implications for human service agencies and programs are the American Institute of Certified Public Accountants, the comptroller general of the United States, the federal Office of Management and Budget, and various titles of the *Code of Federal Regulations.* Some of these auditing standards, cost policies, and financial management requirements apply to all types of

FIGURE 15.1   **Sources of Auditing Standards, Cost Policies, and Financial
Management Requirements**

1. **American Institute of Certified Public Accountants**
   Generally Accepted Auditing Standards (GAAS) are established by the American
   Institute of Certified Public Accountants and apply to financial audits of government,
   private nonprofit, and private for-profit organizations.

2. **Comptroller General of the United States (General Accounting Office)**
   Generally Accepted Government Auditing Standards (GAGAS) are established by
   the comptroller general of the United States of the federal General Accounting Office
   (GAO). GAGAS apply to all federal, state, and local government departments,
   agencies, functions, and activities and to all government contractors and grantees.

3. **Office of Management and Budget (OMB)**
   The federal Office of Management and Budget issues a number of circulars that set
   forth cost policies and audit standards and requirements including

   A. OMB Circular A–87:   "Cost Principles for State, Local & Indian Tribal
   Governments"

   B. OMB Circular A–110:   "Uniform Administrative Requirements for Grants and
   Agreements with Institutions of Higher Education,
   Hospitals, and Other Non-Profit Organizations"

   C. OMB Circular A–122:   "Cost Principles for Non-Profit Organizations"

   D. OMB Circular A–133:   "Audits of States, Local Governments & Non-Profit
   Organizations"

4. *Code of Federal Regulations (CFR)*
   The *CFR* contains regulations issued by federal agencies and departments that deal
   with a variety of cost policies, reporting policies, financial management policies, and
   auditing standards and requirements including

   A. Title 41 *CFR:*   Public Contracts and Property Management

   B. Title 24 *CFR:*   Department of Housing and Urban Development

   C. Title 45 *CFR:*   Department of Health and Human Services

      (1) Part 74:   Uniform Administration of Grants
      (2) Part 96:   Block Grants

organizations and to all types of audits. Others depend on the type of organization
being audited (government or private nonprofit), the type of audit, the receipt of
federal funding, and the amount of federal funding received.

American Institute of Certified Public Accountants

Just as there are generally accepted accounting principles (GAAP), there are also
generally accepted auditing standards (GAAS). Like GAAP, GAAS are established by the American Institute of Certified Public Accountants (AICPA). GAAS
prescribe process and quality standards (general standards, standards of field

work, and standards of reporting) that all audits should meet. GAAS also cover standards and practices in the auditing of financial statements. In addition, the AICPA prescribes specific auditing standards and requirements that apply to private nonprofit organizations. These latter requirements are periodically updated and published as the *AICPA Audit and Accounting Guide: Not-for-Profit Organizations* (e.g., AICPA, 1998).

Comptroller General of the United States (General Accounting Office)

A set of related, yet different, auditing standards exist for audits of federal, state, and local government departments, agencies, programs, functions, activities, contractors, and grantees. These auditing standards are called generally accepted government auditing standards (GAGAS) to differentiate them from GAAS. The comptroller general of the United States, housed in the General Accounting Office (GAO), is charged with establishing GAGAS. GAGAS incorporate GAAS, but set forth additional requirements and guidance for the conduct of financial and non-financial (performance) audits of government agencies and programs. GAGAS are periodically updated and published as *Government Auditing Standards* (e.g. GAO, 1994), also know as the Yellow Book because of its distinctive cover.

Office of Management and Budget (OMB)

The federal Office of Management and Budget (OMB) sets forth a variety of auditing standards, cost policies, and other financial management requirements that apply to federal departments and agencies as well as to other organizations that receive federal funds. These requirements are published in a number of OMB circulars. Some of the more important OMB circulars with general application to state and local government and private nonprofit human service agencies are (a) OMB Circular A–87, which sets forth cost principles for state, local, and Indian tribal governments including allowable and unallowable costs, (b) OMB Circular A-122, which sets forth cost principles including allowable and unallowable costs for private nonprofit organizations, and (c) OMB Circular A–133, which sets forth auditing standards and requirements under the Single Audit Act. All OMB circulars can be accessed, and copies can be downloaded, from the Office of Management and Budget's Internet home page (see Appendix).

Code of Federal Regulations

Departments and agencies of the federal government, as well as individual federal programs, frequently have various financial management requirements and standards with audit implications. Examples are individual department and program-specific cost policies dealing with allowable and unallowable costs; matching requirements where recipients must share (e.g., 10 percent, 25 percent) in the cost of a federal program; policies and procedures for dealing with donations, fees, and other program income; the award of subgrants and contracts; property management stipulations including the disposition of equipment and other property acquired in part or in whole with federal funds; financial reporting requirements; cash management practices; and other miscellaneous financial management requirements. These requirements are periodically updated and published in the *Federal Register* as various titles of the *Code of Federal Regulations (CFR)*.

Some of the *CFR* titles (Figure 15.1) that have the most applicability to government and private nonprofit human service agencies are (a) Title 41 *CFR* dealing generally with "public contracts and property management," (b) Title 24 *CFR* dealing with programs of the Department of Housing and Urban Development, and (c) Title 45 *CFR* dealing with programs administered by the Department of Health and Human Services. Part 74 of Title 45 *CFR* sets forth general "uniform administrative requirements for grants," while Part 96 contains some requirements that apply to selected federal block grant programs including the Social Services Block Grant, the Community Services Block Grant, and the Substance Abuse Prevention and Treatment Block Grant. The *Code of Federal Regulations* can be accessed, and sections can be downloaded, through the Internet home page of the Government Printing Office (see Appendix).

Types of Auditors

There are two major types of auditors: internal and external. An *internal auditor* is one who is employed by a government or private nonprofit human service agency. Internal auditors have historically been referred to as the "eyes and ears" of agency management (e.g., McKinney, 1986). In general, internal auditors provide management with financial- and non-financial-oriented reports, studies, and audits dealing with agency, program, and employee compliance with prescribed policies, procedures, and practices. Internal auditors conduct pre-audits, program audits, financial-related audits, grant and contract audits, and performance audits (types of audits are discussed shortly), but generally not financial statement audits or audits covered by the Single Audit Act. Both GAAS and GAGAS require that financial statement audits be conducted by independent external auditors. OMB Circular A–133 requires that audits subject to the Single Audit Act also be conducted by independent external auditors.

An *independent external auditor* is one who is not an internal auditor and one who is not involved in either creating the financial accounting practices of a human service agency (including the development of the cost allocation plan) or maintaining the agency's financial books and records. The requirement that financial statement audits and audits subject to the Single Audit Act be conducted by independent external auditors is necessary in order to preclude situations in which auditors would essentially be auditing their own work.

Independent external auditors usually come in one of three varieties: (1) elected government officials, (2) officials appointed by a unit of government, or (3) certified public accountants (Freeman & Shoulders, 1993). An independent external auditor can be an elected official. For example, it is not unusual for a city or county government to have an elected auditor who performs audits of other city and county departments as well as city and county grantees and contractors. An independent external auditor can also be appointed by a unit of government, but not the unit to be audited. An example is the "auditor general" function that many state legislatures have. Auditor generals perform audits of state executive-branch departments and agencies and can also audit local governments (including local government human service agencies) as well as state and local government contractors and grantees (including private nonprofit human service agencies). Finally, an independent external auditor can be either an individual certified public accountant (CPA) or a CPA firm.

Internal auditors are usually either certified public accountants (CPAs) or certified internal auditors (CIAs). External auditors are generally CPAs. In some cases, an internal auditor may be both a CPA and a CIA. An internal auditor that conducts performance audits may be neither a CPA nor a CIA, but rather may have special education, training, and experience in program evaluation or performance measurement.

Types of Audits

No generally accepted definition of auditing exists because there are several different types of audits, each with a different primary purpose. As Figure 15.2 illustrates, at least six major types of audits can be identified: pre-audits, financial audits, program-specific audits, grant and contract audits, performance audits, and single audits. In addition, the General Accounting Office, which establishes GAGAS, further subdivides financial audits into financial statement audits and financial-related audits and further subdivides performance audits into economy and efficiency

---

FIGURE 15.2   Major Types of Audits

1. Pre-audits
2. Financial audits
   A. Financial statement audits
   B. Financial-related audits
3. Program-specific audits
4. Grant and contract audits
5. Performance audits
   A. Economy and efficiency audits
   B. Program audits
6. Single audits

audits and program audits (GAO, 1994). Pre-audits, financial audits, and single audits are primarily financial in nature. Performance audits are primarily programmatic in nature although they do concern themselves with such financial issues as the efficiency and economy with which a human service agency or program accomplishes its mission and provides its products and services. Program audits and grant and contract audits can have a financial purpose, a programmatic purpose, or both. The following sections discuss these major types of audits in detail.

Pre-Audits

A *pre-audit* is a miniversion of a financial statement audit. The purpose of a pre-audit is to examine, or test, a human service agency's financial accounting system and record keeping practices in order to determine if they are auditable. *Auditability* means that the agency's financial books and records are being maintained according to generally accepted accounting principles and that documentation exists to support various financial transactions and financial management practices. This latter characteristic is sometimes referred to as an *audit trail*. For example, agency revenues would have an audit trail that would lead back to checks, cash receipts, invoices for payments made to governments or foundations, and so on. Expenses would have an audit trail that would lead back to some documentation as to the nature and amount of the expenses. The audit trail for staff salaries might lead back to weekly signed staff time sheets. Expenses for supplies, equipment, and the like might have an audit trail that leads back to invoices documenting the cost and actual receipt of each item. Expenses for consultants might have an audit trail that leads back to a signed contract specifying the work to be performed, the price, and a statement that the work was completed satisfactorily.

It is a common practice of state and local government departments to conduct pre-audits of private nonprofit human service agencies before they receive grants and cost reimbursement contracts. Used in this fashion, the pre-audit determines if the human service agency's financial books and records can adequately account for expenses incurred in the provision of contract or grant services and can adequately distinguish, or separate, reimbursable costs (both direct and indirect) from other agency or program costs.

Financial Audits

Financial audits can be further subdivided into (a) financial statement audits and (b) financial-related audits.

Financial Statement Audits.   *Financial statement audits* have as their purpose the testing of the completeness and accuracy of the information contained in a private nonprofit human service agency's financial statements: the statement of financial activity (profit-and-loss summary), the statement of financial position (balance sheet), the statement of cash flows, and the statement of functional expenses.

The types of activities that auditors generally engage in when conducting a financial statement audit might include reviewing the human service agency's journal and general ledger, checking and confirming bank balances, reviewing and verifying accounts receivable and accounts payable, ensuring that permanently restricted and temporarily restricted donations are being used for their intended purposes, checking capital equipment assets against inventories, and, in general, examining the entire financial management system of the agency.

Upon completion of a financial statement audit, the auditor issues an audit report and an opinion letter. The audit report presents the auditor's findings. The opinion letter presents the auditor's views of the extent to which the financial statements present fairly the financial position of the human service agency. As Figure 15.3 illustrates, there are four basic types of opinion letters: unqualified opinion, qualified opinion, adverse opinion, and a disclaimer of opinion. An *unqualified opinion* means that the financial statements present a fair and accurate financial picture of the human service agency in keeping with GAAP. An unqualified, or "clean," opinion is the type that human service agencies and human service administrators always hope to receive. A *qualified opinion* letter means that the financial statements present a fair and accurate financial picture of the human service agency in keeping with GAAP, but that some minor deficiencies or problems were found by the auditors.

FIGURE 15.3   Types of Independent Outside Auditor Opinions (Financial Statement Audits)

1. **Unqualified Opinion**
   An *unqualified opinion* means that the financial statements *present* a fair and accurate picture of the financial position of the organization in keeping with generally accepted accounting principles.

2. **Qualified Opinion**
   A *qualified opinion* means that the financial statements present a fair and accurate picture of the financial position of the organization in keeping with generally accepted accounting principles, *except* for some minor deficiencies or problems that are specifically identified.

3. **Adverse Opinion**
   An *adverse opinion* means that the financial statements *do not present* a fair and accurate picture of the financial position of the organization in keeping with generally accepted accounting principles.

4. **Disclaimer of Opinion**
   A *disclaimer of opinion* means that the auditor is *unable to determine* if the financial statements present a fair and accurate picture of the financial position of the organization in keeping with generally accepted accounting principles.

The last two types of opinion letters (adverse opinion and disclaimer of opinion) are ones that human service agencies and human service administrators hope they never receive. An *adverse opinion* means that the financial statements do not present a fair and accurate financial picture of the human service agency in keeping with GAAP, while a *disclaimer of opinion* means that the auditors were unable to draw any conclusions because the human service agency's financial books and records were not auditable.

Financial-Related Audits.   The purpose of *financial-related audits* is to review some particular aspect of an organization's financial operations and can include

- The review and verification of segments of financial statements, budget requests, or other financial information (e.g., travel claims, contractor payments, staff time reporting)
- The assessment of internal controls including, for example, cash management practices, compliance with government procurement and contracting policies, and compliance with contract and grant reporting requirements
- The assessment of compliance with specific laws, regulations, policies, or procedures
- The investigation of allegations of fraud or abuse (GAO, 1994:13–14).

Program-Specific Audits

Program-specific audits are concerned with individual government programs. Program-specific audits can involve the assessment of internal controls, compliance with laws, regulations, policies, procedures, cost sharing requirements, the identification of "questioned costs," and follow-up on previous audit findings. A *questioned cost* is any item of cost that a particular government program may treat as unallowable or some item of cost that is allowable, but is considered unreasonable. *Unreasonable* is generally taken to mean that an item of cost is more than a prudent person would generally pay. In terms of allowable and unallowable costs, many federal government agencies and programs publish their own lists, which are not always the same. Identification of allowable and unallowable costs for grant programs administered by the U.S. Department of Health and Human Services (DHHS) can be found in 45 *Code of Federal Regulations* Part 74 and in the DHHS's *Grants Administration Manual*. Both of these documents can be accessed through the DHHS's Internet home page via the "Grants Net" link (see Appendix).

Grant and Contract Audits

Grant and contract audits can be broad in nature (like program-specific audits) or narrow in nature (like financial-related audits). The difference is that this type of audit does not focus on an entire program, but rather on only one grant or contract. Financial aspects that could be covered by a grant or contract audit include verifying that clients served meet prescribed eligibility criteria, that services billed are actually provided, that fees and donations are accounted for and used according to prescribed policies, and that cost sharing requirements are satisfied. A grant or contract audit could also involve verification of cost and pricing data and information used as the basis for a performance contract (cost per output or unit of service, cost per outcome, or both) or verifying that costs billed under a cost reimbursement contract were actually incurred.

Performance Audits

According to the Yellow Book, the purpose of a performance audit is the systematic and objective review of the performance of a government agency, program, activity, or function to provide accountability, to improve decision making, or to initiate or follow up on needed corrective action (GAO, 1994:14). In general, a performance audit is concerned with programmatic issues, although financial issues may also be involved.

The Yellow Book divides performance audits into two subcategories: (1) economy and efficiency audits and (2) program audits. An *economy and efficiency audit* can focus on (a) determining if a government agency or program is using its resources (funds, personnel, facilities, equipment, etc.) appropriately, (b) identifying inefficiencies and uneconomical practices, (c) determining if a government agency or program has complied with applicable laws and regulations, or (d) any combination thereof. A *program audit* can focus on the extent to which a government agency or program is (a) accomplishing its intended results including outputs (or units of service) and outcomes, (b) complying with applicable laws and regulations, or (c) a combination thereof. A private nonprofit human service agency can be involved in either or both types of performance audits by virtue of providing services under a government grant or contract.

Single Audits

The Single Audit Act applies to audits of state governments, local governments, Indian tribal governments, and private nonprofit agencies (contractors and grantees) that receive federal funds in an amount greater than $300,000 in any one year. Organizations subject to the Single Audit Act must have an "annual consolidated audit" that covers the entire agency and all its programs. Figure 15.4 highlights some of the major requirements of these so-called single audits.

As Figure 15.4 demonstrates, a single audit is primarily financial in nature; performance-related issues are generally not addressed. However, a single audit combines aspects of both a financial statement audit and a financial-related audit. A single audit requires that the auditor determine if the financial statements fairly reflect the financial condition of the agency and render an opinion (unqualified, qualified, adverse, or disclaimer) as would be the case in a financial statement audit. But, a single audit must also address such issues as the extent to which the agency has complied with applicable laws and regulations and the issue of questioned costs as would be the case in a financial-related audit.

FIGURE 15.4   Auditing Requirements under the Single Audit Act

1. **GAGAS.**   The audit must be conducted according to generally accepted government auditing standards.
2. **GAAP.**   The audit must determine if the agency's financial statements are presented fairly and in conformance with generally accepted accounting principles.
3. **Internal control.**   The audit must examine the agency's internal control system to determine the level of risk involving over federal funds.
4. **Compliance.**   The audit must determine if the agency has complied with applicable laws, regulations, and other contract and grant requirements.
5. **Questioned costs.**   The audit must identify any questioned costs.
6. **Audit follow-up.**   The audit must follow up and comment on the action taken by the agency to correct deficiencies noted by previous audits.

As the preceding discussion makes quite clear, a variety of types of audits exist. Consequently, for human service administrators to know that their agency or program is going to be audited is not to know very much; one needs to know what type of audit is to be performed. If a human service agency or program is going to be subjected to a performance audit (which is increasingly common), one knows that the focus will be on results, accomplishments, outputs, and outcomes, with only a tangential concern with financial issues. Likewise, if a financial statement audit is to be conducted, one knows that the focus will be on how the agency maintains its financial books and records, its internal control, and the extent to which the financial statements accurately reflect the financial condition of the agency. Armed with this knowledge, experiencing an audit should be less anxiety producing for human service administrators because they will have more of a general sense of what to expect.

Selecting An External Auditor

Just as a human service administrator needs to know about the various types of audits and their differences, so too do the certified public accountants and CPA firms that conduct financial statement audits, financial-related audits, and single audits of government human service agencies and programs. Not all CPAs and CPA firms are equally knowledgeable about the requirements of government audits. Consequently, human service administrators need to exercise care when selecting an external CPA or CPA firm to conduct an audit, especially financial statement audits and single audits. Figure 15.5 presents a set of suggested criteria that might be considered when selecting an external auditor to conduct a financial statement and/or single audit of a human service agency.

An external auditor should be knowledgeable about government and/or nonprofit accounting depending on the status of the agency. An external auditor also needs to be well versed in GAGAS and applicable OMB circulars. Finally,

FIGURE 15.5 **Considerations in Selecting an External Auditor**

1. Knowledge of government accounting (if a government human service agency) or nonprofit accounting (if a private nonprofit human service agency)

2. Knowledge of generally accepted government auditing standards

3. Knowledge of the requirement of the Single Audit Act as specified in OMB Circular A–133

4. Knowledge of other applicable Office of Management and Budget financial management standards and requirements as enumerated in OMB Circulars A–87, A–102, and A–122

5. Previous experience in conducting financial statement audits of government and private nonprofit human service agencies

6. Previous experience in conducting single audits of government and private nonprofit human service agencies

there is no substitute for actual experience. When selecting an outside auditor, it is preferable to choose one that has prior experience in conducting government audits in general and single audits in particular. It is also a good idea to consult other government and private nonprofit agencies that have used the services of any external auditors being considered to conduct a financial statement audit or a single audit. Were these other government and private nonprofit agencies satisfied with the work performed by the external auditors? Were federal funding agencies satisfied with the auditors' work?

Summary

This chapter looked at the subject of audits and auditing. Sources of auditing standards, cost policies, and other financial management requirements applicable to government and private nonprofit human service agencies were identified. The differences between internal and external auditors were discussed and the major types of audits identified. The chapter also briefly discussed some of the more important factors that human service administrators should consider when selecting an external auditor to conduct a financial statement audit or a single audit.

APPENDIX

Sources of Financial Management Information on the World Wide Web (WWW)

American Institute of Certified Public Accountants (AICPA). For news articles and other information related to private nonprofit accounting rules. <http://www.aicpa.org/index.html>

American Public Human Services Association (APHSA). For information on human service reports and studies (financial and nonfinancial). Gateway to all fifty state human service agencies. <http://www.asphsa.org>

Better Business Bureau (BBB). For information on the BBB's financial management standards for private nonprofit organizations. Select "Charity Reports & Standards." <http://www.bbb.org>

Charity Village. For a variety of articles on such topics as "Financial Management & Investments" and "Capital Campaigns." <http://www.charityvillage.com/charityvillage/research>

Commerce Business Daily. For daily listings about all federal government contracts, grants, and cooperative agreements. <http://www.ld.com/cbd/today/index.html>

Council on Foundations. For information about various foundations nationally. For community foundations, Select "Links & Networking" and then "Community Foundations." <http://www.cof.org>

FinanceNet. For downloadable copies of financial management reports and studies. Also a gateway to other financial management sites. <http://www.financenet.gov>

Financial Accounting Standards Board (FASB). For information about FASB rules governing private nonprofit accounting standards. <http://raw.rutgers.edu/raw/fasb>

Grants Etc. Financial-management–oriented home page maintained by a professor at the University of Michigan's School of Social Work. Serves as a gateway for information on government and private grants. <http://www.ssw.umich.edu/grantsetc/funding/html>

Guidestar.   For financial information on some 620,000 IRS 501(c)(3) organizations developed from IRS 990 forms. Originally set us as a resource for donors. <http://www.guidestar.org>

Idea List.   For a variety of information (financial and nonfinancial) about private nonprofit organizations in the U.S. and in other countries. <http://www.idealist.org>

Innovation Network, Inc.   For information on fundraising, preparing grant applications, and interactive grant budget templates. <http://www.inet.work.org>

Internal Revenue Service (IRS).   *The Digital Daily.* For information about IRS rules, guidelines, and pronouncements governing 501(c)(3) private nonprofit organizations. <http://www.irs.ustreas.gov/prod/cover.html>

Internet Nonprofit Center.   For a variety of information (financial and nonfinancial) about private nonprofit organizations. Large section on FAQ (frequently asked questions). <http://www.nonprofits.org>

National Charities Information Bureau (NCIB).   For information on NCIB's standards (financial and nonfinancial) for private nonprofit organizations, select "NCIB's Standards in Philanthropy." <http://www.give.org>

Non-profit Resources Catalogue.   Over 2,500 web links to private nonprofit organization-related web sites. Compiled by Phillip A. Walker of the United Way of America. <http://www.clark.net/pub/pwalker/home/html>

North Carolina Association of Community Development Corporations.   For web links to a variety of sites dealing with the management of private nonprofit organizations. <http://www.ncacdc.org/orgdevelop.html>

The Beacon Project.   For a gateway to numerous web sites that deal with financial management issues relating to government and private nonprofit organizations, select "Grantsweb." <http://www.beaconproject.org>

The Chronicle of Philanthropy.   For news stories and feature articles on financial management issues relating to private nonprofit organizations. <http://www.philanthropy.com/articles>

The Evergreen State Society (Seattle, Washington). *Information for Nonprofits.*   For a variety of frequently asked questions (FAQs) related to financial and other management issues important to private nonprofit organizations. <http://www.nonprofit-info.org>

The Foundation Center.   For information (financial and nonfinancial) about private nonprofit organizations. One of the nation's largest clearinghouses. <http://www.fdncenter.org>

The Non-Profit Resource Center.   For explanations of AICP, FASB, and OMB statements and documents. <http://www.1800net.com/nprc>

The Peter F. Drucker Foundation for Non-Profit Management. For information (financial and nonfinancial) on private nonprofit organizations. Many links to other web sites. <http://www.pfdf.org>

United Way of America. For access to the National United Way of America home page and a gateway to local United Ways. <http://www.unitedway.org>

U.S. Department of Health and Human Services (H&HS). *Grants Net* for information about federal grants administered by H&HS and access to the *Grants Administration Manual.* Select "Grants Net." <http://www.os.dhhs.gov>

U.S. General Accounting Office (GAO). For information and downloadable copies of GAO reports including *Government Auditing Standards,* 1994 Revision (the Yellow Book). <http://www.gao.gov>

U.S. General Services Administration (GSA). For online searchable access to the *Catalogue of Federal Domestic Assistance.* <http://www.gsa.gov>

U.S. Office of Management and Budget (OMB). For information about and downloadable copies of OMB circulars, select "Circulars." <http://www.whitehouse.gov/OMB>

World Wide Web Resources for Social Workers. Gateway for access to information (financial and nonfinancial) and web sites of interest to social workers and other human service professionals. <http://www.nyu.edu/socialwork/wwwrsw>

REFERENCES

American Institute of Certified Public Accountants (AICPA). (1998). *AICPA Audit and Accounting Guide: Not-for-Profit Organizations.* New York: Author.

Billitteri, T. (1998, February 12), "Goodwill Looting: California Scam Yields Lessons for Charity Managers." *The Chronicle of Philanthropy*, p. 39.

Billitteri, T. (2000). "United Way Seeks a New Identity." *The Chronicle of Philanthropy.* XII(10), 1, 23–25.

The Chronicle of Philanthropy. (1998). 11(1), 8.

The Chronicle of Philanthropy. (1999). "Community Foundations' Assets, Gifts and Grants in 1998." 12(3), 14–15.

Cirincione, C., Gurrieri, G., & Van de Sande, B. (1999). "Municipal Government Revenue Forecasting: Issues of Method and Data." *Public Budgeting and Finance, 19*:26–46.

Council on Foundations. (1999). <http://www.cof.org> (11/02/99).

Dalsimer, J. (1995). *Understanding Nonprofit Financial Statements: A Primer for Board Members.* Washington, DC: The National Center for Nonprofit Boards.

Drucker, P. (1990). *Managing the Nonprofit Organization: Principles and Practices.* New York: HarperCollins.

Drucker, P. (1992). *Managing for the Future.* New York: Truman/Talley Books.

Drucker, P. (1999). *Management Challenges for the 21st Century.* New York: HarperBusiness.

Eggers, W. (1997). "There's No Place Like Home." *Policy Review: The Journal of American Citizenship, 83*:1–7.

Elkin, R., & Molitor (1985). "A Conceptual Framework for Selecting Management Indicators in Nonprofit Organizations." *Administration in Social Work.* 9:13–23

Ferit, M., & Chei Li, P. (1998). *Financial Management in Human Services.* New York: The Hawthorn Press.

Forester, J. (1993). "Use of Revenue Forecasting Techniques." In Lynch, T., & Martin, L. (Eds.), *Handbook of Comparative Public Budgeting and Financial Management.* New York: Marcel Dekker.

Freeman, R., & Shoulders, C. (1993). *Government and Nonprofit Accounting: Theory and Practice.* Englewood Cliffs: Prentice Hall, Chapter 20, "Auditing," pp. 775–806.

Garland, S. (1997, May 19). "A Rich New Business Called Poverty." *Business Week*, pp. 132–134.

General Accounting Office (GAO). (1994). *Government Auditing Standards.* Washington, DC: U.S. Government Printing Office.

General Accounting Office (GAO). (1996). *Tax Administration: Issues in Classifying Workers as Employees or Independent Contractors.* Washington, DC: Author.

General Accounting Office (GAO). (1997). *Social Services Privatization: Expansion Poses Challenges in Ensuring Accountability for Program Results.* Washington, DC: Author.

Ghere, R. (1981). "Effects of Service Delivery Variations on Administration of Municipal Human Service Agencies: The Contract Approach versus Agency Implementation." *Administration in Social Work, 5*:65–78.

Governmental Accounting Standards Board (GASB). (1994). *Concepts Statement No. 2 of the Government Accounting Standards Board on Concepts Related to Service Efforts and Accomplishment Reporting.* Norwalk, CT: Author.

Graham, C., & Hays, S. (1993). *Managing the Public Sector.* Washington, DC: CQ Press.

Gross, M. (1974). *Financial and Accounting Guide for Non-Profit Organizations.* New York: Ronald Press.

Hairston, C. (1985). "Using Ratio Analysis for Financial Accountability." *Journal of Contemporary Social Casework, 66:*76–82.

Hall, M. (1982). "Financial Condition: A Measure of Human Service Organizational Performance." *New England of Human Services, 2:*25–34.

Hay, L., & Engstrom, J. (1993). *Essentials of Accounting for Government and Not-for-Profit Organizations.* (Third Edition). Burr Ridge, IL: Irwin.

Hertzlinger, R. E., & Rittenhouse, D. (1994). *Financial Analysis, Financial Accounting and Managerial Control for Nonprofit Organizations.* Cincinnati: Southwestern Publishing, pp. 133–170.

Hildreth, W. B. (1991). "Federal Financial Management." In Lynch, T. (Ed.), *Federal Budget and Financial Management Reform* (pp. 151–169). New York: Quorum Books.

Horngren, C., Foster, G., & Datar, Sr. M. (1997). *Cost Accounting: A Managerial Emphasis.* Englewood Cliffs, NJ: Prentice-Hall.

Hyman, A. (1994). "The Principles of Risk Management." *Issues and Options, 2* (10); 1–15.

Jenkins, P. (1977). *Guide to Accounting for Nonprofits.* Los Angeles: The Grantsmanship Center.

Johnson, B., & Ross, B. (1991). "Risk Management." In Peterson, J., & Strachota, R. (eds.), *Local Government Finance: Concepts and Practices* (pp. 355–367). Washington, DC: Government Finance Officers Association.

Johnson, D. (1998, August 16). "United Way Receives $3.4 Billion." *The New York Times,* p. 20.

Kamerman, S., & Kahn, A. (1998). *Privatization, Contracting, and Reform of Child and Family Social Services.* Washington, DC: The Finance Project.

Kelly, J. T. (1984). *Costing Government Services: A Guide for Decision Making.* Washington, DC: Government Finance Officers Association.

Kennedy, E. (1996). "A Proposal for a Dissertation Tentatively Entitled, 'Non-Profit Executive Director Board-Work and Its Relationship to Organizational Financial Performance.' " Unpublished dissertation proposal, Columbia University.

Kettner, P., & Martin, L. (1987). *Purchase of Service Contracting.* Beverly Hills: Sage Publications.

Kettner, P., & Martin, L. (1995). "Performance Contracting in the Human Services: An Initial Assessment." *Administration in Social Work, 19*(2): 47–61.

Kettner, P., & Martin, L. (1996). "Purchase of Service Contracting Versus Government Service Delivery: The Views of State Human Service Administrators." *Journal of Sociology and Social Welfare, 23*(2): 107–119.

Kettner, P., & Martin, L. (1998). "Accountability in Purchase of Service Contracting," In Gibelman, M., & Demone, H. (Eds.), *The Privatization of Human Services: Policy and Practice Issues* (Volume I). New York: Springer.

Kettner, P., Moroney, R., & Martin, L. (1999). *Designing and Managing Programs: An Effectivenes-Based Approach.* (Second Edition). Thousand Oaks, CA: Sage Publications.

Keyes, W. N. (1990). *Government Contracts.* St. Paul: West Publishing Company.

Kramer, R. (1994). "Voluntary Agencies and the Contract Culture: Dream or Nightmare?" *Social Service Review, 68,* 33–60.

Lauffer, A. (1997). *Grants, etc.* Newbury Park, CA: Sage Publications.

Lee. S., & Shim, J. (1990) *Micro Management Science.* Boston: Allyn & Bacon.

Lohmann, R. (1980). *Breaking Even: Financial Management in Human Service Organizations.* Philadelphia: Temple University Press.

Lynch, T. D. (1995). *Public Budgeting in America.* Englewood Cliffs, NJ: Prentice-Hall.

Martin, L. (1998). "The Rush to Measure Performance." *Journal of Sociology and Social Welfare, 25*(3), 65–76.

Martin, L. (1999). *Contracting for Service Delivery: Local Government Choices.* Washington, DC: InternationalCity/County Management Association.

Martin, L. (2000a). "The Environmental Context of Social Welfare Administration." In Patti, R. (Ed.), *Handbook of Social Welfare Administration.* Binghamton, NY: The Hawthorn Press.

Martin, L. (2000b). "Performance Contracting in the Human Services: An Analysis of Selected State Practices." *Administration in Social Work* (forthcoming).

Martin, L., & Kettner, P. (1996). *Measuring the Performance of Human Service Programs.* Newbury Park, CA: Sage Publications.

Martin, L., & Menefee, D. (2000). "Costing Government Services," In Gauthier, S. J., & Miranda, R. (Eds.), *Handbook on State and Local Government Finance: Concepts and Practices 2000.* Chicago: Government Finance Officers Association.

McKinney, J. (1986). *Effective Financial Management in Public and Nonprofit Agencies.* New York: Quorum Books.

McMillan, E. (1994).*Budgeting and Financial Management Handbook For Not-for-Profit Organizations.* Washington, DC: American Society of Association Executives.

Melia, R. (1997). *Public Profits from Private Contracts: A Case Study in Human Services.* Boston: Pioneer Institute for Public Policy Research.

Moore, J., & Williams, G. (1999, December). "Ringing Up a New Way to Give." *The Chronicle of Philanthropy, 12*(5),1, 23–25.

Murdick, R., Render, B., & Russell, R. (1990). *Service Operations Management.* Boston: Allyn & Bacon.

National Association of Social Workers (NASW). (1997). "Preparing Social Workers for a Managed Care Environment." (monograph). Washington, DC: Author.

National Charities Information Bureau (NCIB). (1998). *NCIB's Standards in Philanthropy.* <http://www.give.org.> (3/13/2000).

Nonprofit Risk Management Center. (1996). *State Liability Laws for Charitable Organizations and Volunteers.* Washington, DC: Author.

Premchand, A. (1993). "A Cross-National Analysis of Financial Management Practices." In Lynch, T., & Martin, L. (Eds.), *Handbook of Comparative Public Budgeting and Financial Management* (pp. 87–99). New York: Marcel-Dekker.

Rapp, C., & Poertner, J. (1992). *Social Administration: A Client Centered Approach.* New York: Longman.

Smallwood, S., & Levis, W. (1977). "The Realities of Fund-Raising Costs and Accountability." <http://www.nonprofits.org>, (11/2/99).

Starling, G. (1993). *Managing the Public Sector* (4th Edition). Belmont, CA: Wadsworth.

Stehle, S. (1998, September 10). "Study: Americans Confident in Charities' Integrity." *The Chronicle of Philanthropy,* p. 12.

Support Center. (1999). "What Is the Unrelated Business Income Tax?" <http://www.igc.org> (10/18/99).

Swiss, J. (1991). *Public Management Systems.* Englewood Cliffs, NJ: Prentice Hall.

Tempe Community Council. (Undated). *Guide to Non-Profit Corporations.* Tempe, AZ: Author.

The Pew Charitable Trusts. (1999). <http://www.pewtrusts.com> (10/28/99).

Tremper, C., & Kostin, G. (1993). *No Surprises: Controlling Risks in Volunteer Programs.* Washington, DC: Non-profit Risk Management Center.

United Way of America. (1999). <http://www.unitedway.org> (11/9/99).

U.S. Department of the Treasury. (1998a). "Exemption Requirements—501(c)(3)." *The Digital Daily* <http://www.irs.ustreas.gov/prod/bus_info?eo/exempt-req.html> (8/21/98).

U.S. Department of the Treasury. (1998b). "Other Tax Exempt Organizations." <http://www.irs.ustreas.gov/prod/bus_info?eo/oth-orgs.html> (8/21/98).

Wayne, L. (1998, February 27). "The Shrinking Military Complex." *The New York Times*, p. D1.

Weinbach, R. (1998). *The Social Worker as Manager*. Boston: Allyn & Bacon.

Weiner, T. (1994, September 14). "United Way's Ex-Chief Indicted in Theft." *The New York Times*, p. A12.

Wildavsky, A. (1974). *The Politics of the Budgetary Process*. Boston: Little Brown.

INDEX